Al Kaline

The Biography of a Tigers Icon

Al Kaline

The Biography of a Tigers Icon

Jim Hawkins

TRIUMPH
BOOKS

Library of Congress Cataloging-in-Publication Data
Hawkins, Jim.
  Al Kaline : the biography of a Tigers icon / Jim Hawkins.
    p. cm.
  Includes bibliographical references and index.
  ISBN-13: 978-1-60078-314-2
  ISBN-10: 1-60078-314-7
1. Kaline, Albert William, 1934– 2. Detroit Tigers (Baseball team)—History.
3. Baseball players—United States—Biography. I. Title.
  GV865.K3H39 2010
  796.357092—dc22
  [B]
                    2010004005

This book is available in quantity at special discounts for your group or organization. For further information, contact:

Triumph Books
542 South Dearborn Street
Suite 750
Chicago, Illinois 60605
(312) 939–3330
Fax (312) 663–3557
www.triumphbooks.com

Printed in U.S.A.

ISBN: 978-1-60078-314-2

Design by Sue Knopf

To Penny, who has made
everything possible

Contents

Foreword

Al Kaline has never wanted the attention of a biography.

From that day on June 23, 1953, when he first joined the Detroit Tigers team at Shibe Park in Philadelphia, a scrawny 18-year-old high school kid from Baltimore suffering from a foot deformity and weighing only 150 pounds—so skinny he had to wear the batboy's uniform on his first few nights in the big leagues because that was the only one that fit—Al has always been a very private person.

Yet no big-league star deserves a biography more.

Baseball biographies now seem to be hitting the bookstores at the rate of one or two a month. Some are warranted and well done, but many are merely pedestrian career recaps pasted together with reheated stories from old newspaper files.

This one is different. It's much more in-depth. It is a true picture of a superstar who, despite his great talent and reputation, has somehow escaped the spotlight.

Kaline's story is fascinating. A kid with only high school experience becomes one of the superstars of the game. It is a story that has never been accorded a much-deserved, in-depth biography. But now we have one by Jim Hawkins, the best possible writer to relate the Al Kaline story.

I have known Al Kaline for 50 years, and I have known Jim Hawkins for 40. I am delighted that they have teamed up to bring you this story that is so long overdue.

When Al joined the Tigers in 1953, he was lonely, scared—even terrified. Certainly he had no idea what the world of professional baseball held for him.

Little did he, or anyone else, dream that half a century later he would be Mr. Tiger. The Consummate Professional. A Hall of Famer and the most famous of all Tigers, with the exception of Ty Cobb.

When Cobb joined the Detroit team in August 1905, he had already played two years in the minors. Almost all the other Hall of Famers served minor-league apprenticeships. I am talking about Babe Ruth, Walter Johnson, Christy Mathewson, Lou Gehrig, Willie Mays, Joe DiMaggio, Stan Musial, Rogers Hornsby, Jackie Robinson, Hank Aaron, and Ted Williams— the greatest of the greats.

But not Al Kaline. Al never spent one day—not one minute—in the minor leagues.

That makes his story all the more remarkable.

You will enjoy the down-to-earth, straightforward writing style of Jim Hawkins, who has known Al for 40 years, both as a player and as a close friend and confidant.

Like Kaline, Jim, who grew up in Wisconsin, came to Detroit from Baltimore. He joined the *Detroit Free Press* as the Tigers beat writer in 1970 and later authored books about Tigers stars Mark "the Bird" Fidrych and Ron LeFlore, as well as writing *The Detroit Tigers Encyclopedia* with former Tigers executive Dan Ewald.

Hawkins, who is still part of the city's sports scene, has not only covered the exploits of Al Kaline but has also closely followed the ups and downs of the franchise for which Al has served as a player, television analyst, and front-office advisor for 58 years.

Nobody can tell this story better than Jim Hawkins. And nobody deserves to have his story told more than Al Kaline.

—*Ernie Harwell*
September 1, 2009

Acknowledgments

The author would like to thank Willie Horton, Mickey Lolich, Jim Northrup, Gates Brown, the late Earl Wilson, John Hiller, Joe Colucci and all of the others who so graciously shared their insight and memories of Al Kaline and the era in Detroit Tigers history that he embodies.

Thanks also go to those who preceded me on this subject and provided valuable background, including my mentor for many years, Joe Falls; my predecessor at the *Detroit Free Press*, George Cantor; and author Hal Butler.

Thanks also to the *Detroit Free Press*, the *Oakland (Mich.) Press*, and the Detroit Tigers, who put me in a position and gave me the access necessary to chronicle much of this story firsthand; and to Baseball-Reference.com, which filled in the gaps when Kaline's memory, or mine, failed.

Special thanks go to Ernie Harwell, who graciously took the time to write the foreword for this book at what had to be the most trying time of his storied life.

Most of all, the author would like to thank Al Kaline for his cooperation on this book and for his four decades of friendship.

CHAPTER 1

Mr. Tiger

They don't make baseball players like Al Kaline anymore. That is what is wrong with the not-always-so-grand old game today.

No salacious scandal has ever tainted his name. Never has there been the slightest suggestion that he ever used steroids to juice up his statistics. No mind-numbing eight-digit salary or cushy multi-year contract, nice as that might have been, ever drove a wedge between Al and reality.

His has just been a long life filled with baseball. How boring. How beautiful. How rare. One team. One wife. One life. Al Kaline never asked for or dreamed of anything more.

What are the odds that a shy, skinny 18-year-old kid with a deformed left foot could go straight from high school and the sandlots of blue-collar Baltimore to the bright lights of the big leagues, win the American League batting title in just his second full season in the show, and last 22 years before ending up a first-ballot choice for baseball's Hall of Fame and becoming forever synonymous with the storied franchise that discovered him?

Incredible.

"I think about that so much," Kaline admitted one sunny summer afternoon during the 2009 baseball season as he sat in the dugout at soon-to-be-packed Comerica Park, watching the Detroit Tigers take batting practice.

"I put so much effort into becoming a baseball player. It's almost scary. What if I had failed? What would I have done with my life? What if I had

had to do what my dad did, which was to quit school at 16 and go to work? He went to work as a broom maker. Can you imagine? They don't even make brooms anymore, I don't think. It could have been a nightmare."

Instead, Kaline's story became a fairytale.

Baseball is America, and Al Kaline is baseball. Ten Gold Gloves, 18 All-Star Games, 3,007 base hits, 399 home runs, a batting crown, and a World Series championship.

Al Kaline may not have been the best ballplayer ever to wear the Olde English D. That distinction rightfully belongs to Ty Cobb. But to this day, after six decades in the organization, he remains the most beloved, the most revered hero that Tigers fans have ever known. The world has changed. People have changed. Baseball has changed. But Al Kaline has not changed.

Kaline's 22-year playing career with the Tigers—which featured so many clutch hits, so many marvelous catches, so many rifle-like throws—began in the era of day games, bonus babies, and Knot Hole Gangs, when baseball truly was our national pastime and the country worshipped its flannel-clad heroes from afar, via radios or on snowy black-and-white TV screens.

He is a throwback to a simpler time. A time before computers, cell phones, or the Internet. A time before blogs and text messages and, God forbid, Tweets. A time before playoffs, wild cards, and interleague play. A time when every big-league player had a roommate on the road and teammates regularly went out to dinner or to a movie together. A time when players had to find jobs during the winter months to support their families and make ends meet. A time when there were eight teams in the American League and eight in the National, none located west of St. Louis. A time when ballplayers had magical nicknames like Pee Wee and Yogi and great debates raged over who was better—Willie, Mickey, or the Duke.

It was a time when baseball teams rode trains from town to town, wore scratchy wool uniforms, and sang songs on the late-night bus rides from the ballpark. A time when even the biggest stars worked under one-year contracts, and pay cuts—yes, pay cuts—were commonplace. A time when holdouts were rare and agents even rarer.

A time when guys truly did play for the love of the game.

In Kaline's day, especially during Al's early years, players accepted whatever salary a team was willing to offer them—take it or leave it. And they did so until that team decided to trade them or cut them loose.

There was no free agency, no arbitration, and no alternative—except, of course, getting a job in the real world, packing a lunch, and going to work.

And Kaline loved every minute of it. He still does. "I hate to think about those people who have to go to work every day who really regret going to work," Al said softly, thoughtfully, as he exited the dugout and headed upstairs to the Comerica Park press box where, as a special assistant to Tigers president and general manager Dave Dombrowski, Kaline now watches game after game, night after night, year after year, from one of the executive suites. "And I know there are a lot of people like that.

"There I was, at 18 years old, doing exactly what I wanted to do with my life. And I'm still doing exactly what I've wanted to do, ever since I was 13 years of age. How lucky can you be!"

For 22 years, Kaline personified perfection in the outfield. Right field at recently demolished Tiger Stadium became known as "Kaline's Corner." And for 58 years, Kaline has personified the Detroit Tigers.

The story of Al Kaline—like the stories of fellow icons Ty Cobb, Hank Greenberg, Charlie Gehringer, and Alan Trammell—is the story of the Detroit Tigers. The history of the team can be neatly cubbyholed into four eras, each highlighted by a pennant or a world championship.

The Tigers won back-to-back-to-back American League titles in 1907, 1908, and 1909, soon after the irascible Cobb arrived in Detroit. Thanks to Greenberg and Gehringer, they again claimed pennants in 1934 and 1935 and won the franchise's first World Series in 1935. The year 1968 belonged to Kaline, along with Denny McLain and Mickey Lolich. And the Tigers went wire-to-wire in 1984, led by Trammell, the World Series MVP.

Kaline's tenure has spanned 11 United States presidents, from Dwight D. Eisenhower to Barack Obama; 11 Tigers team presidents; a dozen general managers; and 22 managers, from Fred Hutchinson to Jim Leyland. Since 1953 Al Kaline has been the one constant in the Detroit Tigers organization.

"Everything is different now," Kaline admitted. "Only the game itself is still the same."

Al Kaline was never a headline grabber or a money-grubber. In his mind, the game was never about him. He was a ballplayer's ballplayer.

Kaline didn't knock you over with his numbers. At least not until you added them all up, as the veteran members of the Baseball Writers Association of America did in 1980 when they examined Al's 22-year body of work and overwhelmingly—and surprisingly—elected him to the Hall of Fame on the first ballot, just the 10th player in the history of the game, at that time, to be so honored.

Neither a slugger nor a speedster, Kaline was a complete ballplayer, adept at every aspect of the game.

"I call Al our Abraham Lincoln," declared Willie Horton, the popular former Detroit star and Kaline's longtime Tigers teammate, who, like Al, today serves as an advisor in the team's front office.

"He was our leader. He was the man with the tie on. He always set the tone for our team."

Leave it to Horton who, like Kaline, has grown more eloquent with age, to put the career of the Greatest Living Tiger into perspective.

"Al has forgotten this, but I met Al when I was just a kid hanging around Briggs Stadium," recalled Horton, who grew up in a housing project in Detroit's inner city, not far from the old ballpark.

"Then all of sudden, I was there playing with him. Coming up, I watched him a lot. I loved talking about the game with Al. If you went to him, he'd speak from the heart. He had quiet leadership.

"I saw how he went about his business and prepared for games. I watched him in batting practice. He made me a better hitter. He made me a better outfielder. It was an incentive just to come up to his level of expertise."

In 1963 Charlie Dressen—who had managed the Cincinnati Reds, Brooklyn Dodgers, Washington Senators, and Milwaukee Braves before joining the Tigers—was asked to name the greatest player he had ever managed.

"Jackie Robinson was the most exciting runner I ever had," Dressen declared. "He couldn't be equaled on the bases. He could rob a team blind. Pee Wee Reese was the gustiest little infielder I ever had. I'd have to put Roy Campanella in a class with Mickey Cochrane, Gabby Harnett, and Bill Dickey. And Hank Aaron is the best hitter I ever had.

"But in my heart, I'm convinced Kaline is the best player who ever played for me. For all-around ability—I mean hitting, fielding, running, and throwing—I'll go with Al."

No less of an authority than Boston Red Sox great Ted Williams, who humbly considered himself the greatest hitter who ever lived, declared in his book *My Turn at Bat*, declared, "If I had to pick an All-Star Team of those players that I have played with and against, limiting it to the American League, [Joe] DiMaggio would certainly head it up. With him in the outfield, I would go with [Mickey] Mantle and Al Kaline."

When Williams, who batted .406 in 1941, was asked in the mid-1950s who the next big-leaguer to hit .400 might be, he named two: Mickey Mantle and Al Kaline.

Nevertheless, in 2002, as Kaline was beginning his 50th season with the Tigers organization, I asked him what he would change if he could change one thing about his Hall of Fame career.

"I should have been a better ballplayer than I was," confessed the man who played in more games (2,834), hit more home runs (399), and drew more walks (1,277) than any other Tiger who ever lived.

"I had a lot of tools. I could do a lot of things. I think losing with bad teams, year in and year out, knowing every year, going into September, that we had no chance to win, finishing down near the bottom every year, beat me down.

"If you look at my record, when I played in All-Star Games, I did really well. When I played in the World Series, I did really well. If I was challenged, I usually did pretty well.

"Maybe it was my fault," he humbly suggested. "Maybe if I had elevated my game, we would have been a little bit better."

5

Suddenly, it dawned on me: Al Kaline, the greatest player to don a Detroit Tigers uniform in the last half-century, was actually apologizing for his stellar Hall of Fame career.

Kaline never dazzled anyone with his dialogue. He was never a guy who lit up a room simply by walking through the door.

He wasn't colorful like his teammate and close friend Norm Cash. He wasn't controversial like pitcher Denny McLain. He wasn't cantankerous like Ty Cobb or powerful like Hank Greenberg. In fact, Al was barely quotable, especially in his early years.

Kaline believed that playing the game well, and playing it the right way, should be enough. Al didn't wear an earring or dangle bling around his neck. He never had a posse. His life was never a burlesque, never a freak show. Kaline made certain of that; that wasn't his style.

"You know how much I hate talking about myself," he protested when I first approached him a couple of years ago with the idea of writing his first and only complete biography.

"I've had a pretty boring life, really," Al insisted.

And he was right. Which is precisely what makes his story so special.

Kaline never wowed anybody with his physique. In 1964 *Sports Illustrated*'s Jack Olsen noted, "Kaline is one of the last of an almost prehistoric type of ballplayer, the kid who makes it, not because of physique, but in spite of it."

Al was hardly a hardy specimen. He was born with a bone disease known as osteomyelitis. When little Al was eight years old, a surgeon removed a two-inch piece of bone from his left foot, leaving it scarred and permanently deformed. It would haunt Al throughout much of his career.

But Kaline largely suffered in silence. Few ever knew that the man who hit a baseball so consistently, who ran the bases so well and so fast, and who roamed right field with such excellence and grace was playing on a crippled, often painful left foot.

Kaline didn't resort to performance-enhancing substances that are so much in the news today—although there certainly were times, coming back from his myriad major injuries, when he could have used a boost.

Kaline never bet on baseball—not on his team or on the opposition. He was never charged with perjury. He was never investigated by the FBI or called to testify before Congress. He never filed for bankruptcy.

Rarely did he argue with umpires, although he certainly didn't always agree with their calls. "He was a gentleman," umpire Larry McCoy once said. "It would have to be a real borderline pitch for him to even turn his head."

As Al himself noted during his acceptance speech when he was inducted into the Baseball Hall of Fame in 1980, "If there is one accomplishment for which I am particularly proud, it is that I've always served baseball to the best of my ability. Never have I deliberately done anything to discredit the game, the Tigers, or my family."

In 1973 Kaline received the Roberto Clemente Award, presented annually by the commissioner to the player who best exemplifies baseball, on and off the field. He also received the Bill Slocum Award from the New York Baseball Writers for "long and meritorious service to baseball."

Kaline was special. He was unique.

Can you imagine a star player today waiting 15 years to get to the World Series, then telling his manager—and the media—to keep him on the bench because the younger guys on the team, guys who hadn't paid anywhere near the dues that he had paid, deserved to play more than he did?

Can you imagine a skinny kid who was supposedly all glove and no bat suddenly leading the league in hitting at the tender age of 20?

Can you imagine any of today's mega-millionaire ballplayers turning down a salary of $100,000 a year, as Kaline did prior to the 1971 season, informing management that he didn't believe he deserved that much money?

Of course, none of today's players would ever think of accepting a $100,000 contract. Today the rawest and most unready rookie makes four times that amount simply for showing up and taking up space on the bench. The Yankees' Alex Rodriguez makes more than that every time he pulls on his pin-striped pants.

Sitting in the Tigers dugout, watching the team's budding 26-year-old superstar, Miguel Cabrera, clown around with his teammates during batting practice before a game in 2009, I asked Al if he could imagine what it must be like to be that good, that young, and that rich?

Kaline smiled. "I knew a little bit of that," he said wistfully. "But not all of it."

Certainly not the money part.

Kaline, so good, so young, led the American League in hitting in 1955 at the unprecedented age of 20—one day younger than Ty Cobb had been when he led the league in batting in 1907—yet he never made more than $103,000 in any one season in his 22-year Hall of Fame career. And that didn't happen until his final two years, in 1973 and 1974.

"And I was very happy to get it," Al pointed out, "because I wasn't the player I had been previously."

Kaline was never able to pad his paychecks through salary arbitration. He was never allowed to sell his skills to the highest bidder on the open market as a free agent. He never knew the security of a seven-digit salary or a 10-year contract. With Kaline, it was always one year at a time.

When Al broke into baseball, nobody made a lot of money. At least the players didn't. And everybody worried about their jobs. Players didn't make waves; they didn't rock the boat. They didn't dare.

"I have no regrets about the money I made, and I don't begrudge the players today getting the money they're getting," Kaline insisted. "But I do object when I see a player who doesn't appreciate the game. However, in most cases they do. And the owners, obviously, think they can afford to pay those salaries.

"I've never been jealous of anybody making money. Money is great. Everybody needs it. But to me, if you love what you're doing, that's the important thing."

Then a smile spread across Al's face. He couldn't help himself.

"I could have been a free agent four times," he said, grinning, as he whimsically pondered that possibility. "Imagine, teams bidding for my services every five years!"

The money Al might have made if he was playing today would be staggering.

In 1955, still more than two months shy of his 21st birthday, Kaline won the American League batting championship. No player so young had ever done that. And none have done it since. Then Kaline spent the next two decades trying to live up to the image that he had unwittingly created for himself.

At first, Kaline was compared to the famous, or infamous, Cobb, who was merely The Greatest Detroit Tiger of them all. Al was also likened to Joe DiMaggio, the New York Yankees legend who embodied the essence of baseball elegance and grace. Such comparisons were both unrealistic and unfair.

For a shy young man who was uncomfortable around strangers to begin with, often afraid to speak for fear he might say the wrong thing, it was almost too much to bear.

A decade later, Kaline admitted, "The year of 1955, when I won the batting title, was the worst thing that ever happened to me.

"It put an awful lot of pressure on me," Kaline recalled. "I think the writers were responsible. They began comparing me with Cobb and DiMaggio, and the fans read it and they believed it. First thing you know, there was all this pressure on me.

"The comparisons were foolish, especially comparing me with Cobb. I hadn't been around long enough to be compared to him in that way, or any way. Cobb was the greatest player who ever lived. Nobody has come near him.

"As for me, well, they were throwing all this pressure on me, and I didn't think it was fair or even justified. I probably would have had better seasons right after 1955 if the pressure hadn't been applied. Instead, I had a hard time living up to the reputation others were giving me."

Kaline's playing career bridged the gap from the golden era of Al's boyhood heroes, Ted Williams and Stan Musial, through the glory days of his contemporaries—Mickey Mantle, Willie Mays, Hank Aaron, and Roberto Clemente. In all of baseball history, only Baltimore's Brooks

Robinson (1955–1977) and Boston's Carl Yastrzemski (1961–1983) lasted longer with one team.

But Kaline was no Cobb, no DiMaggio, no Mantle, no Aaron, no Mays.

He never said he was. He never would. "I wasn't meant to be a superstar," Kaline insisted early on.

However, some of Al's peers disagreed. "There have been a lot of great defensive players, but the fella who could do everything was Al Kaline," declared Baltimore Orioles third baseman Brooks Robinson, who himself became synonymous with defensive excellence. "He was the epitome of what a great outfielder is all about—great speed, catches the ball and throws the ball well."

"You almost have to watch him play every day to appreciate what he does," observed veteran pitcher Johnny Podres, the hero of the Brooklyn Dodgers' World Series triumph in 1955, who joined the Tigers in 1966 at the end of his career. "You hear about him, sure, but you really can't understand until you see him. He just never makes a mistake."

In Al's mind, simply being the best player that Al Kaline could possibly be was always good enough for him. However, he would accept nothing less than that. "I was never satisfied with just average," Al said.

"I never worried about being patted on the back or stuff like that," Kaline later insisted, when I suggested his accomplishments had been underappreciated by some. "I just appreciated playing. I just wanted to be one the guys, even though I knew I had skills that were better than most of them. I just wanted to be one of the guys, that's all."

But that could never happen. Because Al Kaline was special. "He never really was one of the guys," recalled Gates Brown, the former Tigers pinch-hitter deluxe, who was Kaline's teammate for a dozen years.

And The Gator meant that as a compliment. "The rest of us, Norm Cash and myself and some of the others, we would be goofing around and laughing," Brown remembered. "But Al was always all business. He was always in the game.

"He took a lot of pride in his work. He didn't ever want to screw up. And he never did. He made everything look so easy. I would watch him hit those curveballs, and I'd say to myself, 'Damn, I wish I could hit like that.'

"The guy was gifted," Gates added. "He was just a helluva man."

Kaline never had a flashy nickname. His teammates called him "Line." Others respectfully referred to him by his uniform number, "Six." To his fans, he became "Mr. Tiger."

Today, Kaline is as much at home in the Tigers clubhouse as the organization's elder statesman, mingling with current stars, including Miguel Cabrera and Justin Verlander, as he was in the days when he lockered alongside Norm Cash, Rocky Colavito, and Harvey Kuenn.

It is there, in the locker room or in the dugout or leaning against the cage during batting practice, that Kaline feels most comfortable. In his heart and in his soul, he is still what he has always been, the only thing he ever wanted to be—a ballplayer.

The only difference is Al can't hit or run or throw anymore.

However, the baseball player in him will never die. The game is his life.

"I owe everything to baseball," Kaline once admitted with typical modesty. "Without it, I'd probably be a bum."

As fellow Hall of Famer George Kell, Kaline's TV broadcast partner for 21 years, once declared, "Al Kaline knows baseball like no one else knows the game."

No man—not tempestuous Ty Cobb, not Hammerin' Hank Greenberg, not underappreciated Alan Trammell—has ever personified the Detroit Tigers as well or for as long as Kaline has.

Al Kaline, the father of two and grandfather of four, is Detroit, as respected and revered at the plebeian summer picnics on Belle Isle in the middle of the busy Detroit River as he is at the prestigious, patrician Oakland Hills Country Club in tony Bloomfield Township, where they take their golf seriously and where Kaline has been an active, prominent member for nearly three decades.

"Everybody loves him—everybody," declared former business exec Joe Colucci, who first met Al in a pickup basketball game and who has been his close friend for more than 40 years. "People laugh at us because we're together all the time. We just hit it off.

"I had a chance to sign a pro contract, too, when I was a kid. But my dad told me, 'Don't bother. You're not good enough. Go to college.' I was at Michigan State when Al won the batting title. We're about the same age—Al's four days older than I am—and I was jealous of him. I followed his career from the time he first came up with the Tigers.

"He is truly a great man," Colucci added. "He was a fabulous baseball player—but he's an even better person."

Near the conclusion of Kaline's playing career, I received a letter from a young lady who explained she was writing a high school term paper about Al and asked for any insight I might offer. I replied that perhaps the greatest compliment I could pay him was to say that I had never, not once, heard anyone say anything derogatory about the man.

Even after all these years, those who knew or know him, those who actually saw him play, and those who have only heard or read about what he did speak respectfully about the player he was and the person he still is.

Today, Dave Richards owns and operates his own golf marketing company. But he remembers how, when he was growing up in Ecorse, Michigan, in the 1960s, whenever he did something wrong or was disrespectful, his father would admonish him by saying, "Al Kaline would never do that" or "That's not the way Al Kaline would do it."

"And I knew exactly what he was talking about," Richards remembered.

Even from afar, Kaline set the standard against which young Richards and countless other baseball-minded Michiganders were measured.

Al has been a hero and a role model for generations.

"I never wished I was playing anywhere else but in Detroit," Kaline said. "There were many times when I wished I was playing for a winning team. But I think Detroit was the perfect-size city for me. I don't know if I could have survived playing in New York or Chicago."

But because Kaline played in Detroit, rather than in, say, New York, he didn't always receive all of the media attention and acclaim that he deserved.

"I got to be pretty good friends with Mickey Mantle over the years," Kaline recalled. "We would sometimes have a beer or two together after the game at the Lindell AC when the Yankees were in town, and he used to say to me, 'It's too bad you don't play in New York because people don't even know who you are.'

"Actually, I thought I got more recognition than I deserved," Al insisted. "Honestly, I felt I was treated very fairly. I had writers come up to me, especially when we played National League teams, and tell me, 'Gee, I didn't realize you were this good of a player.' And I'd always say, 'The people in Detroit treat me great.'"

In 1969 when Tigers fans celebrated baseball's centennial by selecting their all-time team, Kaline was, of course, included along with fellow outfielders Ty Cobb and Harry Heilmann, slugging first baseman Hank Greenberg, second baseman Charlie Gehringer (aka the Mechanical Man) catcher/manager Mickey Cochrane, third baseman George Kell, shortstop-turned-politician Billy Rogell, and pitchers Hal Newhouser and Denny McLain.

When the sports-memorabilia market exploded in the mid-1980s, Kaline, not surprisingly, became a popular autograph guest on the baseball-card-show circuit, particularly in the Detroit area. I was putting on such card shows at the time and regularly employed Kaline as an autograph guest at least once a year.

Al charged $2,000 an hour for his services, and his appearances usually lasted three hours. No matter how many times Kaline appeared, year after year, he never failed to attract a crowd. It was amazing.

Al made money, I made money as the show promoter, and the fans and collectors, whose insatiable appetite for autographs never ceased to amaze me, went home happy.

Kaline can sometimes be prickly when people approach him for autographs, especially if he feels he is being taken advantage of or taken for granted. Like most former players, especially those who never made big bucks on the ballfield, Kaline resents it when he thinks people are making money off his name and his fame by selling his signature.

But as long as Kaline felt he was being fairly compensated for his time and his trouble, he was fine.

At one such show in 1993, a 40-something fellow, who appeared to be on the verge of hyperventilating, approached the autograph table clutching a 1968 Tigers pennant in his trembling hands.

"Mr. Kaline," the fan asked excitedly, "do you remember me?"

Kaline looked at the man for a moment and said, "I don't think so. Should I?"

The man appeared deeply disappointed.

"At the parade, after the '68 Series, I ran up to your car," the guy gushed. "I was right next to you. I yelled, 'Al! Al!' You looked right at me and waved. You must remember."

Kaline pretended to study the fan's face for a moment, then said, "I thought you looked familiar. Yeah, from the parade in '68. You ran up to the car. You've changed a little bit. I mean, it's been 25 years. But, yeah, I remember you."

The guy was grinning from ear to ear. He picked up his pennant that Al had just autographed and walked away, still smiling. I swear, his feet barely touched the ground.

Kaline had just made this guy's day, his week, his month, indeed, his whole year. The guy would rush home and tell his wife and his kids and phone every one his friends. *Wait 'til the guys in the office hear about this*, he was surely thinking. *I talked to Al Kaline—and he remembered me!*

My son, Mark, who was sitting alongside Kaline, doing his best to speed along the line filled with fans and collectors who had waited, some for hours, to secure the Hall of Famer's signature, turned in his chair and stared at Al incredulously. Kaline sensed my son's puzzlement and his quizzical stare.

Kaline shook his head. Without looking up, Al quietly said, "Of course not." Then he began signing his name again, with the same smooth, distinctive strokes, for maybe the 10-millionth time in his life, making the next guy in line feel as if he, too, was the most important person in the world.

CHAPTER 2

"Life Was a Baseball Game"

Looking back on it now, from his seat in one of the executive suites high above the field at Comerica Park in recession-ravaged downtown Detroit, Al Kaline is more appreciative than ever of the fact that his parents, Nicholas and Naomi, who contributed so much to Al's development as a person and as a ballplayer, were both still alive and able to be present at the two crowning moments in his career. The first came on September 24, 1974, when he collected his 3,000th hit, making him, at the time, just the 12th player in baseball history ever to reach that prestigious plateau. The second was on August 3, 1980, when he was awarded the game's ultimate honor and ushered into the Hall of Fame, just the 10th man to ever make it on the first ballot.

"I've had a lot of different guys, Hall of Famers, say to me, 'You're so lucky your parents were able to be there,' because a lot of theirs weren't," Al declared.

Kaline was born, humbly enough, on December 19, 1934, the third child and only son of a working-class couple of German and Irish descent. They lived in a modest row house on Baltimore's blue-collar south side, a neighborhood more famous for its factories than its fine homes, where the smell of cinnamon from the McCormick plant, located on Baltimore's then-undeveloped Inner Harbor, spiced the air.

"My mom worked all of the time until maybe my last year in high school," Kaline recalled. "My dad worked all the time, too. My dad walked to work every day. From where I was born, it was maybe six or seven blocks. When I was in elementary school, I would hustle home to meet him for lunch. I would eat a fast sandwich, and then I would hightail it right back to school so I could play a little softball before lunch period was over."

The family, which included Kaline's two older sisters, Margaret and Caroline, lived at 2222 Cedley Street in a neighborhood known as Westport, on the wrong side of the tracks, so to speak, and not far from historic Fort McHenry, where "The Star-Spangled Banner" was born.

Suffice to say, it was not the fanciest of neighborhoods.

"Where I was born, I didn't live close to any ballpark," Kaline said, looking back. "I couldn't walk to a ballpark if I wanted to play ball. And I couldn't ride my bicycle there, because I didn't have a bicycle for a long time. I had to be driven. The closest ballpark was the one my school used. But it was about three miles from my house.

"When I went to high school, I had to take a trolley from our neighborhood first, then catch a bus just to get to my school, which was near Baltimore's Inner Harbor. And we didn't have a baseball field at my school, either. So, after school, we had to catch another ride to get to the ballpark where we practiced.

"My dad would have to pick me up after practice. Or I would have to walk home. That was scary because it would always be dark by then, and it was a bad neighborhood in those days between the ballpark and my house. In those days, the Inner Harbor was all wooden shacks, and they always warned us never to go downtown because downtown Baltimore was terrible.

"Whenever I walked home, I had to walk past a junkyard. That was where I learned how to run. Those junkyard dogs would be barking and snarling. Even though they were behind the fence, I would really be running when I went past that junkyard."

In the closing days of Kaline's career, whenever the Tigers would travel to Baltimore on a road trip, Al always made it a point to sit on the right side of the team bus during the ride downtown from what was then known as Friendship Airport.

As the Tigers' bus passed Westport, Al would gaze out the window at the three smokestacks just beyond Cedley Street and say to his teammates, "There it is, guys, my old hometown. We lived right over there behind the power factory. A great place to grow up."

During the off-season, whenever Kaline and his growing family would visit his parents, Al would drive past the smokestacks so that his two sons, Mark and Mike, could see where their famous father had grown up.

"I wanted them to know that life was not always easy," Kaline explained. "I wanted them to know you had to work hard to get ahead."

Hard work was a way of life on the Kaline household. Al's dad worked in a broom factory while his mom worked in a whiskey distillery by day and scrubbed floors in a downtown Baltimore office building a couple nights a week.

For fun, the elder Kaline had played baseball as a young man. Nicholas and his two brothers, Bib and Fred, Al's uncles, along with his grandfather, Philip, had all played semipro ball. They had all been catchers. Kaline's dad and two uncles were convinced that young Al, with his strong arm, would make a fine pitcher.

Since before the days of Babe Ruth, another of Baltimore's famous native sons, that has been the preferred position of the best ballplayers in the land. "I guess all kids interested in baseball first want to be pitchers," Kaline said.

By the time Al was eight, his dad was squatting behind an imaginary home plate, holding up his catcher's mitt and urging his son to fire the ball into it, harder and harder and harder.

Al loved it.

"Dad used to teach me how to throw the different pitches," Kaline recalled. "By the time I was nine, I knew how to throw a fastball, a curve, and a change-up. A few years later, I pitched for Westport Grammar School and won 10 straight games. That gave me a thrill. Ten thrills, I guess."

As Kaline would declare more than five decades later when he was inducted into the Hall of Fame, "When I was a youngster, life was a baseball game. There was nothing more exciting than a good old game of ball."

During a summer youth festival, Kaline threw a softball 173', six" to shatter the Baltimore Elementary School record. The judges were astounded. Surely they must have measured wrong. No kid so young and so skinny could possibly throw a ball so far. So they ordered young Al to try again, to set the record straight. The second time, Kaline heaved the ball 175 feet.

"My dad never graduated high school, my mom never graduated high school, neither of my sisters ever graduated high school, either," Kaline said. "Out of all my cousins and my family and everybody, I was the first Kaline ever to graduate from high school.

"And I was a very poor student," he admitted.

Baseball, not biology, was young Al's first love. And his family was as determined as he was to see that Al succeeded in that endeavor.

"I put all of my effort into playing baseball," Kaline recalled. "In high school, I played as much baseball as I could possibly play. I was playing five days a week and doubleheaders on Sunday. I had no other skills.

"I was a very poor student in school because I didn't apply myself. Plus the fact that I didn't have anybody at home who could help me. Both of my sisters were older, and they were out dating or married and gone. My mom and dad both worked all the time. When you put it all on my shoulders, a person like me is going to go out and play ball and forget all about schoolwork.

"But I was a good kid," he continued. "All my teachers would tell me, 'We know you're going to be a baseball player.' I guess they knew more than I did. But they'd tell me, 'Just do your work, don't cause any trouble.' And they all passed me through.

"But if I had it to do over again, I certainly would have paid more attention to my schoolwork," Al said.

In the ensuing years, as Kaline's stature and reputation grew, much has been made of his modest upbringing. But in many ways, Al's childhood in Baltimore was every boy's dream.

"I can look back now and see how little my parents had when I was a kid," Kaline told Detroit sportswriter Joe Falls in a 1975 interview. "But when you're growing up in a neighborhood, you don't know what's poor and what's rich. Everyone was just the same.

"I didn't have any money, but I never needed any. I just never thought about it. We were too busy playing. Once in a while, on a Saturday maybe, we'd go to the movies. But the rest of the time we were always playing something.

"Looking back, I had it pretty nice. I had two great parents, and they gave me everything I needed. My dad worked in a broom factory. At the time I was going to elementary school, my mom was also working. She worked in a whiskey distillery, rolling barrels up into freight cars. She filled the freight cars, and she would empty them. I was aware of all this because my dad and I would pick her up after work. She would be wearing overalls, and we would pick her up at 5:00.

"My mom was very strong. She never complained about anything," Al said. "She was always the strongest of the bunch. Even though she was a little woman, she was even stronger than my dad. Actually, she had two jobs. She would come home and cook dinner for us, and a couple of nights a week she would go downtown with some other women and scrub floors in bank buildings and big office buildings. We would pick her up again at 11:00, and she was always so happy to see us.

"My parents always helped me. My parents knew I wanted to be a major-leaguer, and they did everything they could to give me the time to play baseball.

"I thought maybe I should get a job in a drugstore or take a paper route, but my dad and mom didn't want me to work," Al remembered. "Even though the family could have used the money I might have made working at odd jobs, my father would never let me earn a dime. I just played ball.

"I used to talk to them about it, and I remember them telling me, 'You'll be old for a long time and you'll have to work for a long time, so enjoy your games now.' I guess they wanted me to enjoy being a kid. They encouraged me to play baseball.

"Looking back now," he said softly, "I can see how much my parents meant to me."

Down the street from the Kaline family home, there was a vacant lot where the men who toiled at the neighborhood gas and electric company regularly gathered on their lunch break for a friendly 30- or 40-minute game of softball. That was an urban way of life in those days.

Even before Al was old enough to attend school, he was drawn to the makeshift diamond in that vacant lot. There, alone in his fantasies, he would sprint around the make-believe bases, all arms and legs, sliding safely home just ahead of phantom throws that would, of course, never come.

"He'd get a stone and a stick and play all by himself, running the bases, even sliding home," Kaline's mother, Naomi, recalled in 1980 when Al was elected to the Hall of Fame. "That's how it started."

By the time he was six, young Kaline was shagging fly balls in the outfield and playing catch with the workmen as they quickly warmed up for their pickup games.

Before long, impressed with his ability and his enthusiasm, the grown-ups invited Al to join them.

"They were always a man or so short, and I'd be standing under the trees to see if they were," Kaline recalled. "They'd say, 'Come on, Al. Play.' They got to know me by my first name. I was only 10 or 11 at the time, but they would put me in the lineup. That's how I got started.

"I'd stand under those trees waiting for the guys to come out, and I'd just about cry whenever it rained and they had to stay inside. But I'd stand there anyway, waiting.

"I was pretty good at playing," he continued. "The men would encourage me. They'd pat me on the back and say, 'You played a good game today, Al. See you tomorrow.'

"It's strange, but even when I played with the men, I never felt nervous. I just enjoyed it so much, I guess, I did good naturally.

"Our elementary school was a mile from home. We didn't have a cafeteria in those days. Well, they had one, but it was always closed. They couldn't afford to pay people to work there. I used to run home all the way and meet my dad. He'd be just getting home ahead of me. He'd have a sandwich ready for me. I'd say, 'Hi, Dad,' and take off right back to school. Sometimes I'd be running back to school eating my sandwich. That's so I could get in on the pickup games there. We didn't get to play but for about 40 minutes, and I didn't want to miss any of it."

Always small for his age and slender, almost frail, young Kaline was also shy and introverted. He idolized Ted Williams and Stan Musial.

Although it was often overlooked during the course of his career, Kaline suffered from a chronic bone disease known as osteomyelitis. When Al was eight years old, doctors removed a two-inch piece of diseased bone from his left foot, leaving behind jagged scars and a permanent deformity that would haunt him throughout much of his career.

The surgery left him with a set of sharply swept-back toes on his left foot. Only two of those toes touched the ground when he walked. As a consequence, Kaline learned to run on the side of his left foot.

It wasn't easy at first, but Al did it with such ease and speed that most who watched him play never guessed he suffered from what could have been a career-curtailing deformity.

However, he never complained or used that as an excuse. "It's like a toothache in the foot," he once admitted when questioned about the pain.

Those who knew the suffering he endured marveled at his perseverance and performance.

"Al Kaline has had more reason to jake it than almost any player I know," Tigers general manager Jim Campbell admitted midway through Al's playing career. "But I've never seen him give less than everything he had. That's the way he learned to play baseball. And that's the only way he knows how."

In October 1965, Kaline underwent surgery to correct the deformity in his left foot that had caused him almost constant pain.

In the fall of 1949, although he stood just 5'7" and weighed only 115 pounds, 14-year-old freshman Al Kaline tried out for the Southern High School football team. Kaline made the team, but a broken cheekbone midway through his first season ended Al's adventures on the gridiron. It was the first of many injuries that would haunt Kaline throughout his athletic career.

Al also played basketball. He led his team in scoring as a freshman and averaged 22.5 points per game on the hard court during his senior year to lead Southern High to the Maryland State Basketball Championship. There were those who said Kaline was one of the best basketball players ever developed in south Baltimore.

But Al's first love was always baseball. He played any time, anywhere, against anybody he could.

"In those days, amateur baseball in Baltimore was divided into age groups," Kaline recalled. "I started playing when I was 10 years old in the 10–12 age group on a team right there from my little neighborhood. The drugstore on the corner would sponsor us. They gave us each a T-shirt. That was a big deal for us, to have a T-shirt with your team's name on it.

"Then I moved up, into the 12–14, 14–16, and 16–18 age groups. And I got involved in American Legion ball."

When baseball season at Baltimore's Southern High rolled around in the spring of 1950, Kaline naturally went out for the team. But Southern High coach Bill Anderson thought Al, who still weighed less than 120 pounds, was too small to play.

Young Kaline persisted, showing up at practice day after day until Anderson allowed him to try out. Al's strong arm caught the coach's eye. Despite his lack of size, Kaline could throw a ball hard and accurately.

Nevertheless, Anderson thought Kaline was too small to be a pitcher. Besides, the coach already had three proven pitchers on his squad. So he tried Al at shortstop, where his strong arm would offset his lack of size. Still, Anderson worried that Kaline might be too fragile to play the infield.

When the team's regular center fielder broke his leg, Al got his opportunity. And he made the most of it. "Switching to the outfield was the best break I ever got," Kaline later admitted.

Initially, Anderson intended to place Kaline on the junior varsity for his first year. But after Kaline delivered the game-winning hit in an early practice game, Anderson pulled Al aside in the locker room and said, "Son, you're on the varsity now."

In the summer of 1951, Kaline, who by now stood 5'11" and weighed all of 130 pounds, was selected by his hometown *Baltimore News-Post* to play in the annual Hearst Sandlot All-Star Game at the historic Polo Grounds, home field of the New York Giants. It was quite an honor.

Kaline, still only a high school sophomore, belted a home run into the upper deck in left field, singled twice, and was named the game's Most Valuable Player, which earned him the coveted Lou Gehrig Trophy.

The next afternoon, Kaline witnessed his first big-league game, which featured the New York Yankees against the St. Louis Browns.

"Our All-Star Game was at the Polo Grounds, but they took us to Yankee Stadium to see a big-league game," Kaline recalled.

"Before the game, they took us downstairs to the Yankees' locker room. They paraded us through, in one door and out the next. That was Joe DiMaggio's last year. Joe was sitting there in front of his locker, getting ready for the game. They told us to keep moving, but everybody kept stumbling over one another because everybody wanted to stop to stare at him. Just to get a chance to see Joe DiMaggio, we kept bumping into one another, stepping on each other's feet."

Of course, DiMaggio never acknowledged the young players' presence. After all, he was the Yankee Clipper.

Kaline never noticed another young player in the Yankees' locker room, a kid not much older than himself. That kid's name was Mickey Mantle. It would not be the last time that their paths would cross.

Later that summer, Kaline starred in the playoffs of the All-American Amateur Baseball Association in Johnstown, Pennsylvania. Suddenly the big-league scouts who scoured the country in those days searching for talent began paying attention to him. At one time or another, scouts from every team in Major League Baseball saw young Kaline play. Soon every scouting director was familiar with his name.

One scout who took particular note was a burly former schoolteacher named Ed Katalinas, who worked for the Detroit Tigers.

"To me, he was the prospect that a scout creates in his mind and then prays that someone will come along to fit the pattern," Katalinas later declared.

Nevertheless, when skinny young Kaline showed up at a Brooklyn Dodgers summer tryout camp in Baltimore, the Dodgers scout in charge of the tryouts told him to go home and gain some weight.

Charley Johnson, a neighbor of Kaline's, introduced Al to Walter Youse, the manager of the Westport American Legion team. There, Kaline got the chance to play baseball during the summer months as well as with his high school team in the spring. He batted .333 in his first season with the American Legion Post Number 33 and was named to the Legion Junior League All-Star team. In 1951 Kaline batted an incredible city record .609 in Legion ball.

"Back in those days, he didn't look like he'd be big enough or strong enough to play the outfield," Youse later recalled. "But as a teenager he could throw hard, and he had a nice curveball. He would definitely have been a professional pitching prospect if he didn't become such a great outfielder."

In his four years of high school baseball, in addition to his circus catches and rifle throws, Kaline batted .333, .418, .469, and .488. That gave him a four-year batting average of .427. He was named to the All-Maryland Team all four years. No player had done that since the New York Yankees' Charlie Keller.

"Al was the best high school hitter I ever coached," raved Southern High coach Bill Anderson years later. "He would have hit even better except for the size of our ballpark. We had a big field, and a lot of the long outs he hit would have been home runs in most big-league parks.

"He was a fine fielder, too. No one dared take an extra base on his throwing arm. His ability to cut down men at home plate with fast and accurate throws from the outfield won at least a half-dozen games for us. And as for his base-running, stealing second and third on successive pitches was a common feat. Only once in his career was he thrown out, and that was on a highly debatable call."

While still in high school, Kaline also played in a semipro league. "That was where I really learned to play ball," he said.

"There I was, playing against older guys, some of them former professional players who had gone away to play minor-league ball. The name of my team was United Iron and Metal, and we played doubleheaders every Sunday. At different times, I also played with Leone's Tavern and with Gordon Stores, sometime in the same season.

"Some of the guys on the team actually got paid to play, $25 or something like that, a game. Of course, I was just a kid in high school, so I didn't get paid. I didn't even realize until later that some of the guys on the team were getting paid to play.

That was where I learned how pitchers were pitching to me, what they were trying to do to me, things like that. I really learned how to play at a higher level than most kids my age because I was 15 or 16 years old, and I was playing against guys who were 23 and 24 years old. I really appreciated the fact that they gave me a chance to play."

By Al's senior year in high school, he had been scouted by every team in the major leagues. Four teams—the Philadelphia Phillies, Brooklyn Dodgers, St. Louis Cardinals, and Detroit Tigers—were particularly interested.

Most of the other kids in Al's neighborhood took summer jobs if they could find them. But Nicholas Kaline encouraged his son to play as much baseball as possible in the recreational and industrial leagues that flourished around Baltimore at the time, as well as in pickup games whenever and wherever Al could find them.

That made for a busy schedule. Kaline often played for four or five teams in the same summer, which sometimes meant as many as three games, on three different fields, on the same day. Since Al was not yet old enough to drive, his dad and his uncles Bib and Fred took turns chauffeuring him from field to field, team to team, game to game, with young Kaline often changing uniforms in the backseat of the car.

"I'd play a game at one end of town, then my father or an uncle would drive me to another game," he remembered. "I would change uniforms in the car on the way. Sometimes, I'd play three games a day. I never got enough."

All of that experience against top-caliber competition came in handy in 1953 when Kaline went straight from Southern High School to the big leagues.

But it wasn't all joy and bliss.

"I suffered a lot as a kid, playing in all those games," Kaline later admitted when a writer from *Sports Illustrated* asked young Al about his early years. "You know how Baltimore is real hot in the summer? When everybody was going on their vacations, going swimming with other kids, here I was on Sundays playing doubleheaders and all, because I knew I wanted to be a ballplayer.

"My dad always told me, 'You're gonna have to work hard, and you're gonna have to suffer if you're gonna be a ballplayer. You're gonna have to play and play all the time.'

"There were a couple of times when I told my dad I wasn't gonna play on Sunday. I was gonna go down to the beach with my girl or with a bunch of the guys and go swimming. And he said, 'Now look, like I told you in the beginning when you agreed to play for these people, they're gonna be counting on you. So if you're not gonna play, tell 'em to tear your contract up.'

"So I would go play. It was these things he did that showed me the right way and pushed me the right way."

"The Best I Ever Saw"

When 40-year-old Detroit Tigers scout Ed Katalinas, a Pennsylvania high school teacher and football coach by trade, first laid eyes on young Al Kaline in 1950, what he saw was a string bean—and every scout's dream.

Kaline was, without a doubt, the find of Katalinas' life.

"He was one of those golden boys," Katalinas later recalled. "He had a great thing that we all look for as we develop ourselves as scouts. We look for a boy with instinct. Al had the obvious intangibles.

"He was only 15 then, and I had heard about him the spring before, in 1949," Katalinas continued. "I had gone down to Baltimore to sign a boy named Charley Johnson, who was an all-star. Charley never made it, but I won't forget him.

"I was about to leave his house, when he said, 'Ed, there's a boy around the corner by the name of Al Kaline who is going to be quite a ballplayer.' I said, 'How old is he?' He said, 'Oh, he's going to be a freshman in high school.'

"That was the first time I heard the name Al Kaline. I didn't do anything about it until the next year when I went back to look at Johnson's brother. The moment I saw Kaline, I forgot all about the brother."

That was the same Charley Johnson who had introduced young Al to American Legion coach Walter Youse.

A Baltimore "bird dog," a newspaper reporter and baseball aficionado named Murray Wieman who scoured the sandlots and high school fields searching for diamonds in the rough, also alerted Katalinas to Kaline.

Nearly 20 years later, I worked with Wieman at the *Baltimore Evening Sun*. He was still claiming credit for discovering Al Kaline.

"Murray Wieman was around all the time at my games when Katalinas couldn't get there," Al recalled.

The first time Katalinas laid eyes on Kaline, he was sold.

"Kaline was the best I ever saw as a young player," Katalinas declared years later. "And I've seen a lot of them. I've seen thousands of them.

"After the game, I spoke to the kid and introduced myself," Katalinas remembered. "The poise came through in conversation, too. He was shy, always had been, but there was no doubt about what he wanted to do. He wanted to play baseball, period. I made a point right away of meeting his family. His father, Nick, worked in a broom factory, and he had several baseball-mad uncles who followed him around from game to game. I got to be friends with all of them.

"I saw him twice that year and came back again the next year. He had begun to put on some weight and was hitting the ball harder and longer. He was playing in the outfield then, and his arm was stronger than ever. By the middle of the season, he was the most touted and scouted boy in Baltimore.

"He was playing ball constantly, on the high school team, with the Westport Post No. 33 of the American Legion, and in the recreational leagues. Baltimore had a splendid recreation program that provided baseball for boys of all ages. This made it possible for Kaline to play with four or five different teams all the time.

"I'd be there, as often as I could," the Tigers' talent sleuth continued. "I felt that every time Al saw me, I'd make him believe in Detroit as much as I believed in him. Pretty soon, I started driving him around from park to park myself. I began to figure what he'd be worth. The family wasn't too well-off, and it was obvious they'd want bonus money."

By the time Kaline was a senior at Southern High, Katalinas knew the Philadelphia Phillies and St. Louis Cardinals were also interested. And the

Brooklyn Dodgers, realizing their earlier mistake when they turned Al away at one of their tryout camps, had jumped on Kaline's bandwagon. Katalinas worked hard to make certain he maintained the inside track on Al.

"Ed Katalinas got real close to my family, my father in particular," Kaline recalled. "He told my father not to sign anything until he had a chance to talk with us."

Katalinas was determined not to let young Kaline slip away. He asked his boss, Tigers farm director John McHale, to travel to Baltimore to see the skinny young phenom for himself.

"We can't afford to miss this boy," Katalinas wrote in a memo to McHale back in Detroit. "Just thinking about him is keeping me awake at night."

Katalinas informed the Tigers front office, in no uncertain terms, that Kaline was already better than any of the guys playing in their big-league outfield. At the time, that included Bob Nieman, Jim Delsing, and Don Lund.

In 1952 the Tigers had finished in last place in the American League for the first time in the history of the franchise, which dates back to 1901. The team had few players of note, and their fans and the Detroit media were becoming increasingly and openly disenchanted with the hometown team.

The Tigers had shelled out $55,000 to sign bonus-baby shortstop Harvey Kuenn off the campus of the University of Wisconsin in 1952. But Kuenn alone wasn't enough to placate the fans and jump-start ticket sales. The Tigers needed more.

At Katalinas' continued urging, McHale, who had actually set his sights on signing a pitcher named Tom Qualters, flew to Baltimore to see Kaline for himself. Al cooperated, collecting two hits, missing a home run by inches, and demonstrating his finesse in the field, the power and accuracy of his arm, and his speed on the base paths—all on one May afternoon.

"I've seen enough," a convinced McHale told Katalinas before boarding a plane for the flight back to Detroit.

Qualters eventually signed with the Philadelphia Phillies a couple of days before Kaline graduated from high school. He appeared in one game in 1953, then spent the entire 1954 season on the bench, never once throwing a pitch. Qualters' Philly teammates called him "Money Bags." In 34 appearances over three years, he never won or lost a big-league game.

"In June 1953, I told Johnny McHale, our farm director, that I was going to put all my eggs in one basket and concentrate on Kaline," Katalinas recalled. "McHale, who had already sold Spike Briggs, the president, and Muddy Ruel, our general manager, gave me the go-ahead."

Still, Katalinas was worried. There was no amateur draft in baseball in those days. Back in the early 1950s, budding young superstars weren't drafted by anybody except the U.S. Army. Players were free to sign with whomever they pleased—for as much money as they could get.

Baseball didn't introduce its annual amateur free-agent draft until 1965. Instead, promising young players and their parents were wooed by scouts whose sole mission in life was to try to sign as many kids as cheaply as possible in the hope that one or two of them might someday make it to the big leagues.

However, players could not sign until they had graduated from high school. Kaline's graduation day was June 17, 1953, and Katalinas was certain rival scouts were ready to pounce on his pet prodigy—some, perhaps, with bonus offers bigger than the Tigers' offer. It was a very hush-hush, cutthroat business.

"I went up to Baltimore and holed up in a hotel in the lower part of town several days in advance of Al's graduation on the 17th," Katalinas later recalled. "I dropped in on Al and his parents a couple of times and then asked for an appointment at one minute past midnight—the first minute of the morning of the 18th—when I could legally tender him a contract.

"'Ed,' Nick Kaline said, 'you won't be able to do that. Al has got a date with his girl, and he won't be home then. Around 10 in the morning will be okay.'"

Katalinas admitted he "didn't sleep much" that night. After tossing and turning and rising early, he arrived at 2222 Cedley Street at 10:00 sharp, hoping for the best—but, like all good scouts, fearing the worst.

Father and son were waiting in the living room when Katalinas entered the Kaline family home. Kaline didn't have an agent. Agents were unheard of in those days.

Immediately, Nicholas Kaline stood up. "I'll leave you two alone," he said. "It's up to Al to choose his club."

"We talked in general first, and then specifically," Katalinas recalled. "I mentioned taxes, and somewhere along the line I dropped a figure of $30,000. I sensed that Al had about that much in mind. McHale was waiting at the phone in Detroit if I had to go higher."

Young Al was well aware of the rules regarding bonus money that were in place at the time. He knew that if he accepted more than $6,000 in bonus money for signing, he would have to spend the next two years in the big leagues with the Tigers, presumably riding the bench, instead of gaining valuable playing time and experience in the minors.

If Kaline took the bonus bucks, it could actually set his career back because he would probably be shipped to the minor leagues for a year or two of seasoning after he had served his mandatory two-year stint with the Tigers.

But Al had done his homework. He knew the Detroit Tigers were in dire need of good young players. And he thought that maybe, just maybe, under those circumstances, he might get an opportunity to play more often with the Tigers than he would get on a club that was better stocked and stronger. Of course, Kaline realized, that would depend upon his doing well.

In addition, Al wanted to pay off the mortgage on his parents' modest home, to repay them for their years of sacrifice while he was learning to play the game. Al also knew his mother needed cataract surgery to save her failing eyesight.

That was why he wanted the bonus money. "I figured the least I could do was get as big a bonus as I could and give it to my parents," Kaline later explained.

The press reported then, and throughout the years, that the Tigers gave Kaline a $35,000 bonus to sign. It's absolutely untrue, and that distortion of the facts has long rankled Kaline.

"It was a $15,000 bonus, plus two year's salary of $6,000 each, which was the major-league minimum at the time," Al revealed, finally setting the record straight.

The total value of the contract was $27,000.

Today, that sounds like peanuts. The minimum major-league salary in 2009 was $400,000. In 2007 the Tigers paid $7.285 million to land their first-round draft pick, pitcher Rick Porcello, who, like Kaline, signed straight out of high school.

But by baseball's standards in 1953, $27,000 was a significant sum.

"Al said, 'Let me talk to my parents,'" Katalinas recalled. "Al went back into the kitchen, where his mother was cooking lunch, and I waited with my fingers crossed. When he reappeared, he was smiling that nice kid's smile of his. "'Okay, Ed,' he said. 'We'll accept your offer. When do I have to report?'"

Katalinas pulled the contract out of his suit-coat pocket. Al signed first and then, because he was not yet of legal age, he slid the paper across the table to his dad for his signature.

But just as Nicholas Kaline was about to sign and make the deal official, Al held up his right hand. "Wait a minute," he said. "I just thought of something."

Katalinas' heart skipped a beat. "What's the matter?" the scout asked with a worried frown. "Is there something wrong with the contract?"

"No," Al replied. "But I promised to play in a semipro game with United Iron and Metal on Sunday.

"I'll sign," young Kaline told Katalinas, "but I can't back out on my team."

Katalinas was momentarily stunned. The Tigers were offering Kaline $27,000 and a chance to realize his dream of a big-league career, and young Al was worried about making a farewell appearance on the sandlots.

However, Katalinas was not about to let anything kill the deal.

"Yes," he finally said with a sigh. "You can play. But," he quickly cautioned, "don't get hurt!"

Katalinas returned to his home in Shenandoah, Pennsylvania, for a long weekend, a happy man.

"I watched Kaline throughout his entire high school career," Katalinas later recalled. "I saw him grow, gain weight, attain physical strength, and develop into an outstanding player.

"He showed plus-factors in all departments of the game. For a boy so young, his coordination was amazing. Every action on the field showed perfect baseball instinct. Hustling every minute, he took advantage of every opportunity to take an extra base. His sliding technique was almost perfect. Al was a prospect who didn't fit into any ordinary category."

Like Kaline, Katalinas had grown up poor, the son of a coal miner. And, like Kaline, "Kat," as he came to be known, had long loved baseball. Like Kaline's father and uncles, he too had played some semipro ball.

While enrolled at Georgetown University, where he played tackle on the football team, Katalinas met Spike Briggs, the son of the Tigers' wealthy owner, Walter O. Briggs.

In 1940 Katalinas wrote to his college buddy, Spike, asking for a summer job as a scout. Briggs offered Katalinas a few hundred dollars, plus expenses, to work as a part-time scout, and Katalinas spent his summers wandering from ballfield to ballfield in northeastern Pennsylvania, searching for prospects.

It was there, at Reading High School, that Katalinas spotted a husky 15-year-old high school sophomore named Vic Wertz, who would later play for the Tigers from 1947 to 1952 and again from 1961 to 1963.

"That gave me confidence in my own judgment," said Katalinas, who became a full-time scout for the Tigers in 1945 and was named their director of scouting in 1956, three years after he signed Kaline. "I had never even had minor-league experience, but when Vic started to develop, I knew I could spot a good ballplayer when I saw one."

Later, on Katalinas' recommendation, the Tigers plucked pitcher Denny McLain out of the Chicago White Sox farm system and signed outfielder Jim Northrup, among others.

Ed Katalinas, like Al Kaline, was a product of a different era. A time when baseball-minded men scoured the country, searching for youngsters who could play baseball, possibly even at the big-league level someday.

In earlier years, freelance scouts, sometimes called "bird dogs," had beat the bushes and the backwoods, hunting for talent. When they stumbled across somebody good, they got paid.

During the 1930s and 1940s, when the Tigers won four pennants and two world championships and finished second five times, their staff of bush-beaters was led by a long-forgotten fellow named Ed Goosetree, who flushed out such future big-league stars as Tommy Bridges, Gee Walker, and Pete Fox.

In those days, semipro and rural baseball ruled in America.

By the 1950s, scouting had become more of a science. Recognizing a young man's ability to run and throw and hit was no longer enough. A good scout also had to be able to analyze a kid's mental makeup and character.

Guys like Ed Katalinas, Tom Greenwade of the New York Yankees, and Cy Slapnicka of the Cleveland Indians had to be part diplomat, part salesman, part psychiatrist, part investment broker, and part statistician.

"Above all, a scout has got to be able to look into a boy's heart and mind," explained John McHale, Detroit's astute young farm director shortly after Kaline signed with the Tigers. McHale's own career as a player had been cut short by injury.

"How serious is the boy about baseball? Will he stick it out, keep coming back to Tigertown as long as we want him to? The scout has to be intuitive in many of these judgments, and usually they can be made only by watching a prospect over a number of years. Increasingly, we find the things that count are matters of background—discipline at home, strength of family stock, pride in accomplishment."

By the early 1950s, some 2,000 scouts, about 350 of them full-timers assigned to regional territories, roamed the country hunting for potential big-leaguers. A top scout could make as much as $15,000 a year plus expenses, which, of course, could be considerable, given all of their travel. That was considered decent money in those days.

The Tigers, whose farm system had been allowed to deteriorate during World War II, employed 21 full-time scouts. Katalinas was their eastern supervisor as well as the Tigers' chief scout in the states of Pennsylvania, Virginia, and Maryland.

Given the rising costs of signing and developing ballplayers, even in the days before million-dollar signing bonuses and free agency, mistakes could be costly. A good scout couldn't afford to make many—not if he wanted to keep his job.

If a youngster got homesick and quit or didn't pan out, it reflected poorly on the scout who had recommended and signed him.

"The biggest headache, though," McHale said at the time, "is the bonus rule. A scout gets caught in the middle—between hesitating to recommend paying a price and being afraid to lose a good prospect."

In today's baseball, money is everything. But from 1947 to 1965, significant signing bonuses came with a definite stigma. Young players who received signing bonuses of $6,000 or more were branded "Bonus Babies." It was not a complimentary term nor always in the best interest of a promising young ballplayer or of the team that paid what was then considered big bucks to sign him.

From 1953 through 1957, Bonus Babies, regardless of age or readiness, had to be immediately placed on a team's active big-league roster—and remain there for two calendar years from their signing date.

Baseball had enacted the Bonus Rule in 1947 in response to the costly bidding wars that had heated up again following the conclusion of World War II, when the teams with money—most notably the New York Yankees, Brooklyn Dodgers, Boston Red Sox, and St. Louis Cardinals—sought to sign as many promising kids as possible, then stash them away in their sprawling farm systems until they were needed at the big-league level or as trade bait. Teams that didn't have that kind of cash to spread around were clearly at a disadvantage.

All 16 major-league teams carried at least one Bonus Baby at one time or another. Some carried several. From 1953 through 1957, baseball had 57 Bonus Babies—none of whom, by the way, were players of African American or Latin American descent.

Although baseball's color barrier had fallen in 1947—thanks to Jackie Robinson—and most teams were actively pursuing black and Latino prospects, none were ever given enough money at the time of their signing to cause the Bonus Rule to kick in.

Not surprisingly, the established major-leaguers, many of whom would never make anything close to the money that the Bonus Babies had already received, and most of whom had spent long years in the minor leagues paying their dues, openly resented the kids who were taking up space on the bench, taking jobs and money away from more experienced players who might have actually helped the team win.

That, too, was something young Kaline would have to deal with after he signed.

When Katalinas began courting Kaline, Al had liked him almost immediately.

"I liked him because he was so sincere," Kaline recalled. "He was never a pest, even though he was around so much. I knew he was telling the truth about the Tigers needing outfielders, too, and I figured I'd be playing regular a lot sooner in Detroit than anywhere else.

"There were a lot of teams after me. Quite honestly, two teams, Philadelphia and Boston, offered me more money than Detroit. But both teams were good at the time and had a lot of good outfielders. We wanted to go to a team I might have a chance to make.

"The only reason I signed with Detroit was because I wanted to play right away," Kaline continued. "I didn't want to go somewhere and sit on the bench and not play. That was my one fear. I wasn't worried about money at that time. I just wanted to play baseball. But I knew if I played a lot and I played well, I'd make a pretty good salary."

Kaline never spent a day in the minors—a rarity in baseball, then and now. He went straight to the big leagues, as required by the rules. And he never looked back.

"Before I signed with Detroit, I asked Ed Katalinas, 'Who is Detroit's best minor-league outfielder?'" Kaline recalled.

"He said, 'It's a guy named Bill Tuttle.' I asked Ed, 'What did he hit last year?' Ed said, 'He hit about .280 at Buffalo.' I was stupid enough to say to myself, 'Well, I can hit .280.'"

CHAPTER 4

Batboy's Jersey, and a Locker in the John

Ed Katalinas, the Detroit Tigers' middle-aged talent sleuth who had been on the trail of young Al Kaline for more than three years, was not about to leave anything to chance where his prize catch was concerned. He knew Al was the find of a lifetime.

On Tuesday, June 23, 1953, Katalinas showed up on the stoop of the Kaline home on Cedley Street, ready to personally chauffeur young Al and his father Nicholas from Baltimore to Philadelphia, where the Tigers, in the midst of a 14-day, four-city road trip, would be playing the Athletics.

Al had already said his emotional good-byes to his mother and to his high school sweetheart, Louise Hamilton, and was waiting with his bag packed when Katalinas knocked on the family's front door.

During the three-hour drive north, Kaline didn't talk much. In addition to his natural reticence, Al was lost in thought about the uncertainties of the adventure that lay ahead. The moment he had been preparing for all of his young life had arrived.

The three men reached the Tigers' hotel in downtown Philadelphia a little later than Katalinas had planned, and the team was already aboard the bus, ready to depart for the ballpark, when Katalinas' car pulled up to the curb.

"Everybody who has ever ridden a team bus in the big leagues knows that the bus doesn't wait for anybody," Kaline recalled. "When it's time for that bus to leave, it leaves. And the whole team was on the bus by the time we got to the hotel.

"When we pulled up in the car, the bus was ready to leave. Tigers manager Fred Hutchinson was already on the bus. But when Ed Katalinas jumped on the bus and told Hutchinson we were there, Hutch told the bus driver to hold up for a moment.

"I got out of the car, grabbed my bag, gave it to the bellman, and told him to take it up to my room. And I got on the bus right away.

"I was scared to death," Kaline admitted. "I was just a skinny kid. I didn't even know where to sit. And these were all grown men. I had my high school graduation suit on. It was the only suit I owned. I could feel myself sweating under the arms. I could feel the sweat running down my sides."

Welcome to the big leagues, kid.

"Going to the ballpark on the bus was the hardest 30 minutes of my life," Kaline recalled. "I was the last one to get on, and I had to walk down that aisle between all the players.

"I really didn't know too much about the Detroit Tigers at that time. I just wanted to play baseball. I didn't know who was on the team. But I saw every eye as I walked down the aisle. It looked like a thousand eyes were staring right at me, saying, 'Who is this young punk?'

"Finally Teddy Gray, one of the Tigers' pitchers, grabbed me, and he said, 'Here, sit next to me.' He introduced himself and said he was happy I was on the team. He was the Tigers' player rep. He said if there was anything he could do, just let him know. On the way to ballpark, he kind of filled me in on what to expect, how to dress, tipping the clubhouse man, stuff like that.

"We finally got to the ballpark, and I kind of followed the other players along, walking behind them," Kaline continued. "I walked into the locker room and looked for my locker. I didn't know what number I had or anything."

As Kaline walked through the cramped visitors' clubhouse at ancient Shibe Park in north Philadelphia, he saw lockers bearing names such as

Dropo, Kuenn, Boone, Garver, and Hoeft. But Al didn't seen any locker that said Kaline. He wasn't sure what he should do. Finally the clubhouse attendant showed Al where he was to dress for his big-league debut.

"My locker was in the john," Kaline recalled, smiling at the memory that seems so incredibly ironic in retrospect.

"There was a nail in the wall, and that was where I hung up my clothes," he said. "On a nail. In the john."

"I was told that was what a new person coming into the big leagues had to do," Kaline added.

And there was another problem, an even more humbling problem. The Tigers didn't have a uniform small enough to fit their new bonus baby from Baltimore.

"I was so skinny they had to get a uniform made up for me, but that first night or two, I had to wear a batboy's uniform," Kaline admitted.

Al Kaline, future first-ballot Hall of Famer, spent his first day in the big leagues wearing a baseball jersey and trousers that belonged to the batboy.

"I'd brought my glove and my spikes and my sliding pads with me," Al recalled. "That was all I had. I didn't know how to start getting dressed, so I kind of sat there and watched the others. I saw how they'd put on their white socks first and then the oversocks, and I'd do the same thing. I was trying to be casual about the whole thing. I didn't want them to know I didn't know anything at all. I noticed that none of them had sliding pads. I didn't know whether I should use mine. Finally, I made a big decision. I'd wear them. That made me feel good. I'd made a decision on my own.

"I was one of the last ones out of the clubhouse. I didn't know what I was supposed to do. The guys were playing catch, but I couldn't just go out there and start playing catch with them. So I sat on the bench for a while and watched the other team take batting practice. I didn't dare go near the batting cage, so I just watched from there. The Tigers had signed up another bonus player that day, a 17-year-old pitcher named Bob Miller, so when he came out, the two of us played catch.

"Fred Hutchinson was the manager of the team, and he was a big gruff guy who always seemed so serious all the time," Kaline continued. "He's got that long face, and he says to me, 'So you're our new bonus player, huh? I hear good reports about you. I don't know when we'll play you, but I want you to sit next to me on the bench. If I'm too busy, I'll tell you what player to sit next to. All I want is for you to give me 100 percent.'

"I didn't know what he was talking about," Kaline admitted. "A hundred percent? I had never heard that before. I had always just played.

"Hutchinson told me the regulars hit first. He told me to go shag some flies, and when the regulars were finishing hitting, I'd come in and hit with the other guys.

"Once I got in the field, I felt very comfortable," Kaline recalled. "When I took fly balls with the other outfielders, I knew I could do what they did, only better. I could run, and I could catch the ball. That was no problem. When I saw them throw, I knew I could throw better than the other outfielders the Tigers had, unless they weren't really trying. So that eased my mind, right there. I started to relax a little.

"Now hitting, that was another story. It was scary to even think about it. Here I was, an 18-year-old kid. How was I going to hit major-league pitching?

"Back in those days, the pitchers who needed to get in more work used to throw batting practice to the extra guys," Kaline continued.

"Hutch had told me, 'Go up there, and the other guys will tell you when to hit.' Sure enough, as soon as a big side-arming right-hander came in to pitch, the veterans said, 'OK, kid, it's your turn. You can take five swings now.'

"I wanted to hit the ball hard on my first swing. I remember that. I didn't want to miss it, but I wanted to swing hard. I hit a ground ball to second base.

"Fortunately, even when I first came up, I didn't strike out much. I usually put the ball in play. It might have been weak, but I got my bat on the ball. I didn't strike out. In those days, it was embarrassing to strike out.

"When the game started, I sat next to Hutchinson like he said I should," Kaline said.

"I was still scared to death. But it was a good scared. I'd have to say the first day in Philadelphia, the first time I put a major-league uniform on, that was my greatest thrill—even if it was a batboy's uniform."

The Tigers' outfield at the time consisted of Bob Nieman, Don Lund, and Jim Delsing with Steve Souchock and Pat Mullin in reserve. It was hard to see exactly where the skinny young bonus baby from Baltimore would fit in, particularly in the beginning. But Kaline was confident in his ability. And he was determined to be ready to make the most of any opportunity that came his way.

Kaline knew he was entering a whole new world. He knew he had a lot to learn, and he knew he was probably destined to ride the Tigers' bench for most of the next two years.

What Kaline didn't know, what Katalinas had never told him during all of their courtship conversations or on the ride from Baltimore to Philadelphia, was that the Tigers' front office was already looking five years down the road where young Al was concerned.

They would keep him around for the next two years, as required by the Bonus Rule, using him sparingly as a pinch-hitter or pinch-runner and occasionally as an outfielder, then ship him to their Triple A farm club at Buffalo, where he could play every day for two or three years of minor-league seasoning. Then in 1957 or maybe in '58, Kaline would hopefully be ready to play in the big leagues.

On June 25, 1953, a week after Al had picked up his diploma at Baltimore's Southern High School and signed his first contract, he made his major-league debut before a crowd of 2,368, none of whom took more than passing notice of the skinny kid wearing uniform No. 25. Kaline was 18 years, six months, and six days old at the time.

While the Tigers were up at bat in the top half of the eighth inning of a game against Connie Mack's Athletics, Hutchinson turned to the anxious young man sitting alongside him on the bench in the dugout and said simply, "You play right field when Philadelphia bats."

Again there was a problem: Kaline had been a pitcher and a shortstop and a center fielder in high school and sandlot ball. However, he had never played right field in his life, not for one game. Nevertheless, that was where he was going to make his big-league debut, replacing Jim Delsing.

But Kaline didn't dare tell Hutchinson he'd never played there before. He had been given his first opportunity, and he was determined to make the most of it. He never said a word. "The outfield was the outfield to me," he recalled more than half a century later.

Al grabbed his glove and trotted out to right field, where he looked to center fielder Don Lund to position him for each batter, gesturing at him to move closer to the line or over toward center.

Kaline completed the half-inning without incident. Mercifully, no balls were hit his way.

When he ran back to the dugout, Kaline realized he was scheduled to be the leadoff hitter in the top half of the ninth.

Mickey Mantle was 19 years old when he took his first big-league swing. Willie Mays and Hank Aaron were both 20. Joe DiMaggio was 21. Al Kaline was 18. Things were happening so fast, they almost became a blur.

"I didn't have a bat," Kaline recalled. "I didn't bring one with me. So I just grabbed the first one near me and went out into the on-deck circle. The funny thing is, the next thing I remember, I'm standing there at home plate. I don't even remember walking up there or anything. Harry Byrd is pitching for them. He was a big guy, about 6'4", with square shoulders. He was a beer drinker, a gruff-looking guy, and on top of it, he threw sidearm.

"I couldn't think. My whole mind was a complete blank. I was scared, white as a sheet. I couldn't wait to get out of there. There must have been only three or four thousand people in the ballpark, but I thought a million eyes were on me. I could actually feel them.

"I hit the first pitch, and it went out to center field for a fly ball. It wasn't too shallow, but it wasn't too deep. The guy caught it easily. I don't remember getting back to the dugout. I don't remember sitting down. I don't remember anything except swinging at that first pitch."

Kaline's mother, Naomi, had joined her husband in Philadelphia for Al's big-league debut.

"We were shaking all over, and he said later he was, too," Naomi later recalled. "He was white as a sheet. But he hit the ball."

After the game, Detroit newspaper reporter Hal Middlesworth, who would later become the Tigers' public-relations director, approached Hutchinson and asked, "What do you think of your new boy?"

"He's got great wrists," the Tigers manager replied. "He'll be a good one." Kaline had passed his first big-league test, but there were many, many more to come.

A couple of days later, Kaline was again sent into a game as a defensive replacement.

"I don't know whose place I took," he recalled, "but I went to right field. We were ahead by a run in the ninth. They had guys on second and third, Ted Gray was the pitcher, and the batter hit a line drive out to right. I started in for the ball, but I just couldn't get to it. It sort of short-hopped me. It bounced off my glove and rolled away, and both runs scored. We lost the game.

"I thought I should have caught it because I was used to catching everything on the sandlots. But they hit the ball a lot sharper in the major leagues, and I just couldn't reach the ball this time.

"I had to go into the dressing room, and who was sitting there next to me? Teddy Gray. I was sitting there, and I felt like crying. I really thought I should have had it. But before I knew it, he put his arm around my shoulder and said, 'Don't worry about it. You made a helluva effort. A lot of guys wouldn't have even tried for the ball.' Teddy Gray. The pitcher. He was sitting there trying to make me feel good when I just cost him the ballgame."

Before long, it would look as if right field had been invented for Al Kaline.

Late on the night of June 28, following a Sunday doubleheader in Washington, the Tigers returned to Detroit by train to begin Kaline's first homestand.

More than five decades later, on September 27, 1999, the day Tiger Stadium closed its doors forever, Kaline recalled his first glimpse of the storied gray fortress at the intersection of Michigan and Trumbull.

"It was 3:00 or 4:00 in the morning, and we were coming on the team bus down Michigan Avenue from the old train station," Kaline remembered.

"I was sitting next to Johnny Pesky, and he leaned over to me and said, 'Look out the left window. That's going to be your home for the next two or three years.'

"It was dark, but I peeked out. I thought it looked like a great big battleship."

I asked Al if he recalled the first time he ever set foot in the ancient ballyard, then known as Briggs Stadium, that would in fact be his stage for the next 22 years. How could he ever forget?

Eighteen-year-old Al Kaline didn't know anybody in Detroit. Nor did he know anything about the city. The ballclub had arranged a room for him in the Tuller Hotel on Bagley in downtown Detroit, and, after getting directions to the ballpark, on June 30, 1953, Kaline walked alone for the first time down Michigan Avenue to the fabled corner of Michigan and Trumbull.

But again there was a problem. The guard on duty at the gate wouldn't let Kaline—who had grown to 6'1" but who still weighed only 155 pounds—into the ballpark.

"He said I didn't look like a ballplayer," Kaline recalled. "He said, 'Where do you think you're going, kid?' I said, 'I'm a new player.' And the guard said, 'Yeah, sure you are,' something to that effect. I was real skinny, 155 pounds. I'm sure I looked just like a lot of the kids off the street."

Somehow, Kaline finally convinced the guard that he was legit.

"It was a sunny day," Al recalled, "and after I turned the corner in the corridor on my way to the clubhouse, I ducked down one of the walkways to sneak a look at the field.

"I remember thinking, *This is the greenest grass I've ever seen.* The magnitude of the stadium and the greenness of the seats, it was amazing. It was the prettiest place I ever saw in my life. On that day, I was awestruck.

"That memory has always stayed with me. I was only 18, but I thought, *This place looks like a big-league ballpark is supposed to look.* I thought, *This is the most beautiful ballpark I've ever seen.*" Of course, at that point, young Kaline had only seen four other big-league ballparks in his life.

Longtime Tigers general manager and club president Jim Campbell was the assistant farm director when Kaline first joined the team in 1953. Years later, I asked Campbell if he could remember the first time he had laid eyes on the skinny 18-year-old outfielder.

"We heard he was on the field working out, so Ed Katalinas, John McHale, and I went down to have a look," Campbell recalled.

"There he was—at second base. Hutch [Tigers manager Fred Hutchinson] took one look at him, saw he was so skinny, and didn't think he would be able to hit enough to play the outfield," Campbell admitted.

It wasn't the first time somebody had underestimated young Kaline's ability—or his determination.

At the time, Steve Souchock was the Tigers' right-fielder-in-waiting. It appeared likely it would be Souchock's job that young Kaline, the bonus baby, might someday take.

Nevertheless, Souchock often sat next to Kaline on the bench, advising him on how to position himself in the outfield when different batters were at the plate and on what pitches they liked to swing at.

During the daily pregame practice sessions, veteran Pat Mullin, who was approaching the end of his career, and Souchock—two of the guys Kaline had felt staring at him on the bus that first day in Philadelphia—helped Al with his outfield play, coaching him on how to hit the cutoff man and other such intricacies.

Another veteran, second baseman Johnny Pesky, showed Al how to place the ball to left or to right with his bat, and he sharpened his bunting skills.

Years later, Kaline would say that Pesky, who later became a player and longtime coach with the Boston Red Sox, taught him as much as anyone about the game.

On July 8, 1953, in a 14–4 loss, Kaline collected the first of his 3,007 big-league hits, a single to left field off Chicago's Luis Aloma. But Al's first days and weeks in the big leagues were hardly filled with high-fives and hugs.

"I was an outcast," Kaline recalled more than a half-century later. "I took somebody's job who had spent four or five years in the minors getting to the big leagues. And here I come in right out of high school. Somebody had to be let go. The friends of that person didn't know me, but they didn't like me."

Tigers pitcher Ray Herbert remembered the veteran players' reaction to young Kaline that first summer.

"At that time, the minimum salary was $6,000, and a lot of guys on the team were only making $8,500 or $9,000," Herbert recalled. "And here comes Al, right out of high school, with that big bonus, making more money than a lot of the veterans.

"He took a little ribbing from the other fellows. In those days, rookies weren't treated the way they are today. But Al never said a word. He was so quiet. That probably helped him get through that first year or two. If you say something back, you give the other guy a chance to retaliate."

Hall of Fame catcher Rick Ferrell, a longtime Tigers executive, was the team's third-base coach when Kaline broke in. Years later, Ferrell remembered how alarmed he had been when the raw rookie was sent in as a pinch-runner for slow-footed slugger Walt Dropo in the tenth inning of a July 21, 1953, game against the Washington Senators.

The game had been tied at 6–6 at the end of nine innings, but the Senators pushed the potential winning run across the plate in the top half of the tenth. With the Tigers down to their final out in the bottom of the tenth, Pat Mullin walked and Dropo singled.

On the Tigers' bench, Hutchinson hollered, "Kaline, run for Dropo!"

Don Lund was up next, and Hutchinson wanted somebody on first base who might have a chance to score the winning run if Lund came through with a clutch base hit.

"Kaline took the damnedest lead I ever saw," Ferrell recalled. "He was way off the bag at first. I was so sure he was going to get picked off, I called timeout. I stopped the game, went over to first base, and told him he had better stay closer.

"But the next guy up, Don Lund, hit a double to left, and Al scored all the way from first to win the game."

High above the field, in the Briggs Stadium press box, a Detroit sportswriter, impressed by Kaline's display of speed, called Al "the Baltimore

Greyhound." Mercifully, the nickname never stuck. It was but the first of 1,622 runs that Kaline would score in his career.

However, for an 18-year-old who had never been away from home, life in the big leagues was a lonely, unsettling experience—hardly what young Kaline had dreamed about while romping around on the Baltimore sandlots.

"As the days went on, I didn't mind the games," Kaline recalled. "In fact, I looked forward to them. That was the easiest part of all. I couldn't wait to get to the ballpark. I'd be the first one out there, and I was willing to do anything. I think that's why the veterans liked me.

"But the rest of it really scared me," Al admitted. "I just didn't know what to do when we were on the road.

"I used to wear the same clothes every day when I lived at home," he confessed. "I'd wear a pair of jeans three or four days in a row. The same shirt. The same shoes. I didn't know any different. That's how I grew up.

"All of a sudden, I was in the major leagues and we were traveling from town to town, and I saw how the other players were dressing. Different suit every day. A different shirt. A different tie. There I was, I had only one suit, and I kept wearing it over and over, day after day. I was really embarrassed. I didn't even want to leave my hotel room at night to go out and eat.

"If there was a radio in the room, I'd play the radio. But not all the rooms had radios. And, of course, there was no television. I'd just sort of sit there and think until I finally went out and bought myself a couple of sport coats.

"I moved into the Wolverine Hotel in Detroit. That was the first time I had ever lived alone. I didn't know what to do with my time. We didn't play many night games—14 or so—so I was off almost every night. I'd go to the movies a lot and just walk around the streets looking in the store windows. It was 10 or 11 or 12:00 at night, and I had nothing to do. I didn't even know who to talk to. So I was just wandering around the streets feeling pretty lonely."

The ballpark became Kaline's sanctuary. That was the only place he felt comfortable. He was up early, especially when the Tigers were at home. "The toughest time was waiting to go to the ballpark, living in a hotel room by myself, not having anyone to eat with," Kaline recalled.

He was often the first player to arrive at the ballpark. And why not? The other Tigers had lives and wives and families. Kaline was all alone. He had nothing better to do, on the road or at home. "Away from the ballpark, it was a solitary life," he admitted.

Kaline would sit in front of his locker in his underwear, boning his bats or working on his glove, as baseball players have done since the beginning of time.

On September 16, 1953, in Boston, Kaline started a big-league game for the first time, replacing center fielder Jim Delsing, who was down with the flu. All Al did was collect three singles and the first of his 1,583 RBIs as the Tigers downed the Red Sox 8–3.

Before the game, manager Fred Hutchinson took young Kaline across the field to the Boston dugout and introduced him to the legendary Ted Williams, who had batted .406 a dozen years earlier.

Until the day he died in 2002, Williams never tired of talking about hitting, especially with players who spoke the same language. So he was more than willing to share his expertise with the slender young Tigers outfielder, who—as Ted himself told me years later—reminded Williams of himself when he had been a rookie.

For a full 10 minutes the Red Sox slugger, who was famed for his superior eyesight, offered Kaline tips on how to strengthen his arms and wrists by repeatedly squeezing rubber balls during the off-season and how to more quickly identify curveballs and sliders as they neared home plate. Williams also advised Al on the proper approach to take with two strikes against him.

"Go up on the bat and protect the plate," Williams said. "Choke up just a little, but make sure you've got the whole strike zone in range."

Williams told Kaline how to adjust to pitches that were up or down in the strike zone.

"Get a good pitch," Williams preached. "You hear me? Get a good pitch!"

Kaline listened and learned.

"In 10 minutes, he helped me more than anyone I ever talked to," Kaline admitted. "He told me to swing a heavy bat during the off-season to strengthen my arms and shoulders and get snap in my wrists. He told me to squeeze a ball hard, like I was trying to twist the cover off it.

"But I guess the most important thing he told me was how to hit low pitches. He had seen me bat, and he said I was golfing the ball. He pointed out that I wasn't following the ball well enough and wasn't going down with the ball. He told me to use my regular stance on any pitch above my hips, but to go down with the ball if it was low and still in the strike zone. He said that way I could still keep my groove and the bat would come around lower."

A week later, Kaline faced former Negro Leagues legend Satchel Paige, who had finally gotten a chance to play in the major leagues with the Cleveland Indians at the age of 42.

Kaline went hitless in his first three at-bats against Paige but singled to left center in the eighth inning. Kaline's base hit, along with those of Steve Souchock and Jerry Priddy, helped send Paige to the showers. Afterward, Kaline called his single off Paige "a real thrill."

Four days later, sent to the plate as a pinch-hitter in the top of the ninth, Kaline belted his first big-league home run, the first of 399, off Cleveland Indians right-hander Dave Hoskins.

Although the Tigers were routed 12–3 by the Tribe that day, someone had the foresight to retrieve Kaline's home-run ball. It was presented to him in the clubhouse after the game.

Kaline played sparingly, appearing in only 30 games that first season, usually as a late-inning substitute. He got just 28 at-bats from late June through September, and he batted .250 with six singles and that one home run. He played five games in left field that first year, 11 in center, and four in right. He got into 10 games as a pinch-hitter or pinch-runner.

But that was enough to convince Fred Hutchinson that the kid was a keeper. Hutchinson was impressed with Kaline's fielding as well as with his speed on the base paths. "Not only that," the Tigers manager added, "but the kid will hit, too." Al's career was under way.

However, Kaline hadn't heard the last from Ted Williams. "For some reason, Ted took a liking to me early in my career," Kaline recalled. "And he loved to talk hitting with young players. Ted lived in a hotel not far from the one where the Tigers stayed in Boston in those days, and on one of our trips there a couple of years later, he called me up on the phone and invited me to come over."

Of course, Kaline went. "When God calls, you listen," Al said.

"I remember him asking me how I would hit against Early Wynn," Kaline recalled. "I don't remember what I said, but he stopped me and said something like, 'No, no, you dumb so-and-so. You know he's going to throw you that slider away. So here's what you've got to do.' Then he'd ask me about some other pitchers, and I was afraid to answer him because I didn't want to get yelled at again."

Years later, their paths crossed again one day in Boston early in Kaline's broadcasting career, long after Williams had retired.

"Ted had just come back from a fishing trip somewhere in New England, and when he walked into the pressroom at Fenway Park, people were scrambling all over, trying to get to him," Kaline said. "But he ran them all off with that gruff voice of his."

Given Williams' infamous disdain for the media, that certainly was no surprise. But then Ted bellowed, "I'm here for one reason: to say hello to Al Kaline." While the writers who had gathered in the rooftop media dining room stared, Williams headed straight for Kaline, who was eating his pregame meal at one of the tables across the room.

"He walked over, shook my hand, and said, 'Hi, Al. It's good to see you. How ya doing? How's the family?'" Kaline recalled.

"I said, 'Hi, Ted. Everything's great. Thanks for stopping by.' Something close to that. And then he was gone. It couldn't have taken more than a minute or two. But after he left, I felt like I could have walked on air."

Kaline returned to Baltimore at the conclusion of the 1953 season. As promised, Al used his bonus money to pay off what remained on the mortgage on his parents' home. "It wasn't a big house, the house was only worth maybe $15,000 or $20,000," he said.

And he paid for his mother's cataract surgery.

"I went to the hospital to visit her," Kaline recalled. "Back in those days, it was a major surgery. They had her arms strapped down and everything. I wasn't used to seeing my mother like that. I passed out."

"You're My Right Fielder"

As most ballplayers—young or old, rookie or star—did in those days, Al Kaline returned home to Baltimore after the 1953 baseball season ended and found a job. He went to work in a sporting-goods store. Al had given all of his bonus money to his parents and that $6,000 salary he was making would only stretch so far.

With Ted Williams' booming words of advice still ringing in his ears, whenever business was slow and Al got the chance, he would pick up a ball and squeeze it repeatedly, as hard as he could, or slip into the back of the store and swing a bat.

Eager to report to his first spring training with the Tigers, bigger and stronger than he had been the previous June and now knowing better what to expect—and what was expected of him—Kaline made a conscious effort to add some weight to his still-slender frame.

Before Al left for Lakeland, Florida, in February, he gave his girlfriend, Louise Hamilton, an engagement ring. Kaline had met Louise, who had been born in West Virginia, at Baltimore's Southern High School. Unlike many of the girls in school, Louise, who played neighborhood softball, could talk about baseball. That was critical to their relationship, because that was all young Al cared or talked about.

When Kaline arrived in Lakeland, Florida, which, except for three years during World War II, has been the Tigers' spring training home since 1934—the longest such marriage in baseball—manager Fred Hutchinson immediately noticed the difference in his young outfielder. At 6'1" and 165 pounds, Al was still slender, but he was no longer a skinny kid.

"You look in good shape, Al," Hutchinson said when Kaline reported to Henley Field, on the edge of downtown Lakeland. "The added weight will help."

"I followed Ted Williams' advice," Kaline told him.

"That'll help, too," his manager replied.

While Kaline had been busy selling sporting goods during the off-season, Steve Souchock, who was slated to be the Tigers' regular right fielder in 1954, had broken his wrist playing winter ball in Cuba.

For the time being, Hutchinson said, Kaline would fill in for Souchock in right field in the Tigers' Grapefruit League exhibition games. However, Hutchinson made it clear that once Souchock's wrist healed, hopefully in time for Opening Day, he would get his old job back. For Kaline, it meant another opportunity, and he was again determined to make the most of it.

Although he still appeared to lack the power that teams like to see in their outfielders, Kaline hit enough during spring training to convince Hutchinson he could handle the job.

When Souchock's wrist was slow in mending, Hutchinson decided Kaline would open the regular season in right field—even though some in the Tigers' front office weren't yet convinced young Al could hit with enough authority to justify a place in the every-day lineup.

"He's a great fielder," Hutchinson argued, "and he's got an arm like I've never seen before. And he'll hit. I'm sure of it." Eventually the front-office skeptics gave in to the manager. After all, it was his neck that was on the line, not theirs.

Hutchinson sought out Kaline at Henley Field one March afternoon to give him the good news. "You're my right fielder," Hutchinson told him, "until somebody else shows me they can take the job away from you."

Kaline had a new number, too; no more No. 25. Pat Mullin, one of Al's early mentors, had retired following the 1953 season and handed his uniform No. 6—the number that Stan Musial, one of Al's childhood heroes, had worn with the St. Louis Cardinals—down to Kaline.

"I went to Pat at the end of my first season. I knew he was going to retire, and I asked him if I could wear No. 6," Kaline recalled.

"I said, 'Pat, is it okay if I wear your number?' And he said, 'I'd be more than happy to have you wear it. When my son gets bigger, he can get No. 6 from you.'

"Which, of course, never happened," Al added. No. 6 would never again be worn by any Tiger except Kaline.

Two weeks into the 1954 season, Kaline's doubters in the Tigers clubhouse, upstairs in the front office, and in the stands at Briggs Stadium were shaking their heads, saying, "I told you so."

Kaline was batting just .220. And all nine of his base hits had been singles. There were those who seriously wondered if Al was destined to be just a singles hitter, a good player whose lack of power would prevent him from ever stepping up to the level of stardom.

To be perfectly honest, Kaline's fielding was all that was keeping him in the lineup. He caught just about everything that was hit his way, grabbing sinking line drives at his shoetops and climbing the fence in right field to pluck would-be base hits out of the air.

Hutchinson kept raving about his right fielder. "Kaline keeps making the kinds of plays we haven't seen in right field in years," the manager declared.

Finally, in early May, Kaline began to find himself at the plate. On May 8, he delivered three singles and a double in five at-bats in a 12–1 rout of the Chicago White Sox. Against Philadelphia 11 days later, he cracked a clutch bases-loaded single in the bottom of the ninth inning to win the game.

His batting average, which had briefly risen above .300, was a respectable .290, although Al still owned only one extra-base hit.

By this time, Steve Souchock's broken wrist had healed. But Hutchinson, who had fallen in love with Kaline's defense, didn't want to remove Al from right field.

"He's coming around," the manager insisted whenever the question of Kaline's hitting arose—as it often did, both in conversations with the media and with the Tigers brass. "His potential is so great, I can't take him out now."

A pulled groin muscle in late May put Kaline on the bench for one game, but Al talked his way back into the lineup the very next day, and with good reason. The Tigers were playing a doubleheader in Baltimore, and Kaline's parents, his two uncles, and his fiancée Louise all had tickets to the May 31 games.

Kaline put on quite a show for his family, banging out a double and a single and scoring three runs in addition to making two sterling catches in the outfield in the first game, then collecting three singles in three at-bats in the nightcap.

Eleven days later, Al belted his first home run of the season, a grand slam that helped the Tigers trounce the Philadelphia Athletics 16–5.

It was only the second home run Kaline had hit in the majors and, at 19, it made him, at the time, the second-youngest player in baseball history ever to belt a grand slam.

But it was still Kaline's glove and his arm that had people talking. In 1954, Kaline's first full season in pro ball, he threw out nine enemy runners who tried to grab an extra base on balls hit to right field.

In a game against Cleveland, Kaline tried to make a diving catch of a sinking line drive off the bat of Dale Mitchell. But the best that Al could do was to trap the ball. When Mitchell saw Kaline on the ground, he rounded first base without slowing down and headed for second, convinced he had an easy double. Kaline saw him running and realized he didn't have enough time to get back on his feet. So, from a sitting position in shallow right field, Al fired a strike to shortstop Harvey Kuenn, who was covering second on the play. Mitchell was out.

"My God, what an arm that kid has," Mitchell muttered after he had trotted back to the Indians dugout, shaking his head.

A couple of weeks later, in a game against the speed-minded Chicago White Sox, Kaline cut down Fred Marsh trying to score from second on a Nellie Fox single, threw out Jim Rivera attempting to advance from first to third on a base hit by Johnny Groth, and gunned down Minnie Minoso seeking to stretch a double into a triple.

Al's three assists in the game were just one shy of the major-league record. "That was a fair day, real fair," Kaline acknowledged with a small smile afterward. "I liked it."

After that, opponents stopped testing Al's arm.

"I was there because I was a fielder," Kaline later admitted. "That's what kept me in the league. The question was, did I have enough bat?" Kaline would answer that question, too, soon enough.

In addition to Kaline, the 1954 Tigers team included another bonus baby, shortstop Harvey Kuenn, who had been signed off the campus of the University of Wisconsin in 1952 for $52,000. In 1953 the tobacco-chewing Kuenn had batted .308 with a league-leading 209 hits and was named the American League's Rookie of the Year.

The press, always on the lookout for a catchy phrase, labeled Kuenn and Kaline the "K-K Kids."

Attorney Mickey Briggs, the grandson of longtime Tigers owner Walter O. Briggs and the son of Spike Briggs, who had inherited the team by the time Kaline signed, grew up around the ballpark that bore his family's name and often hung out in the dugout before games.

Mickey Briggs fondly remembered young Kaline's first years with the team. "He was a skinny kid out of high school, he was my age," Briggs recalled. "It marveled me to see a kid who was my age play like he could.

"When he was 19, you knew he was an All-Star. The two greatest days of my father's reign were when he signed Harvey Kuenn and Al Kaline. Kaline is the quality, class player that epitomizes Detroit Tiger baseball at its best."

When the Tigers' schedule took them to New York to play the Yankees, Kaline, no longer a wide-eyed high school kid being hurried through the Yankee Stadium locker room, was able to take his time and soak in all of the history and atmosphere in the fabled House That Ruth Built in the Bronx.

"I took the subway out to the ballpark with our trainer, Jack Homel, early in the afternoon," Kaline said. "I walked out to center field to look at the monuments."

Al was beginning to feel more at home in the big leagues. By the end of August, his batting average had climbed to .283, even though the Tigers were again going nowhere in the American League pennant race.

But late in the 1954 season, Kaline suffered the first of many injuries that would hamper him throughout the course of his career. Racing into foul territory down the right-field line at Briggs Stadium in hot pursuit of a fly ball, he crashed into a wall that jutted out toward the foul line in front of a section of box seats. Kaline caught the ball just as he ran into the barrier, whirled, and rifled it back to the infield. Then he passed out.

Al was hospitalized for five days. "I had water on my knee," he recalled.

After the season ended, Tigers president Spike Briggs ordered those box seats removed. "We don't want Kaline to get hurt there again," Briggs explained.

Although he hit only four home runs, Kaline played in 138 games in 1954 and batted a credible although hardly convincing .276. However, all but 25 of his 139 hits had been singles. And his 18 doubles and three triples had been due more to his speed on the base paths than to his actual power at the plate.

The fact that he had driven in only 43 runs—far from an acceptable total for an every-day outfielder—raised more than a few eyebrows in the Tigers' front office, which was growing increasingly desperate for a winning team and a slugging star who would give them a much-needed draw at the box office.

On October 16, 1954, two weeks after the season ended, 19-year-old Al Kaline and Louise Hamilton were married at St. John's Lutheran Church in Baltimore.

There were many people, in Detroit and elsewhere, who felt Fred Hutchinson, a burly, no-nonsense former pitcher and the youngest manager in the American League at the time, might have become one of the finest Tigers managers ever. He certainly would have been good for Kaline's career, especially in those formative years.

But Spike Briggs, the Tigers' playboy owner, stubbornly adhered to the policy of his late father, automobile industry tycoon Walter O. Briggs, who, as a matter of principle, had never granted any manager more than a two-year contract. When Hutchinson's contract expired at the end of the 1954 season, Hutch asked for a new three-to-five-year agreement. When Briggs balked, Hutchinson quit.

The Tigers brought back 58-year-old Bucky Harris, who had been managing big-league teams since 1924 and who had preceded Mickey Cochrane as the manager of the Tigers more than two decades earlier, from 1929 through 1933—never finishing higher than fifth and only once posting a winning record. It was a peculiar hire, to say the least.

Hutchinson, who moved on to manage the St. Louis Cardinals and Cincinnati Reds—piloting the Reds to the National League pennant in 1961—had been one of Kaline's staunchest supporters when he had struggled at the plate and when some in the Tigers' front office as well as many in the media and in the grandstand believed Al should have been benched.

"I've lost a backer," Kaline told Louise before the couple departed for Lakeland, Florida, and the start of spring training in 1955.

"You'll find another," she assured him.

CHA**6**TER

"Everything I Did Was Right"

The silver bat, symbolic of batting supremacy in the American League in 1955, still hangs in Al Kaline's den in his suburban Detroit home. More than half a century later, it remains one of his most prized possessions. Kaline has never been a trophy guy, but that one is a keeper.

"That's one of the few trophies I still have," Al admitted. "That, and one Gold Glove. I gave all my other Gold Gloves and stuff to my parents and kids and the grandkids."

Who needs the metal when you have the memories?

Ironically, under today's rules, skinny young Al Kaline would probably not have been in the big leagues, batting third for the Tigers in 1955 when he hit .340 and won his one and only batting crown.

Instead, Kaline, straight out of high school, would most likely have been sent directly to the Tigers' farm system in 1953. And he probably would have still been there in 1955, honing his skills as young players did in those days, impatiently waiting, worrying, wondering when his time and his turn to come.

When the Tigers signed Kaline as a bonus baby in 1953, their plan, although never publicized or publicly acknowledged, called for Al to spend the requisite two years riding the bench in the big leagues, getting his feet wet and taking a ribbing from envious veterans, then spend two or three seasons developing into the ballplayer the organization believed he could be by playing every day in the high minors. That was the way things were done in those days. It was standard operating procedure.

However, because of baseball's restrictive Bonus Rule, Kaline had been immediately force-fed into the major leagues where, with little more than one full season in the big leagues under his belt, he suddenly exploded with the season of seasons in 1955, slugging his way to the coveted American League batting title when he was still nearly three months shy of his 21st birthday.

No one so young had ever led the AL in hitting before. And no one so young has done it since. Ironically, Kaline edged out former Tigers legend Ty Cobb, who won the first of his 12 batting titles in 1907, by a single day for that distinction. Cobb was born on December 18, 1886; Kaline on December 19, 1934.

By the start of the 1955 season, Kaline had bulked up to a solid 175 pounds and had become a fixture in right field. But his future big-league stardom was still far from a certainty.

As Kaline prepared himself physically and mentally for the 1955 campaign, he knew he needed a breakout year.

Armed with a new $9,000 contract—he had gotten his first pay raise in the big leagues—Al knew he needed to hit with more power, with more authority, to establish himself as a bona fide big-league hitter. He needed to hit more home runs, more doubles, more triples. He needed more RBIs. He wanted to hit .300.

"Near the end of the 1954 season, all of the other players kept saying, 'You've got to go upstairs and ask for a raise because you're a regular now,'" Kaline recalled. "At the time, I was still making the major-league minimum, which was $6,000.

"So I went up and talked to Muddy Ruel, who was our general manager. He gave me a $2,000 raise for 1954. After the season, when I went in to talk about my contract for 1955, he said, 'We already gave you a raise.' So I made $9,000 in 1955."

Kaline was worried about how he would get along with his new manager, Stanley Raymond "Bucky" Harris, a baseball lifer who had been in the big leagues since 1919, first as a player and later as a manager.

But Al found Harris to be a quiet man who had seen it all in his 45 years in the game. The well-traveled Harris, who had previously served three separate stints as manager of the Washington Senators in addition to managing the Tigers, Red Sox, Phillies, and Yankees, believed in letting his players alone as long as they did their jobs. Al liked that.

"I went to spring training knowing I had to fall on my face not to be a regular," Kaline recalled. "And I had a good spring."

The Tigers opened the season on the road, and Kaline collected a couple of hits in each of the first two games. Then the team came home—and Al really got hot.

"I remember the first game, Opening Day in Detroit. We were playing Cleveland, and I hit two triples off Mike Garcia of the Indians, who was a very good pitcher in those days, and drove in three runs," Kaline recalled. "And it just snowballed after that."

"I don't think the kid knows what pressure is," manager Bucky Harris told reporters after the Tigers' home opener, which they lost 5–3 in spite of Al's efforts. "That crowd of 42,000 didn't bother him a bit.

"Al has a combination of everything it takes to be a good hitter—good eye, strong arms and shoulders, quick wrist action, and an even temperament," Harris added. "He's got it all."

And, bear in mind, it was only Opening Day.

"For whatever reason, that game gave me so much confidence," Kaline recalled. "I found myself thinking, *Maybe I do belong here. Maybe I do belong here.* After that, I just kept on going.

"It wasn't until later in the season, maybe until July, that the pitchers started taking me seriously, really working on me. Even then, they'd be thinking, *I'll challenge this young kid. I can get him out.*

"I was still a skinny kid. I had played the year before and hit .276. But most of that came at the end of the year, when I got more maturity, maybe. Anyway, I built off of that. I had put on 10 or 12 pounds, so I was a little stronger. Plus, I had gotten married during the off-season."

Five games into the season, Kaline, the kid who supposedly couldn't hit, was batting .500. On April 17, 1955, Kaline went 4-for-5 against the Kansas City Athletics at Detroit's Briggs Stadium, batting in six runs as he became the first Tiger in history and the first American Leaguer since Joe DiMaggio in 1936 to hit two home runs in the same inning. Earlier in the game, Kaline had also homered off Kansas City's John Gray in the third inning, giving him three homers for the day.

Teammate Fred Hatfield was aboard via a single in the third inning when Kaline belted a hanging curveball in the green left-field seats to end what, up until that point, had been a scoreless stalemate between Gray and Tigers pitcher Steve Gromek.

An inning later, the bases were loaded with Gromek, Harvey Kuenn, and Hatfield when Kaline knocked in his third run of the afternoon with a base hit to right.

In the sixth, with the Tigers comfortably on top 7–0, Kaline led off the inning by lining a pitch from rookie Bob Spicer into the left-center-field stands for his second homer and fourth RBI in the game.

Tigers hitters continued to hammer the hapless Athletics pitchers, batting around and bringing Kaline back up to the plate for the second time in the sixth inning.

This time, Al found Kansas City's Bob Trice on the mound and Kuenn waiting on third base. Again Kaline connected, reaching the seats in left center. The young man who had managed only four homers and 43 RBIs the previous season had just belted three home runs and batted in six runs in one game.

Following his final blast, a grin spread across Kaline's face after he rounded the bases and returned to the Tigers dugout. He couldn't help himself.

"Wake me up, somebody," said Al, still a man of few words, as he slumped down on the bench in disbelief. "I think I'm dreaming." It was, indeed, the beginning of what for Kaline would be a dream year. So much for the need for more seasoning.

In Kaline's fifth and final at-bat, in the eighth inning that afternoon, he had a shot at a fourth home run. But he popped up to shortstop. Even so, Kaline was the story of the day as the Tigers routed the Athletics 16–0.

In the jubilant Tigers clubhouse after the game, Steve Souchock, the man who had lost his right-field job to Kaline through no fault of his own a year earlier, shouted across the room, "Hey, Al! Don't you think you need a little extra batting practice tomorrow?"

"Nobody ever gets too much," the unassuming Kaline fired back with a grin.

When the reporters crowded around his locker, Kaline credited his newfound power to his added weight and strength. "When I went home last fall, I weighed 155 pounds," he explained. "I'm around 175 now."

"Your wife must be a good cook," one of the writers said.

"She is," Kaline replied.

When Kaline was told that the last American Leaguer to hit two home runs in the same inning had been DiMaggio in 1936, when Al was 18 months old, he grinned again.

"Gosh," he said, modestly understating the significance of what he had just done. "I guess that's really something."

It was, by far, the biggest game yet in Kaline's brief career. But it was merely a harbinger of hits and heroics to come. Al was on his way.

When Kaline hit safely in 25 of his first 26 games, including seven home runs, the whole country suddenly began talking about the skinny 20-year-old in Tigers flannels.

The comparisons with Joe DiMaggio, while embarrassing to Kaline, were inevitable. Both players were smooth and graceful. Both made the game look easy. Even DiMaggio jumped on the bandwagon. "This kid can't miss," the retired former Yankees great declared.

"Kaline can do more things well than most players in the league today," cautioned the Baltimore Orioles' sage manager Paul Richards. "Kaline's a helluva ballplayer, and he has tremendous potential. But let's wait a little while before we put him in a class with DiMaggio."

Nevertheless, the accolades kept coming.

"He's going to be one of the great right-handed hitters of baseball—if he isn't that already," predicted Ted Williams.

"Isn't he something to watch?" exclaimed Kaline's manager, Bucky Harris. "Before Al picked up a bat this year in spring training, it was easy to see that he was more mature and was going to be a stronger hitter. Everybody keeps asking me whether he's as good as he looks. I believe he is."

"He's a wonder to watch," agreed Al's Tigers teammate Ray Boone.

"He's just one of those naturals," offered Tigers pitcher Ned Garver. "Nobody expects a kid to step out of high school right into the big leagues. Kaline is an exception to the rule."

However, the more that people talked about him, the more that people sang his praises, the more that reporters rushed to his locker in pursuit of a pithy quote or a good story after the game, the more the naturally shy, reserved Kaline retreated into his shell.

He kept his answers short, in part because he hoped the reporters would just go away and in part because he honestly didn't know what to say. When fans mobbed him for his autograph, Al would sign quickly, often without making a comment or eye contact.

"I know it's wrong, but it's just the way I am," he told his wife. "I can't be any other way."

But the hits kept coming and, thanks in no small part to Kaline, the Tigers kept winning. By the end of April, Al was hitting .429 and the Tigers were in first place. Could this finally be the year that the Tigers and their long-suffering fans had been waiting for? How long could the kid and the perennial second-division team keep it up?

"We're still rubbing our eyes, wondering if this boy is as good as he looks," admitted Tigers president Spike Briggs.

When the Tigers traveled to Al's hometown of Baltimore in mid-May to play the Orioles at the end of a 13-day, five-city road trip, Kaline was honored before a game as the Baltimore Young Man of the Year.

However, Kaline refused to rest on his laurels—or even pay them much mind. He continued to push himself, working harder than ever during batting practice before each game. "He wants to be the best, that's all," noted Tigers farm director John McHale, who understood from firsthand experience what it takes to be a successful big-league hitter.

"I've always had a lot of desire," Kaline recalled. "When I first came up to the Tigers, I was scared stiff, but I had pride and I was determined to make good. Desire is something you have to have to make it in the majors. If you have two players of equal talent, the one with the most desire will become a good player, and the one who doesn't might turn out to be just average. I was never satisfied with 'just average.'"

When it came time for the nation's baseball fans to select the players for the annual midsummer All-Star Game, to be played July 12 in Milwaukee, Kaline was elected by a landslide. Only popular New York Yankees catcher Yogi Berra in the American League and the Brooklyn Dodgers' Roy Campanella in the National received more votes than Al did.

It was Kaline's first of 18 invitations to the All-Star Game, where one of his boyhood idols, Ted Williams, had stolen the show at Detroit's Briggs Stadium with a game-winning, two-out home run in 1941 when Al was six years old.

In Kaline's All-Star debut in 1955, batting sixth behind sluggers Ted Williams, Mickey Mantle, and Yogi Berra, Al more than held his own against baseball's best, playing the entire 12-inning game in right field, collecting a double off Harvey Haddix, and fielding everything that was hit his way.

Ironically, Stan Musial, another of Kaline's childhood heroes, won the 6–5 game for the National League with a twelfth-inning homer over Al's head and deep into the right-field seats.

Years later, Kaline continued to insist that his first All-Star Game, playing alongside Williams, Mantle, and the others as a 20-year-old kid, was one of his biggest thrills.

Less than a week later, after Kaline hit his 20th home run of the season to help beat the Yankees 6–3 in the opening game of a Saturday afternoon doubleheader, New York manager Casey Stengel, never at a loss for words, raved about Al, too.

"That kid in right field murders you with his speed and his arm," Stengel observed. "And he's made some catches I still don't believe. I sorta hate to think what will happen when he grows up."

By the end of July, Kaline was leading the league in batting average (.352), RBIs (77), home runs (23), base hits (141), and runs scored (91), and Tigers manager Bucky Harris was running out of superlatives where his sensational young right fielder was concerned.

"Anything nice you want to say about him, sign my name," Harris told one writer. "He's the best 20-year-old I've ever seen."

Yet when a Detroit reporter raised the question of a possible batting title, Kaline modestly replied, "There's a guy on this club who will beat me out of it." Kaline was talking about teammate Harvey Kuenn, who was nearly 30 points behind Al at .327 at the time.

When Kaline's comment was relayed to Kuenn, Harvey scoffed, "He'll win the batting title with no trouble. Kaline's got great wrists. He takes the ball right out of the catcher's mitt."

Finally, in early September, the inevitable happened: Kaline lapsed into a slump. Although he continued to hit the ball hard, suddenly it always seemed to go right at somebody. Nothing was dropping in. "I just can't get a base hit," Al groaned.

But on September 17, he snapped out of an 0-for-12 funk with a double and two singles, driving in two runs as the Tigers topped the Cleveland Indians 3–1. The next day, Al collected three more hits, including his 27th and final home run of the season.

Ironically, that home run came off Cleveland's Mike Garcia, against whom Kaline had collected a pair of triples in the Tigers' home opener back on April 14 to launch his unexpected bid for the batting title.

Kaline finished 1955 at .340 with 27 home runs and 102 RBIs. Kaline led the league with 200 base hits, including two on the next-to-last day of the season, and scored 121 runs.

At 20 years, nine months, and six days, Kaline was the youngest American League batting champion ever. The next-best hitter in the AL in 1955 was Kansas City's flashy-fielding Vic Power, who batted .319, 21 points behind the Tigers sensation.

Kaline had outhit Mickey Mantle, who was then in his prime, by 34 points, and Willie Mays, arguably the greatest all-around player ever, by 21.

Ty Cobb, hailed as the "Greatest Tiger of All" and "a Genius in Spikes," was older by one day than Al Kaline when he won his first American League batting title in 1907. Ty went on to win 11 more, nine of them in a row. But Kaline never led the league in hitting again. And he would long be haunted by his breakout performance in the summer of 1955.

"It was a good thing and a great thrill," Al said years later. "But it just happened to me too early.

"Everything I did was right that year. For a long time, the pitchers didn't think I was for real. By the time they found out, the season was over and I had the batting championship."

Kaline was named the 1955 Player of the Year by *The Sporting News*, whose word, in those days, was widely accepted in baseball as gospel.

However, the Yankees' Yogi Berra beat out Al for the American League Most Valuable Player Award by 17 points. Berra, it is worth noting, batted just .272 that season with 27 home runs, the same as Kaline, and 108 RBIs. But the Yankees won the pennant. And the Yankees, of course, were the Yankees.

It was not the first time a player from Detroit had been snubbed by the national media. Nor would it be the last. The failure, decades later, of Mickey Lolich, Jack Morris, and Alan Trammell to be awarded their rightful places in baseball's Hall of Fame comes to mind.

For his efforts, the American League's new batting king received a $6,000 raise—from the $9,000 he was paid in 1955 all the way up to $15,000 in 1956.

"I wasn't real happy about that," Kaline admitted. "But when I questioned it, Muddy Ruel told me, 'If we keep giving you those kinds of raises, we won't be able to afford you.'" That was the logic that baseball employed in 1955.

At a banquet that winter, Kaline bumped into Leo Durocher, who was leaving his job as manager of the New York Giants to work as a TV commentator at NBC.

"I hear you signed your '56 contract," the always blunt Durocher said. "Don't know what they gave you—but it wasn't enough."

Typically, Kaline grinned and said, "I'm not kicking."

However, more than half a century later, Al Kaline can only imagine how much money a 20-year-old batting champion might be worth on today's free-agent market. The money would be mind-boggling.

CHAPTER 7

Shy Guy

Al Kaline had begun the 1955 baseball season, just his second full year on the big-league stage, determined to demonstrate that he deserved to be there, that he could hit with sufficient power and for a high enough average to justify his presence in the Detroit Tigers outfield on an every-day basis.

Six months later, there no longer was any question that Kaline belonged. He wore the crown of the American League batting king. But suddenly Kaline's biggest challenge became the fact that everybody expected him to do it again.

Those lofty expectations would haunt Al for the remainder of his Hall of Fame career as he tried, in vain, to live up to the Al Kaline of 1955.

"I was lucky that year," Kaline would tell people, year after year, when they suggested he had failed to live up to his potential because he was never able to duplicate that fabulous summer of '55. "Everything fell into place."

Nevertheless, from then on, nothing Kaline ever did was quite good enough for his critics—not when it was measured against his excellence of 1955.

"The worst thing that happened to me in the big leagues was the start that I had," Kaline admitted in an interview with *Sports Illustrated*'s Jack Olsen nearly a decade later.

"That put an awful lot of pressure on me. Everybody said, 'This guy's another Ty Cobb, another Joe DiMaggio.' How much pressure can you take?

"It hurt me a great deal," Kaline said.

"What they didn't know is, I'm not that good a hitter. They kept saying I do everything with ease. But it isn't that way. I have to work as hard, if not harder, than anybody in the league. I'm in spring training a week early every year. I've worked with a heavy bat in the winter, swinging it against a big bag. I've squeezed rubber balls all winter long to strengthen my hands. I've lifted weights, done push-ups.

"But my hitting is all a matter of timing. I don't have the strength that [Mickey] Mantle or [Willie] Mays have, where they can be fooled on a pitch and still get a good piece of the ball. I've got to have my timing down perfect or I'm finished.

"Now you take a hitter like me, with all the concentration and effort I have to put into it—I'm not crying about it, it's just a fact—and imagine how it feels to be compared to Cobb?" Kaline continued. "He was the greatest player that ever lived. To say that I'm like him is the most foolish thing that anybody can make a comparison on.

"Do you realize there's old people that come to Tiger Stadium and they saw Cobb play ball and they look at me and they say how can I be as good as Cobb? They threw all this pressure on my shoulders and I don't think it's justified and I don't think it's fair to compare anybody with Cobb.

"I'll tell you something else: I'm not in the same class with players like Mays or [Stan] Musial or [Hank] Aaron, either. Their records over the last five seasons are much better than mine."

Nevertheless, in 1956 everybody suddenly wanted a piece of the quiet, introverted kid from Baltimore, just turned 21, who was wearing the AL batting crown. It was, indeed, a long way from the dirt diamonds and streets lined with row houses that Kaline had known as a boy in Baltimore to the bright lights and fast pace of the big leagues.

Reporters seeking stories for their newspapers and magazines flocked to Kaline's locker at the ballpark, drawn like moths to a flame, clamoring for lengthy, in-depth interviews that would presumably be packed with provocative quotes.

Kids gathered outside Kaline's rented home in the Detroit suburbs, hoping to catch a glimpse of the young superstar and get his autograph.

Advertisers looking to capitalize on Kaline's newfound success and popularity suddenly wanted him to endorse their products. Charitable organizations begged him to donate his money and his time. Following the 1955 season, Kaline found himself going to banquets five and six nights a week until he finally had enough and called a halt.

"I was a big thing there for a while," Al recalled.

Fans and the media can be demanding and cruel—even the long-suffering Tigers fans whom venerable Detroit sportswriter Sam Greene once described as "uncomprehending loyalists." Fairly or unfairly, they create an image in their mind's eye of what they believe a particular ballplayer should be and do. Then they criticize and castigate when the player that they have envisioned fails to behave or perform the way they think he should.

If Al Kaline could win a batting crown at age 20, many reasoned, he surely ought to be able to win another. And another. And another. When that didn't happen, all too often Kaline was labeled a disappointment. And fans don't liked to be disappointed. It was their image, their expectations— but it was Al's fault. Because Kaline was usually very good, although not always great, many fans felt he had let them down.

That was patently absurd, of course. But some Tigers fans, starved since 1945 for a championship team, inexplicably turned against the best all-around player the Tigers had employed since the heyday of second baseman Charlie Gehringer.

There were times in the late 1950s and early 1960s when Kaline, the first batting champion Detroit could call its own since George Kell in 1949, actually heard a few boos in his home ballpark.

"There was a segment in right field that got on me once in a while," he recalled. "When I got off to a slow start in '56, after winning the batting title, you could tell that there were some people who were thinking, *Maybe he was a flash in the pan.*"

Even some of Al's own Tigers teammates resented the way he often seemed to withdraw, to set himself apart from the rest of the team. They considered him aloof.

Many in the Detroit media soured on the Tigers star, too. Kaline was not prepared to cope with the inevitable press attention that his batting title attracted. Young Kaline didn't understand the press, and the press didn't understand him. The writers would rush to his locker with their questions, as they did with the stars on every team. But often Al didn't know what to say. So, in self-defense, he often said nothing.

"I was quiet anyway," Kaline recalled. "And the veteran players told me, 'Don't say anything to the press.' I believed them.

"The thing that scared me the most were the newspapermen," Kaline later admitted. "I didn't even know why they wanted to talk to me. I was not a hotshot or anything. I'd had a few articles written about me in the Baltimore papers, but nobody ever came around to interview me.

"Now the writers were coming around all the time to talk to me, and they were asking me all kinds of things. I didn't know what to say. I think a lot of them thought I was stuck-up. I was just scared."

Kaline sometimes ducked into the trainer's room, which was off-limits to reporters, or lingered in the shower until the writers got tired of waiting and took their notepads and their questions elsewhere.

When the naturally reticent Kaline retreated into a protective shell, preferring not to speak rather than risk saying the wrong thing, many reporters took it as a snub or a sign of arrogance.

Ignoring Kaline's natural shyness, the sportswriters labeled him indifferent, immature, even rude and already full of himself. Some suggested that Al sulked and sometimes loafed. One frustrated scribe nicknamed him "Shy Guy."

"I didn't sulk the way the newspapermen said I did," Kaline later insisted. "I was just quiet, and when a newspaperman came up to me and said, 'Nice game' or something like that, I'd just say, 'Thank you.' I would never prolong the conversation.

"I was just quiet. And the guys who didn't know me would say, 'Look at this stuck-up kid.'

"But it was just my way. I don't talk much. I don't like to make people mad at me, and if you talk too much you're gonna put your foot in your mouth sooner or later."

Privately Kaline often wished he could have been more like his teammate Harvey Kuenn, a fellow bonus baby who also found himself thrust into the spotlight early in his career but who was glib and at ease with the media.

With a chaw of tobacco jutting out in his cheek, the fun-loving Kuenn always seemed to know just what to say when reporters came calling with their endless questions. But Al was embarrassed talking about himself to strangers, whether it was one-on-one with the media in the clubhouse or at a podium before some large civic group.

"It's just that I don't like to talk about myself," he admitted years later. "I don't like people who are boastful, and I didn't want to be one of those kinds of people."

Sometimes Kaline would throw his helmet or his bat. He was often frustrated, and that frustration turned to anger—anger with himself and, in turn, anger toward anyone who approached him off the field.

"I just never thought I should make an out," Kaline later explained, armed with the advantage of years of experience and hindsight. "I thought I should get a hit every time up. I didn't know how to handle it."

As Detroit sportswriter Joe Falls, who observed much of this firsthand, wrote, "There was a time when Al Kaline was not a very pleasant person to be around."

In spite of the ease with which Kaline adjusted to the big leagues on the ballfield, he often experienced difficulty coping with the Tigers' management off it.

Still uncomfortable when he was not in uniform, often uncommunicative—even monosyllabic—in his conversations with reporters, Kaline was repeatedly urged by some in the publicity-minded Tigers' front office to become something he was not.

"They wanted me to be more of a flashy-type player," Kaline recalled.

"They'd call me into the office, and they'd say, 'You've got to be a drawing card.' I thought I did that—on the field. But I guess they wanted more than that. That kind of startled me because I thought just putting up the numbers for the team was enough.

"But they wanted me to do a lot of stuff, like sliding on my face, diving after balls, and cutting up. But how could I change my personality? That just wasn't my nature. I'm just a quiet person. I wasn't a yelling-type guy.

I'd get mad at myself, but I wouldn't get on my teammates. That just wasn't the way I was.

"They told me to be more colorful, that I could bring more people into the ballpark if I was more colorful. But how could I do that? I suppose it's colorful if you argue with the umpires, throw your bat around, and make easy catches look hard. I could jump up and down on the field and make an ass out of myself arguing with umpires, but I'm not made that way. I could have made the easy catches look hard, but I'm not made that way, either.

"Oh, there were times when I'd get mad at myself and maybe throw my batting helmet around in the dugout. But that was a kind of private anger. I just don't like to put on a big show in front of people."

Former Tigers general manager Jim Campbell once told me that young Kaline often wouldn't say a word when he was summoned to the front office, whether to talk contract or simply for a friendly chat.

"He'd just sit there," Campbell recalled. "He wouldn't say a word, unless you asked him a question. Then he'd say yes or he'd say no. But that was about it."

Today, when Kaline speaks, people listen. But Al still avoids the spotlight as much as possible.

"He's getting better now, but when Al first joined Oakland Hills Country Club in the early 1980s, if he showed up at the club and I wasn't there, he'd leave—because he's so damn shy," said Joe Colucci, Kaline's friend of more than 40 years.

"He has turned down more appearances and stuff over the years—he has turned down money after money after money—because he's so shy. I had a deal for him where he could make $10,000 just to play golf in a tournament and say a few words, and he wouldn't do it. He had a chance to go to New York and make some big money for an appearance before some ad people, and he just said no."

Rushed straight from high school, where he had thought only about playing baseball, to the big leagues, where, almost overnight, he became a celebrity and a full-blown star, Kaline never really had a chance to grow up.

More than a decade later, in 1966, when Kaline collected his 2,000th base hit, he was still struggling to cope with the media. When reporters rushed to Al's locker after he reached that milestone against Boston's Jim Lonborg on June 15, 1966, he brushed them off, insisting it was no big deal. In Kaline's mind, all it meant was that he had put on his uniform enough times to get 2,000 hits.

But Al quickly realized he had been rude for no reason. "Damn, damn, damn, I did it again," he said quietly after the writers had moved on in pursuit of their postgame stories on a day when Kaline deserved to be the lead.

A short while later, Kaline approached sportswriter Joe Falls, who was lingering in the locker room, and said, "I should have understood what they wanted. Would you please apologize to them for me?"

The kid was learning.

CHAPTER 8

"He Can't Miss"

After what young Al Kaline had done in 1955 at the tender age of 20, the sky appeared to be the limit for the slender young outfielder who, whether he felt it was warranted or not, suddenly found himself labeled a superstar. Now the trick would be to keep it up, to prove that his batting title was no fluke and that he was no flash in the pan.

The comparisons to Ty Cobb and Joe DiMaggio kept coming. Rather than considering them compliments, they made Al cringe.

The pressure Kaline had felt to prove himself worthy at the start of the 1955 season was nothing compared to the pressure he felt going into the 1956 campaign. In part, no doubt, due to his obligatory off-season tour of the banquet circuit, Kaline weighed 186 pounds when he reported for spring training in February 1956. That was more than 30 pounds heavier than he had been when he signed in 1953 and 11 pounds more than he weighed at the start of the 1955 season.

Not that his manager, Bucky Harris, seemed to mind.

"You look good," Harris told Al on his first day in camp. "You're heavier but not too heavy."

However, spring training had barely begun when Kaline was sidelined with a sore shoulder and sore arm for the first time in his baseball-playing life.

Reporters showed up at the Tigers' camp in languid Lakeland, Florida, that spring determined to write about Kaline, the American League's new batting king, and no one else. They took advantage of Al's down time to pepper him with questions day after day, before, after, and sometimes even during the daily practice sessions.

Kaline complained to his road roommate and friend, infielder Reno Bertoia. But Bertoia, who was largely ignored by the press, told Al that the time to start worrying was when the writers stopped coming around to talk to him.

The pain in Al's right shoulder was eventually traced to two abscessed teeth. Once those were extracted, Kaline soon felt better.

Under the circumstances, it probably was not surprising that Kaline got off to a slow start in 1956. At the end of the first week of the season, he was hitting an embarrassing .143, compared to a robust .560 at a similar stage a year earlier. The pressure was on. Kaline was clearly frustrated, angry, and it showed.

Sensing what his young superstar was going through, manager Bucky Harris—who had been managing big-league ballplayers of all shapes and sizes and skill levels since 1924 when, as the rookie player-manager of a team that included the great pitcher Walter Johnson, he piloted the Washington Senators to their first and only world championship—called Kaline into his office and closed the door.

"Look, Al, don't get discouraged," Harris told him. "No one expects you to even come close to last year. We all realize you're starting this season under a handicap because you missed so many spring games with a sore shoulder.

"But you're developing one bad habit, Al, and you'll be in a lot of trouble unless you correct it. You're reaching for too many bad pitches. You're not that kind of hitter. Last year you made the pitchers come to you with the pitch you wanted. That was your strength. Don't lose it this year."

Nevertheless, the slump continued, and Kaline continued to brood.

He bruised his shoulder trying to make a shoestring catch in right field and was sidelined for three days. He bruised his instep and missed two more games.

The Tigers weren't winning, injuries were mounting, morale on the team was sinking, and Kaline blamed himself for not being able to do more to help.

To make matters worse, Al's roommate and confidant, Reno Bertoia, had been sent back to the minor leagues, and the Tigers assigned young pitcher Paul Foytack to room with Kaline on the road. The front office hoped the talkative Foytack would help draw Kaline out of his shell.

It was a difficult time—both for the team and for its budding superstar.

In a game against Washington on June 27, thinking that a fly ball to the outfield would be caught, the Tigers coaches held up the runners on the base paths. But the ball dropped in for a hit, and Tigers owner Spike Briggs, who had been seated in the stands, exploded. "Even the coaches aren't hustling!" he told reporters with undisguised disgust.

One of those Tigers coaches, Joe Gordon, got so mad he quit. "If he has a squawk, why doesn't he come to us?" Gordon grumbled. "Why does he have to blast us in the papers? It bowled me over to read that my work wasn't satisfactory. Bucky Harris never had any complaints."

Many of the Tigers players were angry at their owner, too, and the atmosphere in the clubhouse deteriorated further.

Finally Briggs, who had fled to Florida after igniting the firestorm, sent a telegram to his team: "From reading down here quotes attributed to me, I feel apologies are due all of you. If you feel the same way, please consider this an apology. All of you know how I feel about you. Be advised from now on, I will not be subjected to a question and answer period during the playing of a ballgame. Good luck."

The next day, after Briggs' mea culpa had been read and posted in the clubhouse, the Tigers rode home runs by Kaline and Charlie Maxwell off future Dodgers manager Tommy Lasorda to a 5–0 victory over the Kansas City Athletics.

Elected to the American League's starting lineup for the All-Star Game for the second year in a row, no doubt more because of what he had done in 1955 than what he was doing in 1956, Kaline again had a chance to sit down and discuss hitting with Boston great Ted Williams.

"You're pressing," Williams told him. "You're swinging at too many first pitches. The pitchers are keeping the ball outside and away from you, and that means you're swinging at bad pitches. You're coming to the pitchers instead of making them come to you. Be patient. When you're up there, wait for the pitch you want." It was basically the same advice Bucky Harris had given Al back in April, but this time Kaline listened.

Over the next month, Al hiked up his batting average 25 points to .308. He also hit 10 homers and knocked in 35 runs. When a reporter asked Al to explain why he was suddenly hitting so well, Kaline answered with two words: "Ted Williams."

Meanwhile, in July 1956, ownership of the Tigers—which had passed four years earlier from the late automotive magnate Walter O. Briggs to a trust managed by his fun-loving son Spike and Briggs' four daughters—landed in the hands of an 11-man syndicate of broadcasting moguls for $5.5 million.

At the time, that was the highest price that had ever been paid for a big-league baseball team. By comparison, the Philadelphia Athletics had sold for $3.5 million in 1954, the St. Louis Cardinals for a record $4.55 million, the St. Louis Browns for $2.475 million in 1953, the Cleveland Indians for $2.2 million in 1949, the Pittsburgh Pirates for $2.3 million in 1946, and the New York Yankees (including valuable real estate in Newark and Kansas City) for $2.8 million in 1945.

Contrast that to the $82 million that Mike Ilitch paid fellow pizza baron Tom Monaghan when he bought the Tigers in 1992 or the $371 million that, according to Forbes.com, the Detroit baseball franchise was worth in 2009, and you get an idea how dramatically the finances of baseball have changed during Kaline's tenure with the organization.

Spike Briggs, who often pampered his players and loved to hang out with them, had tried to retain ownership, offering the family trust fund $3.5 million for the franchise. But Spike's sisters, who reportedly disapproved of their brother's carousing, refused to sell their shares to him.

In order to buy the team, the syndicate, headed by Fred Knorr and John Fetzer—both of whom owned radio stations in Michigan and who were actually more interested in gaining control of the broadcast rights than they were in owning a big-league baseball team—first had to outmaneuver maverick operator Bill Veeck, the gimmick-minded former owner of the Cleveland Indians and St. Louis Browns.

"I had always liked baseball and followed the Tigers and that sort of thing, but the last thing I wanted to do at that juncture in my life was to own a baseball team," Fetzer told me years later.

The bids to buy the ballclub were supposed to be sealed and secret. But Veeck was publicly campaigning for himself through the press, promising to wake up the dormant Tigers and the city of Detroit with a barrage of fireworks and clowns and exploding scoreboards. Veeck openly bragged that he held a $2.5 million line of credit with the National Bank of Detroit.

Fetzer, a businessman first and foremost, knew that banks usually required borrowers to match their credit line with an equal amount of cash. Therefore, Fetzer reasoned, Veeck's bid had to be about $5 million.

Fetzer's group of broadcast-minded baseball novices had intended to bid $4.8 million for the ballclub. But Fetzer convinced them they had to raise their bid to $5.5 million or, as he put it, "get out of the game."

Fetzer and his friends upped the ante, and they won. Veeck, who had bid $5.25 million, cried foul and attempted to increase his offer to $6 million and later to $6.75 million. But the ground rules for the auction stood.

How Al Kaline's career and life might have been changed if the flamboyant Veeck had bought the club, the world will never know.

However, back at the ballpark, Kaline's heroics in the outfield were fast becoming the talk of the league.

On July 18, in the second game of a midweek doubleheader at Yankee Stadium, the Tigers were leading 4–3 when New York put two runners aboard with two out in the bottom of the ninth.

The next batter, a fellow named Mickey Mantle, belted a drive off Frank Lary deep to right field, where the outfield fence was low. In the broadcast booth, New York announcer Jim Woods, Mel Allen's partner, immediately exclaimed, "It's a home run! The Yankees win!"

Inside the still-empty visitors' clubhouse, attendant Mickey Rendine flipped off the radio and waited for the disappointed, tired Tigers to shuffle into the locker room with their heads down.

Instead, moments later, the Tigers burst through the door, screaming and slapping one another on the back.

"What happened?" the stunned Rendine inquired. "You guys lost!"

"No, Kaline caught the ball!" one of the jubilant Tigers shouted.

"Yeah, it was one of those easy catches he always makes," cried out another.

As soon as Mantle had connected for what appeared to be his game-winning blast, Kaline had raced back to the outfield wall, placed one foot on the fence and leaped high in the air to rob Mantle of a home run and the Yankees of a victory with a backhanded grab.

"The New York radio crew couldn't believe I caught the ball," Kaline recalled. "They went off the air saying the Yankees had won the game. The clubhouse man was listening, and he expected us to come off the field all down.

"I remember the look on the clubhouse guy's face when I came in," Kaline said, even as he downplayed the difficulty of the catch.

"I bruised my back when I bumped against the wall," he explained. "But I didn't think it was such a tough catch, really."

On July 31, Kaline, who had finally stopped trying to match 1955 and started concentrating on simply having another good year, contributed a home run, a double, a single, and three RBIs to a 6–4 Tigers win over Boston. That came in the middle of a 12-game hitting streak that would include an 8-for-13 performance with 11 RBIs in an uplifting three-game sweep of the first-place Yankees.

Brushback pitches, knockdowns, even beanballs were an accepted part of the game in those days, much more so than they are today. Pitchers weren't afraid to throw inside, and hitters learned to expect that.

In the National League, for example, Sal Maglie was known as "the Barber" because he specialized in close shaves. Early Wynn was another who liked to keep hitters loose at the plate by pitching inside.

But opposing pitchers soon learned it didn't pay to knock Al Kaline down. It didn't intimidate him; it merely made him mad.

"Pedro Ramos of the Senators used to throw at Al's head all the time," former Tigers pitcher Hank Aguirre recalled years later. "Every time Al stepped up there, Ramos would knock him down. It was vicious. He would knock him down, and Al's bat and his helmet would go flying.

"Al kept trying to hit the ball back at him, to knock Ramos down. Finally one day, Al drilled Ramos in the leg with a line drive. He really stung him. When Al got to first base, he looked over into our dugout and gave us a little grin. That was one of the real satisfying moments in life."

The Tigers, under their new ownership, posted the best record in the league (48–30) during the second half of the 1956 season. Nevertheless, they still finished in fifth place behind New York, a full 15 games off the pace, which gives you an idea how bad the first half of the season (34–42) had been.

In spite of everything, Kaline enjoyed another very productive season, knocking in a career-high 128 runs and again belting 27 homers while batting .314, thanks to a strong, second-half spurt.

"I'm sure 1955 wasn't a flash performance," Kaline insisted, when a reporter raised the question to Al himself. "I got 200 hits that season and 194 the next. Also, I got the same number of home runs (27) each year. If I was a flash in 1955, then I had to be a flash in 1956.

"Am I overrated? Maybe," Al admitted. "But not by me. I never claimed to be a superstar, and I never expected to be one. Thank God I'm not fatheaded. The batting championship in 1955 meant a new responsibility for me, a new standard to maintain. I've tried very hard to do it, even if I've failed."

Away from the ballpark, Kaline and hockey superstar Gordie Howe of the Detroit Red Wings, two of the city's biggest sports celebrities, had become friends. Soon after the 1956 season ended, businessman Frank Carlin invited Al and Gordie to join him in an automobile-parts venture in the Motor City.

All that Kaline and Howe had to do, Carlin explained, would be to contact Detroit's car companies and use their famous names to get their company's foot in the door.

Kaline readily admitted he knew nothing about the automotive or tool-and-die business. And the idea of the shy, withdrawn outfielder working as a salesman sounded incongruous at best.

Howe, from Floral, Saskatchewan, on the outskirts of Saskatoon, in the heart of Canada's wheat-farming prairie, was also a man of action, not naturally given to orations or sales pitches. That was part of the reason he and Kaline got along so well.

But Carlin persisted. "Your job and Gordie's will be to open the doors," Carlin explained. "As sports stars, you two can get in to see anyone.

"You can work in the winter, when you're not playing baseball, and Gordie can work in the summer when he isn't playing hockey. You can't beat it."

Kaline consulted his wife, Louise, who liked the idea a lot more than her husband did. She was looking ahead to the day when Al would be out of baseball and in need of a job to support his family.

Eventually, Kaline and Howe signed on. Their company would be called the Michigan Automotive Products Corporation. Howe would be the president, Kaline would be the vice president, and Carlin would be the treasurer. It was enough to convince the Kalines to make their year-around home in the Detroit area.

Despite Kaline's initial reservations, the company clicked. Al found the businessmen who invited him into their offices much easier to talk to than the prying newspaper reporters. Before long, the trio formed the Howe-Kaline-Carlin Corporation, a separate entity that would serve as manufacturers' representatives. The young ballplayer from Baltimore had become a successful businessman.

Soon Kaline would learn about the business side of baseball, too.

Before departing for Baltimore with his wife after the end of the 1956 season to spend the holidays with their parents, Kaline met with Tigers president Spike Briggs to discuss Al's contract for the coming year.

Briggs, who had been allowed to remain in charge of baseball operations after the Tigers had been sold, acknowledged the fact that Kaline had enjoyed another good year but offered only a modest raise from Al's 1956 salary of $15,000.

Kaline rejected the club's opening offer. Al was in Baltimore when he received Briggs' second offer through the mail. Still not satisfied, Kaline, who had not yet said a word to the press about his stalled salary talks, returned the second contract unsigned.

Days later, when called upon to make an impromptu speech at a banquet at the Statler Hotel in downtown Detroit, about a mile from the ballpark, an obviously irked and possibly intoxicated Briggs mentioned the ongoing salary stalemate with his team's young star.

"Al thinks he's as good as Mickey Mantle and wants more money than Mantle," Briggs told his stunned audience. "I don't agree with him, and he isn't going to get it. After all, his batting average went down last year, and he didn't lead the American League in anything. We have offered Kaline a bigger raise than he got last year. And that's that.

"I sent Kaline a contract over the holidays along with a $3,000 bonus for last year," Briggs continued. "I got the contract back, unsigned. I didn't get thanks for the bonus or even a holiday greeting."

Furthermore, Briggs declared, he had no intention of negotiating any further with Kaline until spring training.

When word of Briggs' provocative statements reached Kaline in Baltimore, he was deeply offended and immediately flew back to Detroit, determined to set the record straight.

"I definitely didn't ask for Mantle's pay," an angry Kaline told a Detroit reporter. "That would have been ridiculous. All I want is a fair raise. I was shocked and surprised that Spike said I thought I was better than Mantle and that I wanted as much money as he gets. I would never say anything of the kind. I know I'm not as good as Mickey. But I do think I deserve a better contract than the one Spike offered me.

"This sort of publicity is bad," Al added. "It makes me look like a heel."

However, when Kaline confronted Briggs in his office at the ballpark, Spike shrugged off the entire incident. "Don't get upset about it," Briggs said. "I didn't mean it the way it sounded."

Then Briggs flew off to Florida on vacation and left Tigers executive John McHale to clean up the mess he had left behind.

Kaline met with McHale and came to terms on a new contract almost immediately—for the same salary Al had initially requested. "We were only $3,000 apart when Spike made the statement anyway," Kaline explained.

However, the public squabble did impact Kaline's off-season business. "I got the money, but the story hurt me," Al admitted later. "I was doing reasonably well as a salesman with my firm, but when the salary story broke, I could see a difference. People seemed a little cooler. It was something I had to live down."

In 1957 the Tigers harbored legitimate hopes of climbing into the first division for the first time in Kaline's career.

Aging manager Bucky Harris, who was suffering from a nervous disorder, had quit over the winter before the team's new ownership could fire him. Harris had been replaced by Jack Tighe, a feisty bald-headed coach and organization man who once took a lie-detector test while managing in the minor leagues to prove that he had not spit on an umpire.

John Fetzer, one of the partners who now owned the team, had wanted to hire highly respected Al Lopez, who would eventually be enshrined in the Hall of Fame. But Briggs, who had remained as the team's general manager after the sale to the 11-man syndicate and who was ostensibly still in charge of baseball operations, insisted on promoting Tighe from within the organization.

"We'll finish second in 1957!" Tighe promptly predicted, parroting the party line.

Catching the mighty Yankees was still out of the question, but the Indians and White Sox were both aging, and the Red Sox boasted little other than the great Ted Williams.

"We want to bring Detroit a pennant as fast as we can!" promised Fred Knorr, the 43-year-old former dance-band piano player, overnight radio disc jockey, and sandlot baseball player, who had become a part-owner of the Tigers and, temporarily, the new team president.

One sunny spring morning in 1957 in Lakeland, Florida, Tighe was watching his players work out at Henley Field, when he suddenly declared, "You know something, he can't miss."

"Who can't miss?" asked Joe Falls, the Detroit sportswriter who happened to be sitting by Tighe's side on the bench.

"Kaline," the rookie skipper replied. "By the time he's done, they'll have him in the Hall of Fame in Cooperstown."

Kaline was optimistic, too. A year earlier, he had demonstrated that his batting title in 1955 was no fluke. Now he looked forward to just playing ball.

"Everybody expected great things from me last season," Al explained early in training camp. "Now I don't have that pressure, and I can concentrate on having a good season and helping the team as much as I can.

"If we win the pennant, I don't care if I hit .250, just as long as I can knock in a run now and then and help out."

Nevertheless, the off-season salary spat continued to haunt Al, even though the controversy was not of his making. Sportswriters from around the country who stopped in Lakeland on their annual tour of the spring-training camps across Florida, had read Briggs' inflammatory comments, and they all wanted to know the same thing: did Kaline really believe he was worth more money than Mickey Mantle?

It made for a good headline—never mind the fact that it had already been debunked as a nonstory.

For Kaline, it was a lose-lose situation.

Day after day, Al heard the same questions. And he had no answers—at least none that would make the endless inquiries stop and the senseless controversy go away. So Al again retreated into his protective shell, which only led to more stories by rebuked reporters about Kaline's uncooperative, sullen personality. However, not everyone took the negative approach

"This fellow is pretty amazing," declared Yankees manager Casey Stengel, who, without prompting, spoke out in Al's defense after a Tigers exhibition outing in St. Petersburg.

"He's only 22, and you ask yourself four questions: Can he throw? And the answer is yes. Can he field the ball? And you answer yes. Is he active on the bases? Yes, you'd have to say yes. And then, can he drive in the runs? The real test. And again, you say yes.

"The kid murders you with his speed and arm. He made some catches I still don't believe. So he's only 22 and he does all those things, and he's getting better. So he is an amazing fellow."

However, Kaline suffered through the worst year yet in his young career in 1957, even though, thanks to a strong finish in August and September, his final numbers were not all that bad.

When Kaline began the season 0-for-13, new manager Jack Tighe pulled Al aside and said, "Just stay in there and keep swinging. You'll come out of it."

On April 26, 1957, Spike Briggs, who had publicly accused the Tigers' new ownership of "trying to run the team like a factory," quit in a huff—or was quietly pushed out the door. The exact details of Briggs' abrupt exit were never made public.

Front-office politics aside, Kaline continued to struggle, plagued by a sore shoulder and his deformed left foot, which had been largely forgotten in 1955 when he was hitting so well.

Now reporters constantly came around, asking the former batting champ about his hitting woes. Kaline didn't enjoy talking about that any more than he had relished talking about his earlier success.

In spite of his prolonged slump, Al was again elected to the American League All-Star team. Kaline, whose wife was expecting their first child, considered that quite a compliment and responded with one of his best All-Star Game performances ever, driving in two runs with a pair of singles and making a couple of outstanding catches in the outfield as the American League narrowly prevailed 6–5.

In August Kaline finally came alive at the plate. By August 26 he was again batting .300. Al belted a dozen home runs during the month of August alone. Led by Kaline, the Tigers, who had been in sixth place earlier in the month, climbed to fourth in the standings.

On August 21, Mark Albert Kaline, the couple's first of two sons, was born.

Kaline also met Tigers legend Ty Cobb, the man against whom he had been so unfairly compared in the wake of his 1955 batting title.

"I had always heard what a fierce man Ty Cobb was," Kaline remarked. "But when I met him, he was very mild-mannered."

However, Cobb couldn't resist the opportunity to offer Kaline some hitting advice. "He told me, 'Always bear down, because there'll come a time when you won't be able to bear down,' meaning there'll come a time when you won't be able to play," Kaline recalled.

The Tigers played spoilers in September. The White Sox were chasing the Yankees, and on September 3, Kaline belted an eleventh-inning home run off Chicago's Gerry Staley to defeat the ChiSox 3–2. After the game, one the Tigers players quipped, "The Yanks ought to vote Kaline a share of their World Series money."

The Tigers finished fourth in 1957, the highest they had been since 1950, before Kaline arrived. But they were still 20 games back, which was the furthest behind they had been since 1954.

Obviously, there still was a lot of work to be done. For everyone.

C H A P T E R

"There Goes Our Pennant"

Although Al Kaline played in Detroit for 22 years and 2,834 games, more than any other Tiger, he enjoyed only two more summers after his banner 1955 season in which he was able to play at least 150 games.

Over the course of his career, Kaline missed more than 500 games, the equivalent of more than three full seasons, more often than not because of one injury or another.

"I never had any little injuries," Al recalled. "It seemed like when I got hurt, I always broke a bone. I didn't pull many muscles or things like that. When I got hurt, it was worth four, five, six weeks at a time."

In 1954 Kaline spent five days in the hospital after he crashed into an outfield wall chasing a fly ball and injured his knee. Early in 1958 it was an irritated nerve in his hip and pain in his back. Later that season, just when Al was coming on strong at the plate, he tore the ligaments in his ankle when he crashed into the railing at Yankee Stadium while making a sensational catch on a fly ball by Mickey Mantle.

On June 18, 1959, Kaline was batting a hearty .351 when an errant first-inning throw by Baltimore second baseman Billy Gardner struck the left side of his face as he ran to first base, shattering his cheekbone. Kaline immediately dropped to the ground, out cold. Medical personnel, including

Tigers trainer Jack Homel, worked on Al for 20 minutes before he was placed on a stretcher and carried off the field to a waiting ambulance.

Quietly, Homel informed manager Jimmie Dykes that he thought Kaline would probably be out of action for at least six weeks.

As the ambulance, its siren blaring, raced through the streets of Kaline's hometown to Baltimore's Union Memorial Hospital, Kaline finally opened his eyes.

Seeing Charley Creedon, the Tigers' traveling secretary, leaning over him, Kaline asked, "When do I play again?"

"We don't know yet, Al," Creedon replied. "The doctors will tell us that."

At the hospital, Dr. Edward A. Kitlowski discovered that the injury was not as serious as first feared. Kaline had suffered a broken bone in his left cheek. After Dr. Kitlowski reset the bone during a 30-minute surgery, he predicted, "He probably will be able to play in a week."

Kaline rejoined the team in Washington and cheered from the bench as the Tigers downed the Senators 7–4 to inch to within half a game of the league-leading Cleveland Indians.

But when the Tigers proceeded to drop three games in a row to fall two and a half back, Kaline sought out manager Jimmie Dykes.

"Put me back in the game," Al pleaded.

"You better wait," responded the stunned Dykes, a concerned look on his face. "Your cheek is swollen, and your eye is bloodshot."

"I don't bat or throw with my cheek," Kaline argued.

Against his better judgment, Dykes put Kaline back in the lineup on June 24—there was, of course, no designated hitter in those days—and although Al didn't get a hit in three trips to the plate, he was happy to be back.

"I felt good out there," Kaline told reporters after the game. "I was going nuts sitting on the bench."

On May 26, 1962, Kaline was off to a fantastic start, batting .345, third-best in the league. He had hit 13 home runs and accounted for 38 RBIs. Another batting title was quite possible. Baseball's storied Triple Crown was not out of the question.

And after winning the opener of their important three-game series in New York, the Tigers were just four games behind the Yankees.

"We are where we are because of Kaline," manager Bob Scheffing told reporters in the dugout during batting practice before the second game of the series. "Where we go from here depends on him."

Then, with the Tigers clinging to a 2–1 lead in the bottom of the ninth inning, with two out and the potential tying run in the person of Hector Lopez on base, Elston Howard looped a fly ball to shallow right field.

Tigers first baseman Norm Cash and second baseman Jake Wood both went running back. Kaline came rushing in. Meanwhile, Lopez was circling the bases as fast as he could in hopes of tying the score.

Realizing he was the only Tiger who had a chance to catch the ball—and then only because he was Al Kaline—Al lunged though the air at the last possible second, his gloved left hand outstretched.

In midair, Kaline twisted his body to get his glove underneath the ball. As the ball nestled into Al's mitt, his right shoulder awkwardly struck the ground. A sharp, stabbing pain shot through his body. The agony was intense. Kaline felt certain he was going to black out.

"Are you okay?" asked Norm Cash, the first Tiger to reach the fallen right fielder.

"I don't know," Kaline whispered through clenched teeth, still clutching the ball in his glove.

"Get Jack Homel. I'm hurt."

Cash turned and frantically waved for help.

When Homel reached Kaline's side, outfielder Billy Bruton and Jake Wood were also there.

"I'm afraid it's broken," Homel said, as he cautiously touched Kaline's shoulder.

Several players anxiously signaled for a stretcher.

"Just get me up," Kaline grimaced. "I can walk. There's nothing the matter with my legs."

Kaline's worried teammates gently helped Al to his feet and, as he walked slowly off the field, the partisan but stunned Yankee Stadium crowd applauded. The Tigers players weren't saying a word.

As Kaline descended the steps into the Tigers dugout, several of his teammates grabbed Al as he collapsed into their arms. He had almost passed out.

Kaline's teammates carried him through the tunnel leading to the visitors' clubhouse. In the locker room, lying on the table in the trainer's room with Homel and Yankees team physician Dr. Sidney Gaynor, an orthopedic surgeon, at his side, Al passed out from the pain.

The players milled aimlessly around what should have been a jubilant locker room. They had won the game. But the Tigers realized their best hope for a pennant lay in anguish on the trainer's table.

Kaline passed out again before the ambulance finally arrived to transport him to Lenox Hill Hospital when it was determined he had broken his collarbone.

As the ambulance pulled away from Yankee Stadium with its lights flashing and its siren blaring, Tigers manager Bob Scheffing was heard to say, "There goes our pennant, riding off in that ambulance."

"He'll be out of the game for two months," Dr. Gaynor predicted. "At least two months."

Kaline had robbed Elston Howard of a game-winning hit and preserved the Tigers' victory, pulling them to within three games of the front-running Yankees—and in the process he had been robbed of what might have been his best season ever.

"I sat on the bench that day hoping Al would catch that ball," recalled Tigers future Hall of Fame pitcher Jim Bunning, who later became a United States senator from Kentucky. "And I spent the rest of the season wishing he hadn't."

Or as Tigers pitcher Hank Aguirre put it, "We won the game today— but we've lost the season.

"That guy meant everything to us," added Aquirre, who, thanks to Kaline, received credit that afternoon for the win in his first start in two years.

"It's a terrible blow," admitted Bob Scheffing, who was surrounded by reporters in the somber locker room. "Al has been our big man all season. We'll find the going rough without him.

"But, you know," the Tigers manager added, "what happened out there today, that's what makes Kaline great. He's an established star, but he tried for that ball like a rookie trying to hold on to his job."

The injury cost Kaline eight weeks, causing him to miss 57 games, more than one-third of the season.

"That was the most devastating year for me, even though I ended up having a good year," Kaline recalled. "It probably would have been my best year ever. I was leading the league in everything. I was having a great year."

Kaline's injured shoulder was placed in a protective harness. He kept his right hand tucked inside his shirt to take the pressure off his shoulder. He couldn't dress himself. He couldn't button his shirt. He couldn't tie his shoes.

On June 30, 1962, midway through Al's depressing convalescence, his wife gave birth to their second son, Michael Keith Kaline. That lifted Al's spirits, as did the fact that Al was named to the American League All-Star team, even though everyone knew he couldn't possibly play in the first game.

Al returned in time to join his AL teammates for that season's second All-Star Game on July 30 at Wrigley Field in Chicago. Although he was used only as a pinch-runner, it felt good to be back. "A guy like Kaline belongs in there," said AL manager Ralph Houk of the Yankees, who would later manage Kaline during Al's final season in Detroit.

Despite missing almost two full months, Kaline finished the year with 29 home runs and 94 RBIs in just 100 games. The Tigers finished the season an unfulfilling fourth, 10½ games behind the Yankees.

But that was not the end to Kaline's serious injuries.

A nagging knee injury, the result of an outfield collision in May, prematurely ended Kaline's season in September 1963 when he was locked in a battle with Boston's Carl Yastrzemski for the batting title. Al finished second in the race, just nine points back, for what would have been his second crown.

Kaline again finished second in balloting for the American League Most Valuable Player Award in 1963, this time trailing the Yankees' Elston Howard, whose fly ball the previous summer had cost Al what could have been his best year ever.

Howard drove in fewer runs, 85 to Kaline's 101, and batted .287 to Kaline's .312. Nevertheless, for the fourth year in a row, a Yankee was named MVP in the league. Slugger Roger Maris won it in 1960 and '61, and Mickey Mantle took home the hardware in '62. It was no coincidence that the Yankees won the American League pennant in each of those seasons.

For the second time in his career, Kaline was named The Sporting News Player of the Year. But again it was small consolation.

In spring training of 1964, while running out a routine ground ball in an exhibition game, Kaline came down hard on his left foot on the first-base bag and felt a sudden jolt of pain.

The osteomyelitis that had caused doctors to remove two inches of bone from Kaline's left foot when he was a youngster, leaving it deformed, had been kept largely in check throughout his career. Suddenly, after years of pounding, the pain was severe.

Kaline didn't say a word. But when he removed his shoe and sock in the clubhouse after the game, he discovered that his big toe was swollen and red. Al dismissed it as a sprain and continued to play, even though each step brought another shot of pain.

Unaware of the problem with Kaline's foot, manager Charlie Dressen continued to write Al's name in the lineup for every exhibition game, knowing that the fans who came to the quaint little spring-training parks around Florida each afternoon wanted to see the Tigers star play.

In early May, with Kaline hitting .224 and in obvious pain, Dr. Russell Wright, the Tigers' team physician, ordered Al off his feet for five days to rest. The tendon in Kaline's big toe was swollen and inflamed. "I don't know how Al's been able to play at all," Dr. Wright declared. "He's just been too proud to let anyone know about it."

That was Al.

In 1965 Kaline missed six games in May after he injured his hand while diving for a ball and another 18 games in August after he tore the cartilage in his ribs making a shoestring catch.

"Well," the dejected outfielder said, "here I am on the floor again."

A strained muscle in his right side caused Al to miss nine games in 1966.

On June 27, 1967, frustrated after striking out in the sixth inning against Cleveland's Sam McDowell, Kaline returned to the dugout and violently slammed his bat into the rack, accidentally striking the wooden bat rack with the side of his hand. Immediately, he felt a sharp pain in his little finger.

Suspecting something was wrong, Kaline walked over to Tigers trainer Bill Behm and quietly said, "I think you'd better look at my hand. I think I just broke something."

Behm immediately escorted Kaline to the clubhouse and informed manager Mayo Smith. Kaline was taken to Detroit Osteopathic Hospital where, after examining the X-rays, team physician Dr. Russell Wright confirmed, "Kaline fractured the metacarpal bone a half inch behind the knuckle of the little finger on his right hand.

"His hand is in a splint and will be put in a cast after the swelling goes down and more X-rays are taken," Dr. Wright announced.

Kaline was hitting .328 at the time, with 15 home runs and 53 RBIs.

"Of all the dumb things I've ever done, this has got to be the dumbest," Al declared at the time, thoroughly disgusted with himself. "I just lost control, that's all. I've been trying to keep it bottled up all season—you know, no bench kicking or things like that—and it all came out at once. This was so unnecessary. I feel like a damned fool." The "dumb" mistake would cost him 25 games.

The following season, on May 25, 1968, in the treacherous twilight at Oakland Coliseum, Kaline was struck on the right forearm by a pitch from the Athletics' Lew Krausse. Kaline lost sight of the path of the ball, which was inside, and at the last instant instinctively threw up his right hand to protect his face. The pitch struck his arm, fracturing the ulnar bone.

At the end of the half-inning, Kaline was taken out of the game. After a painful, sleepless night, Al flew home to Detroit where X-rays revealed the fracture. Diagnosis: Kaline would be sidelined for a month, if not more.

"These are the breaks of the game," a dejected Kaline told Louise. "And I've had my share of them."

The mid-1960s were a troubling time for Kaline and for the Detroit Tigers.

In 1965 manager Chuck Dressen suffered a heart attack during spring training. Dressen returned after three months, but on May 16, 1966, he suffered another heart attack. Dressen, who had managed the Reds, Dodgers, Senators, and Braves before he was hired by the Tigers, died on August 10, 1966.

Former coach Bob Swift was called upon to replace Dressen twice before he himself was diagnosed with lung cancer and replaced by another organization man, Frank Skaff, midway though the 1966 season. Swift, who had been the Tigers' catcher in 1951 when St. Louis Browns owner Bill Veeck sent 3'7" Eddie Gaedel up to bat, passed away on October 17, 1966.

Somehow, despite losing two managers under tragic circumstances, the Tigers finished third in 1966, and Kaline hit .288 with 29 homers and 88 RBIs.

His injuries notwithstanding, Kaline's .296 batting average during the decade of the 1960s was the best by any player who appeared in at least 1,000 games in the big leagues.

Although it attracted little attention at the time and has been all but forgotten since then, Willie Horton may have saved Kaline's life in 1970.

On May 30, during a game against the recently transplanted Milwaukee Brewers, Kaline and center fielder Jim Northrup collided while both were closing in on a fly ball to right-center field, knocking Al unconscious.

"Northrup hit me right in the throat with his elbow, and I swallowed my tongue," Kaline recalled. "I couldn't breathe. I was starting to turn purple. At least that's what they tell me. I don't know because I was out cold."

When Horton, the Tigers' left fielder who had secretly been a successful amateur boxer as a youngster, reached Kaline's side, he immediately realized what was happening. And Willie knew what he had to do.

"Willie was the only one strong enough to separate my jaws and reach into my mouth and pull my tongue out of my throat," Kaline said.

"You put pressure on the nerves on the back of the jaw and that makes the man relax enough to let you pry his mouth open," Horton explained.

Al escaped with nothing more serious than a bad headache. One day later, he was back in the lineup.

Despite all of his injuries, Kaline appeared in 100 or more games for 19 seasons in a row, from 1954 through 1972, tying an American League record held by the legendary Tris Speaker. In his 22nd and final season, Al played in 147 games in 1974.

Who knows what kind of numbers Kaline might have put up in his career if he had been able to remain reasonably injury free?

CHAPTER 10

"Not for Mantle— or Mays"

Aside from the world championship season of 1968 and half a pennant in 1972, Al Kaline's 22-year tenure as a player with the Tigers was marred by the team's perennial mediocrity.

In Kaline's first eight seasons in Detroit, from 1953 through 1960, the Tigers never placed higher than fourth and finished a combined 194 games out of first place.

That tends to get discouraging.

From 1952, when the Tigers finished in last place for the first time in franchise history, through 1960, the team made 37 trades involving a total of 147 players—all to no avail.

The annual plight of the ballclub became a bad joke.

Under those circumstances, it was understandable that the fans and the press would grow increasingly frustrated with the failure of Kaline, the team's leading man, to deliver a pennant, albeit all by himself.

It was inevitable that from time to time there would be suggestions in the newspapers, in the Briggs Stadium grandstand, and even in the Tigers' own front office, that the team might be best served by trading Kaline away and rebuilding without him.

The Tigers hadn't won a title with him, Al's critics reasoned, so maybe they would have a better chance without him. What did they have to lose?

And there were many times when Kaline, who yearned to play on a winner and participate in a World Series, would gaze around the game at the teams and the players who were appearing in the World Series or at least contending, year after year, and wish fate had placed him with a better team.

"In the back of my mind, I would wonder, *Man, am I ever going to get a chance to play in the World Series?*" Kaline admitted.

"Yeah, there were second thoughts. Sometimes I'd think, *Man, if I could only play for the Yankees.*"

That almost happened—several times.

During the 1958 World Series, in which the Yankees beat the Milwaukee Braves, New York general manager George Weiss cornered his Detroit counterpart, John McHale, and asked point-blank, "Is Kaline available?"

"Let's go to lunch, George," McHale replied, sidestepping the question.

When McHale got back to Detroit after the conclusion of the World Series, he summoned the Tigers' beat reporters to his office in an effort to squelch the rumors that, fanned by the New York press, were by then rampant.

McHale admitted the Yankees were interested but attempted to make light of the situation. "Suppose I had told him that Kaline was available," McHale said, coyly. "I wonder who the Yankees would have thrown in besides Mickey Mantle and Bob Turley."

Wink, wink.

However, McHale never said that Kaline was untouchable.

The fact that those were financially trying times for the Tigers further fueled speculation about a possible trade involving Kaline.

During spring training in 1959, when the Tigers threw a 25th-anniversary party for the 1934 American League champions—including Mickey Cochrane, Hank Greenberg, Goose Goslin, and Schoolboy Rowe—the Lakeland, Florida, Chamber of Commerce had to pick up the tab for the food and drinks.

That year, with one eye, as always, on the bottom line, the number of ticket sellers at Briggs Stadium was sliced in half, the assistant public-relations director was lopped off the payroll, the free employee lunch program at the ballpark was reduced, and, as ridiculous as it may sound, the ballplayers themselves were each limited to two clean towels in the clubhouse per day.

In 1959, the year before Norm Cash arrived in Detroit, Mickey Mantle and Whitey Ford pulled Kaline aside and said they had heard that the Yankees had offered the Tigers first baseman Moose Skowron and a couple of minor-leaguers in exchange for Al. Supposedly, the Tigers' front office was interested. At least, they were listening. Then, in July, the injury-prone Skowron broke his wrist, and the trade talks ceased.

An enterprising Detroit sportswriter, searching for a new angle, compared Kaline's first six seasons in the big leagues to Ty Cobb's first six and reported that Kaline had hit more home runs and driven in more runs than the great Cobb had at a similar stage in his career.

"That's where it stops, though," said Kaline, who, having matured in his dealings with the press, found the comparison more amusing than irritating. "In his seventh season, Cobb batted .420. I'll settle for a hundred points less."

Still, as the Tigers continued to play second fiddle or worse to the Yankees, the speculation over trading Kaline persisted.

However, Bob Scheffing, Kaline's manager from 1961 through 1963, and Al's personal favorite, never joined that chorus. "I wouldn't trade him for Mantle—or Mays," Scheffing declared.

Well-traveled Charlie Dressen, who replaced Scheffing as the Tigers' manager in 1963, agreed. When he was asked to name the greatest player he had ever managed, Dressen pondered the question carefully before answering.

"I'm not the kind of manager who goes from club to club, each time singing the praises of a local boy," Dressen said. "I don't want to sound like one of those guys who manages in Chicago and says, 'This Chicago player is the best,' then manages in St. Louis and says, 'This St. Louis player is the best.'

"Jackie Robinson was the most exciting runner I ever had. He couldn't be equaled on the bases. He could rob a team blind. PeeWee Reese was the gustiest little infielder I ever had. I'd have to put Roy Campanella in a class with Mickey Cochrane, Gabby Harnett, and Billy Dickey. And Hank Aaron is the best hitter I ever had.

"But in my heart, I'm convinced Kaline is the best player who ever played for me. For all-around ability, I mean hitting, fielding, running, and throwing, I'll go with Al. He's a cinch for the Hall of Fame someday."

Even so, Kaline never warmed to Dressen.

"Scheffing was a real man, well liked by his players," Kaline said. "He let you alone as long as you did your job. He was a father-type manager.

"Dressen, on the other hand, was a teacher. He had tremendous knowledge of the game and was always teaching us the fine points of play. He didn't rely completely on his coaches to teach batting, pitching, and so on. He would do it himself. He was the most knowledgeable manager I ever had."

In 1964 the New York Yankees offered to trade single-season home-run king Roger Maris to the Tigers, even-up, for Kaline. But general manager Jim Campbell turned them down.

When Campbell was asked by *Sports Illustrated* if he would ever think of trading Kaline under any circumstances, the lifelong Tigers executive replied, "I would consider it. Yes sir, I certainly would.

"If the Giants, say, were to offer me Willie Mays and Juan Marichal and Orlando Cepeda for Kaline, I would have to give it some consideration."

Still the trade rumors refused to die.

In 1966, during the winter meetings in Columbus, Ohio, the Los Angeles Dodgers bundled several of their top young prospects together and dangled them in front the Tigers in exchange for Kaline. This time, Campbell refused to even listen

That same off-season, the Minnesota Twins reportedly rejected Campbell's offer to trade Kaline and pitcher Dave Wickersham for ace hurler Jim Kaat and outfielder Jimmie Hall—although that story was never confirmed.

In retrospect, Kaline is often remembered as a man who could do no wrong. But that was not always the case. The 1950s and early 1960s were turbulent times in Tigers history, and Kaline, as the face of the team, the lone superstar, often found himself caught in the middle.

Today, Kaline is hailed as the man who humbly rejected the Tigers offer of $100,000 in 1971 because he didn't believe he deserved it. However, in 1958 general manager John McHale sliced several thousand dollars off Kaline's salary—even though Kaline had batted .295 with 23 homers and 90 RBIs the previous season.

As a matter of policy, McHale automatically cut the pay of any player who had an off year. However, in Kaline's case, he secretly made a "gentleman's agreement" to give Al a $3,000 bonus, provided he was hitting .300 on June 1. Such provisions were prohibited under baseball rules, but McHale made the offer anyway.

That same year, manager Jack Tighe, who was feeling the heat from the front office for the Tigers' fourth-place finish the season before, moved Kaline from right field to center during spring training on the theory that, with Al's speed, he could cover more ground in center.

Kaline went along with the change, although he didn't like it.

That ticklish situation quickly resolved itself when shortstop Harvey Kuenn, who preferred to play the outfield anyway, went to Tighe and suggested that he move to center field in order to make room at shortstop for Billy Martin, who had been acquired from Kansas City in a 13-player off-season swap, or promising rookie Coot Veal—whom Tigers management favored, at the time, over a young speedster named Maury Wills.

Late that spring, as the Tigers barnstormed their way north for the beginning of the regular season, Kaline, who had been struggling at the plate in the exhibition games, uncharacteristically failed to run out an infield grounder.

Tighe, who was both surprised and angered, pulled Kaline aside and chewed him out. Later the Tigers manager told a reporter, "It's not that Al is loafing. He has worked hard all spring. But he gets so mad at himself when he isn't hitting that he does things like that. He has to learn to get over that habit."

Kaline, who usually played every game as if the pennant was on the line, acknowledged his mistake. "Jack Tighe was right," he said.

But on May 21, with Kaline batting a paltry .217, Tighe benched him and inserted Johnny Groth in right field. "Al is talking to himself. He is worrying too much about his slump. A rest might help him," the manager explained.

Kaline was stunned. Then the story about the $3,000 bonus that John McHale had promised Al if he was hitting .300 by June 1 leaked out in the press. Sportswriters, who were down on the team anyway because of their poor start, suggested the bonus offer had placed undue pressure on Kaline and that the Tigers were paying the price.

On May 22, following a 5–4 loss to the Yankees, the Tigers tumbled into last place in the American League. The next day, in the midst of the team's ninth loss in a row, the public-address announcer at Briggs Stadium, while making a routine announcement about the availability of tickets for future games, was drowned out by a chorus of angry boos.

On June 10, an off day, with the team still in the cellar, manager Jack Tighe, a genuinely decent sort although maybe not major-league-managerial material, was fired and replaced by Bill Norman, who had been called the "minor league Casey Stengel" and who could at least drink beer with the best of them.

At the time, Kaline was in the midst of what would become an 18-game hitting steak, the longest so far in his career, that lifted his average to .310. But it came too late to save Tighe—or for Al to collect that $3,000 bonus. At least it got the Tigers fans on Kaline's side again—and the critics off his back.

"He hasn't reached superstar class yet, but he has the potential," said GM John McHale, who described Al as "one of the most exciting players in the game.

"He's only scratched the surface," McHale added.

"He'll be a superstar when he learns to cut down on strikeouts," observed former Yankees slugger Tommy Henrich, who had been hired as a Tigers coach. "With two strikes on him, he's got to forget everything except to become a goal tender."

On defense, Kaline seemed to be better than ever, if that was possible.

In a tie game against the Yankees, with Yogi Berra on third base, Mickey Mantle lofted a long fly ball down the right-field line. As the ball drifted into foul territory, it became apparent that if Kaline caught the ball, Berra would probably be able to tag up and score the go-ahead run from third.

The smart play, the safe play, would have been to let the ball land foul and keep Berra on third. But Kaline caught the ball deep in foul territory, whirled, and cut down a surprised Berra—who has hardly the fastest man in the game—with a strike to home plate.

Despite his slow start, Kaline finished the 1958 season hitting .313, 15 points behind Ted Williams, who won the batting title for the second year in a row.

Even so, the Tigers finished in fifth place in 1958, a .500 team at 77–77.

For the second season in a row, Kaline won a Gold Glove as the best right fielder in the league. Although enemy hitters rarely challenged Kaline's arm by running on him, he led all outfielders in both leagues with 23 assists.

"The more you look at that figure, the more you marvel," said Tigers general manager John McHale. "That assist figure means Kaline is even better than anyone thinks."

From 1957 through 1967, Kaline won ten Gold Gloves.

In 1959, with the team again reeling, manager Bill Norman moved Kaline to center field in place of Harvey Kuenn, whose arm had been broken when he was hit by a pitch. "He's as good in center as he is in right," declared Norman, who by that time was struggling to save his own job. "I think he's in the same class with Mantle or Mays."

Kaline made the move for the good of the team. But Al did not like playing center field.

When the Tigers lost 15 of their first 17 games, Norman was fired. On May 2, Jim Campbell, then the Tigers' vice president and business manager, accompanied new general manager and future Hall of Famer Rick Ferrell to the locker room to deliver the news.

"Bill," Campbell said, "Rick has something to tell you." Then the soft-spoken Ferrell ushered Norman into an adjacent waiting room just outside the clubhouse door, where the players' families and friends gathered after games, to awkwardly give him the ax.

To replace Norman, the Tigers hired 62-year-old Jimmie Dykes, who had played in the big leagues for 22 seasons, beginning in 1918, and spent

18 more managing four different ballclubs, along the way acquiring a reputation as a guy who knew how to fix floundering ballclubs.

But Dykes, who had seen it all during his four decades in the game, had no delusions about his new job with the Tigers. "I'm no magician, and neither is any other manager," he said. "The players make or break a ballclub. If we're going to climb out of the basement, they'll have to do it."

Dykes quickly came to appreciate the talents of the young man playing center field—so much so that when Kuenn returned to the lineup in early June, the new manager left Kaline in center and played Kuenn in right.

"What a pleasant exposure it is seeing that boy operate every day," Dykes said of Kaline. "What a break putting him in center field. Now he can run and do what he does. What a range he has. There may be others just as fast, but none with better ball instinct. And they don't run on his arm, either. You watch him come in on a fly—he's great at it. I've told him not to play too deep. For every ball hit over his head, he will make 10 catches in front of him. As a matter of fact, it's hard to hit one over his head, too."

The feeling was mutual.

"I don't think Dykes can get too much praise for what he's done with this club," Kaline said when a reporter asked Al's opinion of his new manager after the Tigers had won seven of their first eight games under Dykes. "He's kept the players keyed up. He inspires them. He's with the players a lot. He kids around and he tells you stories about the old-timers. He's a ballplayer's manager."

By late June, under Dykes' direction, the Tigers had climbed from last place to second and trailed the front-running Cleveland Indians by just half a game. A lot of that was due to the hitting of Kaline, who was batting .351.

"I hope it keeps up," said Kaline, who had also belted 12 home runs. "You know, I never expected to be a big home-run hitter. I only hit four home runs in four years in high school. I always thought that I could maybe hit more home runs if I swung up on the ball, but I haven't really tried it. I think I'm a better hitter when I hit the ball on the line."

But on June 18, Kaline was struck on the left side of his face by an errant throw from Baltimore second baseman Billy Gardner, fracturing a bone in his cheek.

When Al returned to the lineup, he was named to the All-Star team for the fifth year in a row and selected to start in center field ahead of Mickey Mantle. There were two All-Star Games in 1959, and Kaline homered in the first one.

Harvey Kuenn won the American League batting title in 1959 with a .353 average, and Kaline placed second at .327. Al also led the league with a .530 slugging percentage, matched his career high with 27 more home runs, and was credited with 94 RBIs. In addition, he won his third Gold Glove in a row, this time as a center fielder—the first man ever to win the trophy, which is annually awarded for defensive excellence, at two different positions.

Nevertheless, the Tigers finished in fourth place, two games under .500 and 18 behind the White Sox. It was an all-too-familiar story.

Kaline, who had moved into a new home in a fashionable Detroit suburb, was convinced he deserved a nice raise. But he dreaded the thought of having to negotiate with the Tigers' flamboyant new president, Bill DeWitt, a notorious tightwad.

After mailing Kaline five contracts, only to have each of them returned unsigned, DeWitt phoned Al. "Come on down, and let's straighten this out," the Tigers president said.

They did. Kaline signed for $42,000, a 30 percent increase over his salary the previous season and just $2,000 less than Al had been seeking. Obviously, Kaline was a better negotiator than he realized.

Prior to the start of the 1960 season, the Tigers traded rookie infielder Steve Demeter to Cleveland for an unproven, nondescript first baseman named Norm Cash.

"I'll give you Cash for Demeter," Indians general manager Frank Lane told Tigers GM Rick Ferrell.

"Norman Cash or cold cash?" Ferrell inquired.

"Norman," Trader Lane replied.

It turned out to be one of the best trades the Tigers ever made.

In 1961 the carefree, fun-loving Cash, who soon became Kaline's close friend, surprised everyone by smacking 41 homers, driving in 132 runs, and leading the American League with a .361 average.

Not until years later did Cash confess he had illegally hollowed out the ends of his bats to help make that sensational season happen. But by then nobody seemed to mind.

On the eve of the 1960 season opener, DeWitt, who fancied himself a wheeler-dealer, stunned everybody by trading Harvey Kuenn, the reigning American League batting champ, to the Indians for home-run king Rocky Colavito.

It was a baseball first. Kuenn had led the American League in hitting the previous season, batting .353, while Colavito had belted an AL-best 42 homers for the Tribe.

Furthermore, Colavito was a matinee idol in Cleveland, very popular with the female fans, while Kuenn was a hard-nosed ballplayer who came to the park every day prepared to play and win.

"A hamburger for a steak," snorted Indians general manager Frank "Trader" Lane, who never tried to hide the fact that he believed he got the better of the deal.

"I was very surprised," Kaline later admitted, when asked about the blockbuster deal. "Harvey was a good friend of mine. And I did well when he was here because he was on base all the time. I got to drive in a lot of runs.

"But they called me in and said, 'Now you get on base, and Rocky will drive you in.' It was a different mind-set."

When the Tigers began the 1960 season by winning their first five games, three of those victories thanks to key hits by Kaline, the Detroit media, happy to be able to write about a winner for a change, began trumpeting the team's new "Murderers Row" of Kaline, Rocky Colavito, and Norm Cash.

But that fantasy was short-lived, and Kaline soon found himself plagued by nagging aches and pains and batting a mere .226 as the Tigers dropped like a rock from first place to seventh.

The last thing Kaline needed right then was to become entangled in an off-the-field controversy.

During the off-season, Frank Carlin, who had entered in those business ventures with Kaline and hockey star Gordie Howe, convinced his partners they should invest in racehorses as a way to legally reduce their tax liability on the profits they were making in the automotive business.

Soon the newly formed HKC Stables owned horses named Stormy Al, Challenge Baby, and Mr. Bruce, which were racing at a track in Toledo, Ohio, some 50 miles south of Detroit.

When the story of their stable broke in the Detroit newspapers in mid-May, Kaline suddenly found himself forced to defend more than just his disappointing batting average.

"Sure, I'm part owner of a string of horses," he admitted. "What's all the excitement about? I happen to like racing. I like horses. I go out to the tracks quite a bit when we aren't playing ball because it relaxes me. For that matter, so do club owners, managers, coaches, everybody. I don't see what all the fuss is about."

Some 50 years earlier, former Tigers owner Frank Navin had been an avid gambler who regularly frequented racetracks in the Detroit area and who reportedly won the money to purchase his initial stake in the ballclub in an all-night poker game.

But ever since the 1919 World Series scandal involving the infamous Chicago Black Sox, Major League Baseball had done everything it could do to distance itself from gamblers and gambling—even when such gambling was aboveboard and perfectly legal. And a decade later Kaline's teammate, Denny McLain, would be suspended for half a season because of his involvement with gamblers and bookmakers.

However, in 1960, baseball commissioner Ford Frick, the former sportswriter, declined to involve himself in the simmering Kaline controversy.

"I don't know anything about it," Frick insisted. "You say he has horses. Maybe they're show horses. Anyway, I'm not going to say a thing until I know more about it."

In Detroit, Tigers president Bill DeWitt sought to defuse the situation.

"I really don't know much about it," DeWitt said. "But I'll say this: I don't think baseball and racing mix. I'll have a talk with Kaline," DeWitt continued. "Perhaps the boy needs a little guidance. I would wonder if it affected his baseball playing. That would be my chief concern—although I don't imagine it has. The objection isn't to racing itself, understand. It's just that the notion has always been that ballplayers might meet and get to know some gamblers through association with it. Of course, we wouldn't like that."

Kaline was stunned by the reaction to what, in his mind, had been a totally innocent, legitimate investment. Nevertheless, not looking for a fight, he quickly severed his relationship with HKC Stables, selling his interest to Carlin. As always, with Al, baseball came first.

"I'm sorry I got everybody so shook up," Kaline told the press. "But I've got nothing to be ashamed of. This was only an investment. But I think it is best for everybody that I drop out of the racing thing. After all, my life is baseball, and I don't want to embarrass anybody connected with the game."

The furor quickly died down, but baseball fans have long memories. When Kaline struggled at the plate, some leather-lunged customer in the stands would inevitably shout, "How's the horse-race business, Al?"

"Those guys in the bleachers even remembered the names of the horses," Kaline recalled. "It took a little time to live down the incident with them."

In mid-June, as Kaline's frustration at the plate continued, he was thrown out of a game for the first time in his career. Al objected to a third strike called by plate umpire Bob Stewart, yelled something, and immediately got the thumb.

Kaline realized he had been wrong and sought out Stewart after the game to apologize. Later, when asked by a reporter about the ejection, Kaline admitted, "I was wrong, and I knew it when I got back to the dugout. I called him stupid and used another word you can't print. That's why I told him I was sorry."

It was not the last time Kaline would lose his temper and be ejected. And it was not the last time he would apologize. "I think the umpires have the toughest job in the world, and I respect them," he said years later.

Kaline's woes at the plate continued until, hobbled by an injured left knee that refused to heal, Al found himself benched by manager Jimmie Dykes.

By then, Kaline had taken to watching movies of himself filmed during his batting championship season of 1955, searching for answers. In a doubleheader against the Washington Senators in late June, Al heard a smattering of boos each time he stepped up to bat. Kaline, who began the day batting .229, went 2-for-8 as the Tigers dropped both ends of the twin bill.

He tried a lighter bat. That didn't work, so he tried a heavier one. He closed up his batting stance. Then he widened it. Nothing worked. The 1960 season was fast becoming the worst year Al had ever known as a pro.

It certainly came as no surprise that when the American League players and coaches elected that summer's All-Star team, Kaline's name was missing from the starting lineup. But AL manager Al Lopez, who had himself been passed over by the Tigers' front office three years earlier when they promoted Jack Tighe, salvaged some of Al's pride by picking him as one of the reserves. "How can you play an All-Star Game without Kaline in it?" Lopez asked.

Kaline's injured left knee still bothered him. He felt pain on nearly every step, especially when he extended himself, running hard after a fly ball or to first base. But Kaline didn't say a word to Lopez.

Mickey Mantle was the American League's starting center fielder, and his knee was hurting, too. When the AL All-Stars took the field in the top half of the sixth inning in the first of what were to be two All-Star Games that summer, trailing the National Leaguers 5–0, Lopez motioned to Kaline and said, "Go in for Mantle."

In the bottom half of the inning, Kaline grounded sharply to third baseman Eddie Mathews. When, out of the corner of his eye, Kaline saw Mathews momentarily bobble the ball, Al dug for first base as hard as he could, even though every step brought more pain. He was safe.

Eventually Kaline worked his way around to third, from which he scored the AL's first run on a bloop single by Nellie Fox.

The next inning, ignoring the pain in his leg, Kaline robbed Hank Aaron of an extra-base hit with a spectacular running catch that brought the crowd at Kansas City's Municipal Stadium to its feet.

And in the bottom of the eighth, Kaline homered to drive in the AL's only other runs in a 5–3 defeat. As he circled the bases, Kaline smiled to himself. At least this time he didn't have to run hard. He could take it easy on his aching leg.

A Detroit sportswriter covering the game, one of the few at the ballpark that sweltering afternoon who was aware of how much pain Kaline was in, began his report with this sentence: "Al Kaline is a good man to have around, even when he only has one leg."

In August Kaline came off the field at the end of an inning at Briggs Stadium and slumped on the bench.

"You look tired," a worried Jimmie Dykes said.

"I'm dragging," Kaline, never one to complain, confessed.

Dykes removed Al from the lineup and ordered him to see the Tigers' team physician, Dr. Russell Wright. Dr. Wright discovered Al's blood pressure was low. "He tires quickly and easily," the doctor said. "But he'll be all right."

Kaline rested on the bench for a couple of days before Dykes wrote Al's name on the lineup card again. "A weak Kaline is better than some of the strong boys in our lineup," reasoned Dykes, whose own job was reportedly in jeopardy.

On August 3, Bill DeWitt, the impetuous president who in late June had publicly absolved Dykes of any blame for the Tigers' slump, traded the Tigers' skipper to Cleveland in exchange for the Indians' manager, Joe Gordon.

For DeWitt, who earlier had swapped batting champ Harvey Kuenn for home-run king Rocky Colavito, it was another baseball first. The deal made headlines from coast to coast.

When Gordon, who had played for 11 years in the big leagues with the Yankees and Indians, walked into the bemused and a bit bewildered

Tigers clubhouse for the first time, he was greeted by first baseman and club comedian Norm Cash, who had himself come over from Cleveland before the start of the season.

"First Frank Lane trades me, then he trades Rocky, and now he trades you," Cash quipped in his Texas drawl. "What's he trying to do, break up the Indians?"

One of the first things Gordon did after taking the job was to sit down with Al Kaline. Gordon knew Kaline was struggling, and he also knew how important Al could be to the team.

"Look, I'm not going to try to tell you how to hit," Gordon said. "All I want to say is, you're all tensed up at the plate. Try to relax, and you might salvage something out of this season yet."

Slowly Kaline, still on medication to treat his low blood pressure, began to come around at the plate. On August 18 he homered, doubled, and delivered two singles to lead the Tigers to an 11–6 win over Kansas City. Little more than a week later, he went 6-for-7 in a doubleheader split against the Yankees. In early September, in a doubleheader sweep over Washington, he tripled and singled in the first game and belted a grand-slam home run in the nightcap.

By the end of the season, Kaline's average had climbed to .278, which was hardly satisfactory, especially alongside his 15 home runs and just 68 RBIs—his lowest such totals since 1954. As Al told Louise, "It was a terrible season, and the best thing I can do is just forget it."

The combination of the Tigers' sixth-place finish and team president Bill DeWitt's insistence on sticking with established players rather than bringing up promising kids from the farm system was enough to convince Joe Gordon that he didn't want to remain as the manager in Detroit. At the end of the season, Gordon locked himself in his apartment and refused to come out. He quit.

When John Fetzer purchased controlling interest in the ballclub in October and assumed the position of president, DeWitt, who was not content to be merely the general manager, resigned. The duties of the remaining front-office executives were rearranged, and the ballpark at the corner of Michigan and Trumbull, originally known as Navin Field and later as Briggs Stadium, was renamed Tiger Stadium.

Needless to say, it was not an atmosphere that Kaline, ever the perfectionist who had always set such high standards for himself and his team, initially relished.

General manager Rick Ferrell was entrusted with the task of finding a new manager. And after an unsuccessful attempt to hire the legendary Casey Stengel, Ferrell picked affable Bob Scheffing, a former National League catcher who had managed the Chicago Cubs for three seasons.

"I hope they'll like me and play for me," said Scheffing. "But one thing is sure—I'll be firm enough to earn their respect."

In fact, Scheffing turned out to be Kaline's favorite manager among the 14 Al played for during his 22 seasons. "He made me a good ballplayer," Kaline recalled. "And I was really devoted to him."

During the off-season, the Tigers traded for Billy Bruton, who had been regarded as one of the best center fielders in the game during his eight years with the Milwaukee Braves, and Scheffing immediately moved Kaline back to right field.

During spring training, the Tigers' new manager urged Kaline to take more of a leadership role on the team.

"When I had a bad year like the last one, how can anyone look up to me as a leader?" Kaline protested.

"That has nothing to do with it," Scheffing told Al. "There's no such thing as a ballplayer who hasn't had a bad year. The point is, you're the key man on this club. This is your ninth year, and the younger players will accept anything you tell them. You have to show them how to play this game, not only by example but by your willingness to help them with their problems."

"I'll do my best," Kaline promised but with reservations.

Kaline's main concern was still the Tigers' annual lack of success as a team. And the future was not looking any brighter.

"Sure, I like my hits and want to build a good personal record in this game," he said, as the Tigers prepared for the 1961 season. "But the most important thing is winning. Hits are not very important if you always lose.

"You know, I've been with the Tigers eight years now, and I don't know what it is to play with a winner. Baseball has given me a lot, but the one thing I've missed is playing in a World Series. I'd like to do that just once."

Nevertheless, Kaline tried to embrace his role as an elder statesman and his responsibility as a team leader.

"Before the season I never thought of myself as being an example to the kids on the team," he said. "But Scheffing convinced me that I'm supposed to set the example for the young players. Tell me, how would it look if I dogged it? Maybe they'd think that's the way to do things in the major leagues.

"Another thing," Al added, "after last year, I'm hustling because I have to prove something to some people—including maybe myself."

When the 1961 season began, both Kaline and the Tigers started off strong. The Tigers lost their opener, then won eight in a row and 17 of their first 22 games to take a three-game lead in the American League.

"Scheffing should get more credit for that than people give him," Kaline, who was hitting .337 at the time, told reporters. "He gets 100 percent out of everybody."

Kaline appreciated the fact that Scheffing had returned him to right field, and he said so. "I feel more comfortable in right field," Al admitted. "I came up as a right fielder, and I had my best years there. I think I have more opportunities to throw men out from right field."

Kaline wasn't the only Tiger pounding the ball. Rocky Colavito and Norm Cash were hitting, too. The team was in first place and on a roll.

On June 20, with infielders Steve Boros and Chico Fernandez both injured, Scheffing asked Kaline to play a totally new position: third base.

Although Al worried he might let his teammates down and cost them a game, he handled his two chances in the field with ease and contributed a single and a double at the plate, driving in two runs and scoring another in a 5–4 Tigers win over Washington.

Surprisingly, the Senators did not try to bunt toward third base as everyone, including Kaline, had expected them to do. "Why should we?" said Washington outfielder Gene Woodling after the game. "That Kaline can throw!"

In July Kaline helped the Tigers win a game another way—scoring from third base on a ground ball back to the mound after first bluffing the pitcher, Boston's Galen Cisco, into thinking he intended to stay put at third.

"Base running like that is instinctive," raved Tigers third-base coach Phil Cavarretta. "Kaline is one of the best. What makes him great is the fact that he can beat you with his bat, his arm, his fielding, and his legs."

Norm Cash's bid for the batting title was big news in Detroit. But the rest of the nation only had eyes for the battle between Yankees Mickey Mantle and Roger Maris to see which of them would break Babe Ruth's storied single-season record of 60 home runs.

The Tigers went into New York for a three-game series on September 1, trailing the front-running Yankees by just a game and a half. It was a do-or-die for the suddenly pennant-minded Tigers. This was their chance. Suddenly, all of Detroit was talking about the Tigers.

But they lost the opener 1–0 despite two singles and a triple by Kaline as the Yankees' Whitey Ford outdueled Don Mossi. Then the Tigers dropped the second game of the crucial series 7–2 as a home run by Rocky Colavito accounted for their only runs. The Yankees completed the sweep 8–5 despite two more hits from Kaline, in effect knocking the Tigers out of the pennant race. They ended the season eight games behind New York.

Cash, by now known as "Stormin' Norman," batted .361 to win the hitting title, while Kaline finished second at .324. And the Tigers, led by Cash (41), Colavito (45), and Kaline (19) belted 180 home runs and won 101 games. Unfortunately, the Yankees, led by Maris' record 61 home runs and Mantle's 54, blasted 240 homers and won 109 times.

Nevertheless, it was the Tigers' best finish since 1950, and their win total matched the team record set in the pennant-winning season of 1934. It marked only the third time in AL history that a team had won 100 or more games and failed to claim the pennant.

For his efforts, Kaline was named the 1961 American League Comeback Player of the Year, a dubious distinction at best, which prompted Al to quip with a wry smile, "I didn't think I was that bad in 1960."

CHAPTER 11

"What Will I Use for Legs?"

For his performance in 1961, Al Kaline received a pay raise to $49,000 in 1962. At the time, it was the largest salary the notoriously tight-fisted Tigers had ever bestowed on any player, other than home-run slugger Hank Greenberg, who had made $75,000 in 1946, his final season in Detroit.

When Kaline reported to spring training in Lakeland, Florida, one of the several reporters who had happily fled the Michigan winter and gone south to cover the team commented that Al, who was about to begin his 10th season as a Tiger, seemed as enthusiastic as he had been when he was a skinny young kid.

"I really think I'm a better ballplayer—more help to the club—today than I was then," said Kaline, rejuvenated by the Tigers' presence in the pennant race the previous summer for the first time since he had joined the team in 1953.

"I think, sometimes, batting averages are overemphasized. I advance more runners today, and I'm stronger defensively. I just hope I can keep it up. I really have two ambitions now. Besides playing in the World Series, I'd like to play in the majors for 20 years."

Detroit had not played in the World Series since 1945, when Kaline was 10 years old. But when asked to assess the Tigers' chances in 1962,

Al said, "We came close last year and folded. Yes, I think we have a good chance this year."

At the time, nobody paid much attention to Kaline's comment about his second goal, playing in the major leagues for 20 years. It sounded nice, but only one player, the incomparable Ty Cobb, had ever worn a Tigers uniform that long. And Al was not yet halfway there.

Surprisingly, Kaline found fault with his performance in 1961 for a strange reason: he had only struck out 42 times.

"That's not enough," Al told one of the reporters covering the team during training camp. "For a batter like myself, someone who goes to the plate more than 600 times a year, 42 strikeouts isn't enough.

"It means that I wasn't attacking the ball like I should. I must have been playing it safe an awful lot of times by taking an easy swing at the ball."

Weeks later, sitting in his Washington hotel room, brooding over going 0-for-4 in the Tigers' April 9 season-opening 4–1 loss to the Senators, Kaline made up his mind he was going to swing harder in 1962 and try to hit more home runs, even if it cost him a few points on his batting average.

It worked. By May 11 Kaline was batting .364—and he already had 10 home runs, compared to just 19 in all of 1961.

"I also think I'm more patient," explained Kaline, after admitting he had, indeed, been making a conscious effort to swing harder. "I'm waiting for my pitch instead of swinging at the pitcher's pitch—something Ted Williams told me to do a long time ago. That's something that's difficult to do.

"I'm taking advantage of pitching mistakes, too. I'm not swinging at the ball that is low and away. I used to do that, and that's no good. But with the exception of swinging harder, I'm not doing anything else that's different."

Kaline was batting .345 with 13 home runs and 38 RBIs on May 25 when the Tigers returned to Yankee Stadium, where their pennant hopes had evaporated the previous September. Again they were within striking distance, just five games out of first place.

Then on May 26, with two out in the bottom of ninth, a New York runner on first, and the Tigers nursing a 2–1 lead over the Yankees, Kaline broke his right collarbone making a game-saving catch on a fly ball off the bat of Elston Howard.

Kaline was lost for eight weeks, and without their leader the Tigers looked like a team that was merely going through the motions. The team fell to seventh place, and general manager Rick Ferrell criticized the club's lackadaisical attitude.

"I hate to use the word 'complacency,'" Ferrell said. "I think most of the players are bearing down. But there are some who are taking defeat too lightly. I don't like that."

With Kaline back in the lineup beginning on July 23, the Tigers salvaged what they could from the rest of the season, eventually finishing in fourth place. "We knew our pennant hopes were over when Al was hurt," manager Bob Scheffing admitted. "But he got us into the first division in the last two months. What a ballplayer he is! I wish every man I ever handled had his spirit and his will to win."

Despite missing 62 games, Kaline batted .304, sixth-best in the league. However, he fell 50 appearances short of the 502 trips to the plate required to officially be part of the batting race. Nevertheless, he smacked a career high 29 home runs and had 94 RBIs, matching his best effort in that department since 1956. His .593 slugging percentage was the second-highest in the AL, and he won his fifth Gold Glove.

That left Kaline, the Tigers, and their fans to wonder what kind of season Al might have had, what kind of numbers he might have put up, if only he hadn't gotten hurt.

Following the 1962 season, Al and Louise joined the rest of the Tigers players and their wives on a baseball junket to Japan. There, Kaline discovered two things: the Japanese fans knew all about him, and the pain in his right arm had gone away.

The trip abroad made him retrospective about his life and his career. "I don't know where I would be without baseball," Kaline told a writer upon his return. "I guess I'd be working with my dad in that broom factory. The game has been good to me. I never fully realized what a good life we all have in this country until we went to Japan. I saw women working on construction crews, down on their hands and knees, working like men from dawn to dusk. I'm more satisfied than ever to be living in America and playing baseball."

When Jim Campbell—who had been promoted from farm director to general manager, replacing Rick Ferrell—sent Kaline a contract that called for a salary of $54,000 in 1963, Al didn't hesitate. He signed.

Early in spring training, Kaline took stock of his situation and decided that, despite his 29 runs during the injury-abbreviated season before, with big boppers Norm Cash and Rocky Colavito on his side, it no longer made sense for him to swing for the fences so often.

"I've decided not to swing for home runs," Kaline told reporters monitoring the ballclub in Florida. "I figure my job is to get on base as much as I can so Colavito and Cash can drive me in. The big thing is to win games, and I think we'll win more if I swing for hits instead of homers."

Kaline was optimistic about the season ahead. "I think the '63 Tigers are the best team I've played on," he observed.

However, in 1963 sluggers Rocky Colavito and Norm Cash got off to sluggish starts, and pitcher Frank Lary, who had been plagued by a sore arm the year before, continued to struggle.

By June 1, Kaline was hitting .314, but the Tigers were buried in eighth place, nine and a half games out of first.

"I thought we were going to do better than this," Kaline told a Detroit writer. "I thought we had a real shot at the pennant. It's frustrating."

By mid-June, Kaline had boosted his average to .353, but the team had sunk to ninth place. In an effort to quiet the fans, the front office traded pitcher Paul Foytack, Kaline's former roommate, and called up outfielder Gates Brown from Syracuse.

Then, on June 17, with the Tigers' latest losing streak at seven, Jim Campbell did what baseball teams always do when all else fails: he fired manager Bob Scheffing and his entire coaching staff and hired 64-year-old pepperpot Charlie Dressen.

The wholesale midseason change was unprecedented. It marked the first time that a major-league manager and all of his coaches had been dismissed at midseason. Although no explanation was given, it was widely believed that Scheffing lost his job because the front office thought he was too easy on the players.

There were protests from the press and from the public—and from some of the Tigers players, including Kaline, who liked Scheffing the best of all of the 14 managers he eventually played for.

"I really can't thank him enough for what he's done for me," Kaline declared as Scheffing departed.

"He [Scheffing] wasn't a good manager," Kaline conceded years later, "but he was the only guy who came to me and told me what he wanted me to do."

"It was a hard thing to do because Bob was a good friend," Campbell later recalled, without any remorse, when asked about the firing.

"But he was fed up with the whole thing, too. Bob was such a nice guy, he couldn't bring himself to discipline the players because they had done well for him two years before. And some of the very guys he was being nice to were the ones kicking him in the tail.

"So when I decided to make a change, I made up my mind I was going to clean the whole thing out," Campbell explained. "Charlie Dressen let me pick the coaches, and I brought them in from our own minor-league system. Bob Swift, Pat Mullin, Stubby Overmire, and Wayne Blackburn. These were guys who knew our minor-league players and what they could do. And I knew that was what we had to do—build from within."

Dressen, who had previously managed the Cincinnati Reds, Brooklyn Dodgers, Washington Senators, and Milwaukee Braves, brought a reputation as a sharp-tongued taskmaster who wouldn't accept anything less than a player's best.

Publicly, at the time, Kaline said, "I think that Charlie Dressen knows more about baseball than any manager I've ever had."

Privately, Al later admitted, "I had some problems with him because he was really a young players' manager."

Of the 14 managers Kaline played for during his career, he liked Dressen the least.

Kaline was again voted to the starting lineup for the All-Star Game, collecting a league-high 226 votes. Minnesota's Bob Allison, Al's closest competitor in right field, received 25 votes.

Kaline continued to be hobbled by persistent pain in his knee, which he had twisted in May, and he worried that playing on it might cause permanent damage. A visit to the doctor relieved Al of that worry. "It's just a matter of how much pain you can stand," the doctor told him.

Kaline went into September locked in a battle with Boston's Carl Yastrzemski for the American League batting title. But the pain in Al's leg was taking its toll. He began altering his batting stance in an effort to ease the pressure on his knee, and his average dipped as a result.

With another batting title now out of his reach, Kaline set his sights on 100 RBIs. "Then I think I'd be willing to call it quits and rest this knee," he said.

But even after Kaline got the four RBIs he needed to reach 100, homering twice and hitting a triple and a single in a 13-inning win over Minnesota on September 19, he was reluctant to call it a season.

"I'd like to rest the knee," he said. "But I might be able to play in some of the last nine games as long as we have a chance for fourth place. I'll play if Charlie Dressen wants me to."

However, the pain worsened and Kaline finished the year with a .312 average—second only to Yastrzemski, who batted .321. It marked the seventh time in ten years as a regular that Kaline had batted .300 or better, and it boosted his lifetime average to .309.

He also knocked in 101 runs, second-best in the AL, and belted 27 home runs in addition to winning his sixth Gold Glove.

To top it off, he finished second behind Elston Howard in balloting for the American League Most Valuable Player Award, despite playing most of the season on an injured knee.

As soon as the season ended, Kaline checked into the Mayo Clinic in Rochester, Minnesota, to have his knee examined. But doctors found only a severe strain, no physical damage, and prescribed rest.

When Jim Campbell mailed Kaline a contract calling for a salary of $70,000 in 1964, Al again signed immediately. He was anxious to get going again.

Now approaching 30 years of age and feeling every minute of it, especially after he injured his crippled left foot during spring training, Kaline could feel his dream of someday playing in the World Series slipping away.

"You can't help but feel a little jealous when you see kids just coming up and getting into a World Series in their first or second year," he admitted. "I've been around for 11, and we've only come close once."

When the 1964 season began, Dressen moved Kaline from the No. 3 spot in the Tigers batting order to fourth, behind Norm Cash.

"Al batted in 94 runs in 1962 despite missing two months with a broken collarbone, and he had 101 RBIs in 1963," Dressen explained when reporters asked. "He's a good RBI man, and I think we ought to take advantage of this."

The idea of batting cleanup appealed to Kaline, too.

"I'm enthusiastic about it," he said. "Batting fourth, you get a lot more chances to drive in runs. I like to hit with men on base, and I think I bear down a little more."

But by early May, Kaline, hobbling on his crippled left foot, was hitting a mere .224. The tendon in Kaline's big toe was swollen and inflamed, and Tigers team physician Dr. Russell Wright ordered Al to stay off his foot for four or five days.

"I don't know how Al's been able to play at all," the doctor said. "He's just been too proud to let anyone know about it."

Kaline returned to the lineup on May 15, but the Tigers continued to flounder. After losing two games to the Washington Senators, the Tigers flew to Cleveland. Always a close-knit group, a number of the players began singing and rocking the bus on their late-night ride from the airport to their downtown Cleveland hotel.

For Dressen, that was the last straw. The volatile little 146-pound manager jumped to his feet at the front of the bus and angrily whirled to face his struggling team.

"Cut out rocking the bus!" Dressen shouted. "The way you're acting, you'd think you won the game. Cut it out, you bunch of clowns!"

The outburst silenced the players but also served to reinforce their opinions of Dressen, a subject on which they were already seriously divided. Some of the Tigers respected their manager's experience and knowledge of the game. Others disliked him and blamed him for the team's failures on the field. Dressen could be charming one minute and caustic the next. Kaline could see both sides of his skipper.

"Dressen was a teacher," Kaline said. "He had tremendous knowledge of the game and was always teaching us the fine points of play. He didn't rely completely on his coaches to teach batting, pitching, and so on. He would do it himself. He was the most knowledgeable manager I ever had."

A week later, the Tigers finally gave up on struggling Frank Lary, who had won 123 games for the team before injuring his arm, and sold him to the expansion New York Mets for $30,000. The pitcher took a potshot at Dressen on his way out of Detroit. "He's too strict. The players can't relax under him," Lary declared.

As the Tigers' losing continued into June, so did Dressen's often profanity-laced tirades—along with the pain in Kaline's left foot. In July Al withdrew from the All-Star Game to rest his aching foot.

Despite the nagging pain, Kaline hit .293 and led his team in doubles, total bases, and slugging percentage as the Tigers stumbled across the finish line in fourth place, 14 games behind the Yankees.

That winter Kaline was finally fitted with a special shoe, complete with padding and a metal plate, designed to protect his crippled left foot, particularly the inflamed big toe.

"I think it will help," Al said hopefully. "Last year, I was putting my left foot too far behind me when I batted. I was always afraid I'd hit it with a foul ball. That threw my stance off-balance, and my hitting suffered."

This from a man who had just batted .293.

When the Tigers asked Al to take a $5,000 pay cut in 1965, down to $65,000, Kaline accepted it without complaint. "They treated me fairly," he said. "When I have a good year, I expect to be paid for it. When I have a bad one, I expect to be cut." It is difficult imagining a player today calling a .293 season "a bad one" and graciously accepting a cut in pay.

As Kaline was about to embark on his 13th season, a Detroit writer again raised the question of how much longer Al might continue to play. After all, he had had more than his share of injuries and aches and pains. And 12 years in the big leagues was a career for most players.

"If I can do it, I want to play for 20 years," Al replied, reiterating a goal he had set years earlier. "And, of course, I want to play in a World Series. Anyone with any pride wants to play in the Series. That's one of my biggest ambitions." Then he added, "I don't know if this club is ever going to make it. There's nothing you can do but keep trying.

"Baseball is tough work now," Kaline continued. "But it always has been, I guess. To make a success of this business, you have to work hard and sacrifice something of your body. I think I've done that. And I'm still doing it.

"My foot is worse now than it has ever been. But I know I have to play on it, and I'll continue to. Baseball is hard work, but I still love it."

Spring training is always a time for optimism. That is true for all teams. And in 1965, Kaline and the Tigers were no exception.

On March 7, following a Sunday intrasquad game, manager Charlie Dressen, an amateur chef who took great pride in his cooking, threw a chili party in the clubhouse for his players. Dressen spent four hours personally preparing the chili feast and stuck around for the party. It was nearly 11:00 PM when the 65-year-old manager finally got back to his hotel room.

At 7:00 the next morning, Stubby Overmire, the Tigers' pitching coach, was awakened by a phone call from the skipper.

"I need you to drive me to the airport," Dressen said.

"The airport?" the surprised Overmire asked.

"Yes. My wife is ill in Los Angeles, and I have to fly out there," Dressen replied.

Then Dressen phoned general manager Jim Campbell, offering the same explanation for his sudden departure. "I'll be back in a few days," Dressen promised. "Bob Swift can handle the team while I'm gone."

It was noon on the following day when Campbell and the Tigers found out the truth about their manager's unexpected hasty exit. Dressen had suffered a heart attack in his hotel room after the chili party in the clubhouse and, upon arriving in Los Angeles, had been rushed to Santa Monica Hospital.

Campbell immediately approached interim manager Bob Swift, who was in the middle of practice at Henley Field. "Get the players in the clubhouse," Campbell ordered.

There, Campbell informed Kaline and the rest of the team of Dressen's condition. "We hope he'll be able to return to the team by Opening Day, but we're not certain," the grim general manager admitted.

As the stunned Tigers returned to the field, Norm Cash turned to Kaline and said, "It's tough. I think the team was just beginning to understand that man."

For a moment, Kaline was lost in his thoughts. "I've learned a lot from Charlie," he said softly.

Even those players who had been critical of Dressen now worried about what his heart attack would do to the team.

"When I first met Dressen, I didn't care for him," admitted promising young pitcher Mickey Lolich. "But he's shown me something. He's got more guts than any man I've ever seen. We ought to go out and win the pennant for him."

Bob Swift, a former catcher with the Tigers in the 1940s and 1950s who had been behind the plate in 1951 when showman Bill Veeck sent midget Eddie Gaedel up to bat for the St. Louis Browns, was a career baseball man who immediately had the respect of his players.

Before the Tigers' season-opener in Kansas City, Swift read a telegram from Dressen to the players.

"Loads of luck to all of you," wrote Dressen, who was recuperating in California. "I want you to know I appreciate the way you have performed for Bob Swift and the coaches during my absence. I hope all the hitters hit .300 and all the pitchers win 20 games. I will be following your play pretty closely now, but don't worry about me if you are thrown out at the plate on a close play. Take chances when the opportunity presents itself."

More than ever, Kaline found himself assuming the role of elder statesman in the Tigers clubhouse.

On May 8, when a Detroit writer who had been particularly critical of the Tigers' play approached Al to ask about his fifteenth-inning, game-winning home run in Baltimore, Kaline bristled. "I don't want to talk about it," Al snapped. "I'm tired of talking to people who put the knock on our players."

The next day, that writer's uncomplimentary story posed the following question: "Is Kaline setting himself up in a new role—clubhouse censor?"

In mid-May, when young Tigers slugger Willie Horton suddenly found himself besieged by members of the media because of his league-leading nine home runs, .406 batting average, and incredible .906 slugging percentage, he sought Kaline's counsel.

"Al, can we talk for a few minutes?" the muscular 22-year-old Horton asked.

"Sure, what about?" Al replied.

"The writers," Horton said softly. "They make me nervous. I don't know what to say to them."

Kaline recalled how he had felt in his early years, especially in 1955 when his pursuit of the batting title had made him the center of attention at age 20.

"I know how you feel," Kaline said. "I was the same way. But I've learned that all you have to do is be honest with them and don't knock any of the other team's players. That's about all there is to it."

In an effort to get the bat of another young Tigers slugger, Jim Northrup, into the lineup, interim manager Bob Swift moved Kaline to center field and played Northrup in right. When Charlie Dressen rejoined the team on May 30, he kept Al in center.

By June 9, Kaline, who continued to bat cleanup, had belted a dozen home runs. "I really don't know what's happened, because I'm not consciously swinging for home runs," Al insisted.

But by July, the ache in his left foot had returned. Kaline, who was hitting .300 at the time, was out of the lineup for the three games immediately prior to the All-Star Game, where American League manager

Al Lopez, who had been made aware of the pain in Al's foot, only used him as a pinch-hitter.

The suits in the Tigers' front office were worried—both about Kaline's status for the balance of the 1965 season and about his future with the ballclub.

However, some of the Tigers fans, frustrated by their favorite team's continued failure to treat them to a pennant and a World Series, again turned against Kaline, suggesting Al only limped when he was in a slump and used his deformed foot as an excuse. That bothered Al.

"When they say things like that, how does it make me look?" he angrily asked a sympathetic member of the Detroit press corps. "Here we're trying to win the pennant, and it sounds like I'm taking a rest. The reason I don't play on certain days is because I can't play.

"Take doubleheaders, for instance. Dressen usually rests me now in the second game because the bad foot just can't take the pounding it gets in two games. I suppose, actually, I could make it through a doubleheader. But then I'd be no good the next day. Or maybe it would put me out of the lineup longer than that.

"I don't want to hamper the club by hobbling around. But you can be sure of one thing: I'll be out there any time Dressen wants me to be and any time I can make it."

After the All-Star break, Kaline had his foot examined at Detroit's Henry Ford Hospital. Doctors indicated he might need surgery after the season ended. Nevertheless, Al continued to play, although he was sometimes replaced in the late innings of games to rest his foot.

And the respect for him around the league had not diminished.

In the first game of a doubleheader against Cleveland on July 21, Indians manager Birdie Tebbetts twice ordered his pitcher to walk Kaline intentionally with first base open—even though the hot-hitting young Willie Horton was due up next.

"Look, Kaline is going to be in the Hall of Fame," Tebbetts explained. "I don't know about Horton yet. So, if I have a choice, I'm not going to let Kaline beat me."

In spite of the pain in his foot, Kaline stole second base for the fourth time in four tries. He also raced from first to third on a single to shallow left field.

"Kaline runs the bases like DiMaggio used to," Charlie Dressen noted. "He goes halfway to the next base on his turn. If he sees he can make it, he keeps going. If he sees he can't, he's got time to go back."

On August 4, Dressen moved Kaline back to right field, where he would have less ground to cover. "Either way suits me, if it helps the team," Al told reporters. "But I do like right field best."

Keeping Kaline in the lineup was critical to the Tigers' slim pennant chances. "Without a healthy Kaline," Cleveland manager Birdie Tebbetts declared, "the Tigers are dead."

In mid-August, Kaline missed three more games after receiving an injection of cortisone in his foot. "If the cortisone doesn't work, I don't know what I'll do," Al admitted.

On his fourth day back in the lineup, Kaline tore the cartilage between his ribs on his right side while trying to make a shoestring catch of a sinking line drive off the bat of Minnesota's Earl Battey. He was sidelined for 18 days and never did regain his batting stroke, finishing the season with a .281 average—Kaline's lowest in five years but still the best by any of the Tigers, who finished fourth for the third time in four years.

On October 11, 1965, Kaline underwent surgery on his left foot at Henry Ford Hospital. Al's big toe was curled almost completely over the toe next to it. Doctors had to break his big toe and reset the bones. He spent six days in the hospital.

"The doctors were shocked when they first saw the X-rays," revealed Tigers vice president Rick Ferrell. "I never doubted that Al had pain, even though he kept going all out. It must have been real misery for him to play as much as he did, and as good as he did, for the last two years."

The timing of the surgery gave Kaline nearly four months to recuperate before the start of spring training. "After that, the foot should be almost as good as new," predicted Kaline, who expected to recover in half that time.

With young sluggers Willie Horton and Bill Freehan in the lineup along with ball hawk Mickey Stanley, and Jim Northrup in reserve, plus a promising young pitching staff that included Denny McLain, who had won 16 games in 1965, Mickey Lolich with 15 wins and Joe Sparma with 13, the Tigers were viewed as up-and-coming contenders in 1966.

And after a winter of rehabilitation, Kaline was looking forward to a season free of any pain in his foot. "It's a great feeling to know I'm in a position to do some things I haven't been able to do for the past two years," he told reporters. "I'm anxious to go all-out during the spring exhibition games to really test the foot. I feel I owe it to the club to find out as soon as possible if the foot is sound.

"There's no way I can expect to have the speed and agility I had when I first joined the club. But right now it feels great."

However, on April 28, Kaline again found himself in the center of a controversy—this time for, of all things, stealing second base in the eighth inning of a 13–5 romp over the Kansas City Athletics.

"That Kaline is bush," Athletics manager Alvin Dark barked to reporters after the game. "Tell me now, do you all steal bases with two out in the eighth inning when you're leading by nine runs? That was bush."

When Dark's comments were relayed to Kaline, Al went on the offensive.

"John Wyatt threw me a spitball," Kaline charged, referring to the Athletics' reliever who would later become Al's teammate with the Tigers. "I don't mind if it means the ballgame, but he was way behind. I would never try to steal normally, but Wyatt got me mad, and I took off against him."

On May 16, the Tigers were taking batting practice before an exhibition game against the National League St. Louis Cardinals when Kaline suddenly noticed that manager Charlie Dressen was nowhere to be seen on the field or in the dugout.

For a moment Al wondered if he might be off discussing a major trade. Then general manager Jim Campbell appeared on the top step of the dugout, waving his team off the field.

Once all of the players were in the clubhouse, Campbell, looking pale and worried, cleared his throat and said, "Charlie Dressen is ill again and has been rushed to Henry Ford Hospital.

Rookie Al Kaline in the Tigers dugout at Briggs Stadium in July 1953.
PHOTO COURTESY OF AP IMAGES.

Al Kaline is presented with the Silver Bat Award for leading the American League in hitting in 1955. Making the presentation (right) is Charlie Gehringer, the Tigers former Hall of Fame second baseman, who became Kaline's close friend. USED WITH PERMISSION BY LOUISVILLE SLUGGER MUSEUM & FACTORY.

Al Kaline, pictured here at 20 years of age in 1955, led the American League in hitting with a .340 average that season, making him the youngest player ever to win the AL batting title. PHOTO COURTESY OF AP IMAGES.

Mickey Vernon (left) of the Cleveland Indians, and Al Kaline (right) pose for a portrait with a representative of Wilson Sporting Goods prior to the MLB All-Star Game on July 8, 1958, at Memorial Stadium in Baltimore, Maryland. PHOTO COURTESY OF GETTY IMAGES.

Al Kaline watches the flight of the ball as he belts one at Tiger Stadium during a 1965 game. PHOTO COURTESY OF GETTY IMAGES.

Tigers pitcher Denny McLain, his head covered in shaving cream, pours a bottle of champagne over Al Kaline's head as they celebrate their American League pennant victory in the Tigers dressing room on September 17, 1968. PHOTO COURTESY OF AP IMAGES.

President Richard Nixon poses in the White House with three sports stars on February 13, 1969. His guests, from left, are Green Bay Packers quarterback Bart Starr, pro golfer Arnold Palmer, and Al Kaline. The three were in Washington to attend a special sports program at the National Press Club. PHOTO COURTESY OF AP IMAGES.

Al Kaline bats against the Cleveland Indians during a game in June 1971. PHOTO COURTESY OF GETTY IMAGES.

Al Kaline connects for a single into left field for the 2,999th hit of his career during a game against the Brewers in Milwaukee on September 22, 1974. Just two days later he got his 3000th hit, becoming the first American League batter since 1925 to reach 3,000 hits and only the 12th in major-league history. PHOTO COURTESY OF AP IMAGES.

Al Kaline and George Kell, right, pose in their broadcast booth at Tiger Stadium on July 3, 1979. PHOTO COURTESY OF AP IMAGES.

National Baseball Hall of Fame inductees Duke Snider (left) and Al Kaline (center) talk with Hall of Famer Ted Williams on stage before inductions on August 3, 1980, in Cooperstown, New York. PHOTO COURTESY OF AP IMAGES.

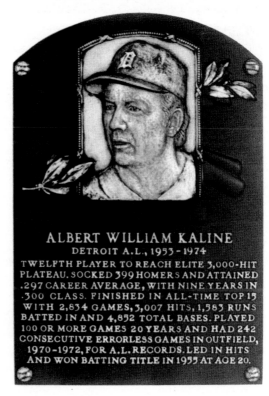

Al Kaline's plaque at the National Baseball Hall of Fame in Cooperstown. PHOTO COURTESY OF AP IMAGES.

ALBERT WILLIAM KALINE
DETROIT A.L., 1953-1974
TWELFTH PLAYER TO REACH ELITE 3,000-HIT
PLATEAU. SOCKED 399 HOMERS AND ATTAINED
.297 CAREER AVERAGE, WITH NINE YEARS IN
.300 CLASS. FINISHED IN ALL-TIME TOP 15
WITH 2,834 GAMES, 3,007 HITS, 1,583 RUNS
BATTED IN AND 4,852 TOTAL BASES. PLAYED
100 OR MORE GAMES 20 YEARS AND HAD 242
CONSECUTIVE ERRORLESS GAMES IN OUTFIELD,
1970-1972, FOR A.L. RECORDS. LED IN HITS
AND WON BATTING TITLE IN 1955 AT AGE 20.

Al Kaline joins the postgame pennant-winning celebration after the Tigers defeated the Oakland A's 6–3 in Game 4 of the American League Championship Series at Comerica Park on October 14, 2006. PHOTO COURTESY OF GETTY IMAGES.

Al Kaline, as popular as ever with Tigers fans, signs autographs before the spring-training game against the New York Mets at Joker Marchant Stadium in Lakeland, Florida, on February 27, 2008. PHOTO COURTESY OF GETTY IMAGES.

"We don't know how serious it is yet," Campbell continued, "but we know Charlie won't be back for a while. Bob Swift will take over management of the team in Charlie's absence." For the second time in less than two years, the Tigers returned to the field with their heads down.

"You can quote me on this: Charlie Dressen has won the respect of this team," Norm Cash told reporters, who were as shocked by the news as the players were.

It was not until two days later that the Tigers would learn that Dressen had suffered his second heart attack in 14 months. Few thought their feisty little skipper would ever wear a major-league uniform again.

After a pulled muscle in his leg cost Kaline four games, he was again asked to shift over to center field because his replacement in right, Jim Northrup, was hitting so well. By early June, the Tigers enjoyed a 31–19 record, their best start since their near-miss in 1961.

On June 15, in an 11–7 win over the Red Sox, Kaline went 3-for-4—including the 2,000[th] hit of his career—and drove in three runs.

In the clubhouse after the game, one sportswriter, hoping to coax a good quote out of Al, suggested, "Maybe you can make it 3,000 hits someday."

"What will I use for legs?" Kaline grumbled in response.

In 1966, infielder Dick Tracewski, who had been Sandy Koufax's roommate during Dick's days with the Los Angeles Dodgers, was traded to the Tigers. Tracewski had played on two world championship teams in Los Angeles, but he quickly came to appreciate the man who roamed right field in Detroit.

"I was at shortstop one day and somebody hit a ball down the right-field line," Tracewski recalled. "I had already conceded the guy a double. I was just standing there when I saw Al charge the ball and throw. Then it dawned on me what was happening. I started running like hell toward second base, but it was too late.

"The ball went by me and down into the bullpen, and a run scored on the play. It was my fault. I had never seen a right fielder make a play like that. Never.

"But they gave the error to Al. He actually got an error because he was so damn good. I felt terrible. I kept apologizing. But Al never said a word."

Kaline kept hitting, but the Tigers kept losing. Then on July 14, two days after the All-Star Game, where Al had gone 1-for-4, interim manager Bob Swift, who has again filling in for Charlie Dressen, was himself rushed to Henry Ford Hospital, suffering from what doctors initially diagnosed as a "virus infection in the lining of the stomach."

No team in big-league baseball history had ever before lost two managers to illness in the same season. Third-base coach Frank Skaff, who had managed for many years in the Tigers' minor-league system, immediately took over for Swift.

"Having three managers in one season will have an effect on this club, no doubt about it," admitted general manager Jim Campbell. "Whenever you change the atmosphere, there is a feeling-out period until the ballplayers get to know just how the new man operates. Things are bound to be rough during times like that."

On July 22, the Tigers were further shocked to learn that Swift was, in fact, suffering from cancer, not a virus.

The team was in turmoil. The front office was still holding out hope that Charlie Dressen, who was convalescing at the Sheraton-Cadillac Hotel in downtown Detroit, would eventually be able to return to the dugout. Meanwhile, rumors were flying that former Chicago White Sox manager Al Lopez or former Tigers infielder Billy Martin, now a coach with the Minnesota Twins, would be named the team's new manager.

And the news got worse. On August 5, Dressen was readmitted to the hospital, this time because of a kidney infection. Five days later, while the Tigers were on the road in Washington, the players learned that their feisty former manager was dead due to cardiac arrest.

"It's a terrible, tragic thing," said Frank Skaff when he was cornered by reporters in the lobby of the Shoreham Hotel. "We're all extremely grieved and heartbroken."

The 55-year-old Skaff, who had played just 38 games in the big leagues in the 1930s and 1940s, had waited all of his life for a chance to manage in the majors. But he certainly didn't want to get that opportunity this way—with one of his predecessors dead and the other dying of cancer.

"I was in the hotel room when I heard the news of Dressen on the radio," Kaline later recalled. "It was hard to believe. I remember later that it had a serious effect on the team. We couldn't concentrate well on the games right after Dressen's death. It seemed a bad thing if you played ball and had a good time doing it. You kept thinking that Dressen was dead and here you were having fun."

The Tigers finished the season in a fog. In early September, Kaline reinjured his surgically repaired left foot stepping on a base, twisted it the next day, and finally fouled a pitch off it.

On September 26, the players learned that Bob Swift had lapsed into a deep coma and was listed in critical condition. He passed away on October 17 without ever regaining consciousness.

Meanwhile the Tigers, who had been fighting to hang on to second place in the American League, slipped to third by losing to Kansas City three times at home on the final weekend of the season. It was their best finish since 1961, but that did nothing to ease the trauma of the year they had just been through.

Immediately after the final game, general manager Jim Campbell dismissed the entire coaching staff, including acting manager Frank Skaff, and hired 52-year-old New York Yankees scout Mayo Smith, who had previously managed the Philadelphia Phillies and Cincinnati Reds and never once in five seasons won more games than he lost.

Everyone in the organization, including Al Kaline, was eager to make a fresh start. They needed one.

CHAPTER 12

So Close

After suffering through 21 seasons without a pennant, the Tigers and their fans felt certain that 1967 was at long last going to be their year. When Al Kaline met with Jim Campbell during the winter to sign his $70,000 contract, he told the general manager, "I want to play in the World Series in 1967."

New manager Mayo Smith was a bit of a bon vivant, fondly known in the ballpark press rooms, where the food and drinks were always free and the liquor often flowed long after the final out, as "America's Guest."

Smith's first challenge would be to rebuild the Tigers' spirits in the wake of the shocking loss of managers Charlie Dressen and Bob Swift the previous season.

Many had expected the Tigers to hire a fiery new field general who would whip the players into line. The laissez-faire Smith, who had played for 17 years in the minor leagues, reaching the big leagues only as a wartime replacement with the Philadelphia Athletics in 1945, was anything but a firebrand. Smith had previously managed the Philadelphia Phillies and Cincinnati Reds. But in five seasons, his teams had never finished above .500.

However, in the wake the unsettling deaths of Dressen and Swift, the Tigers' front office felt that the team needed a calming influence more than it needed a kick in the rear.

Mayo Smith was calm. Mayo was predictable. Mayo was old-school, just like his bosses, Tigers' owner John Fetzer and general manager Jim Campbell. Mayo Smith was a safe pick.

However, Smith did not run a tight ship. And he did not always command the complete respect of his players, who frequently ridiculed him...and not always behind his back.

Late in the ill-fated pennant race of 1967, one of the Tigers scrawled a message on the clubhouse chalkboard for all to see. It read, "Let's win this in spite of Mayo."

In late May when Willie Horton crashed into the left-field fence chasing a fly ball and fell to the ground in a heap, Mayo Smith pulled a muscle in his own leg running out to check on the condition of his star slugger. That caused the Tigers manager to hobble around like the gimpy character Chester on the TV show *Gunsmoke* for a couple of weeks—much to the amusement of his players.

Smith, for the most part, was a hands-off manager, content to let his veteran players do their thing. And most of them responded to him, at least most of the time.

"Mayo has a way of showing confidence in his players," Kaline said then. "He talks to them a lot. He isn't the kind who thinks he knows everything about this club. He listens to people and takes suggestions. But he's the one who decides things."

Al Kaline had started 84 games in center field in 1966 and 60 in center the year before that. But Al had always made it plain to anyone who asked that he much preferred playing right field.

"If I were asked to play center, I'd play it," Kaline said. "But I don't enjoy center field. I do enjoy playing right field. Everything seems to come so easy there. I know, too, that there are a lot of people playing center field in the league who are a lot better there than I am."

Kaline didn't say there was nobody in the American League who was better than he was in right field. He didn't have to. Plenty of other people were saying it for him.

When Smith took command in 1967, he quickly made it clear Al would remain in right. "He made his reputation as one of the best right fielders ever," the new Tigers manager explained.

The Tigers appeared positioned for a long-awaited run at the pennant.

When first baseman Norm Cash, who had become one of the most popular players on the team, struggled early in the season, the colorful, always quotable Texan quipped, "If they have to bat me sixth or seventh, we just might win this pennant by 20 games."

The mound staff, under the coddling of new pitching coach John Sain, who had arrived along with Smith during the off-season, was led by left-hander Mickey Lolich, right-handers Joe Sparma, Earl Wilson, and, of course, the inimitable bespectacled organ player, Denny McLain.

Fred Gladding, a 225-pound bear of a reliever, soon became the late-inning darling of the Tigers bullpen. Naturally, he was known as "the Bear." When Gladding would begin warming up with the game on the line, fans at Tiger Stadium would chant, "We want the Bear! We want the Bear!"

However, by the end of the season, Gladding and his bullpen buddies Hank Aguirre, Larry Sherry, and Dave Wickersham would bear the brunt of the blame for the team's near miss.

Kaline got off to a great start in 1967. By April 29, he had a 13-game hitting streak going and was batting .415. Three times, Al had driven in the go-ahead run, and on three other occasions he had delivered a game-tying RBI.

And Kaline's efforts in right field were still the marvel of friend and foe.

In a game against Boston in May, with the Red Sox's George Scott on first base, Dalton Jones drilled a low line drive to right field. Realizing he couldn't possibly get to the ball in time, Kaline nevertheless jogged in as if he was preparing to make a routine catch. Seeing that, Scott, who didn't want to be doubled off first, stopped a few steps toward second base and turned to watch Kaline in right field. When the ball dropped in for a base hit, which was where it was headed all along, Kaline grabbed it and fired it to second base to easily force Scott. Instead of having runners on first and third with nobody out, the Red Sox now merely had a man on first with one out.

"Al did a magnificent job of faking Scott," Mayo Smith said after the game. "Al's the best I've ever seen."

That was the difference Kaline so often made. He could—and did—win games in so many different ways.

By June 4, Kaline had hit safely in 39 out of 45 games and was leading the league with a .348 average. "I guess I'm bearing down even harder this year," he admitted. "I think we have a good chance for the pennant, and if we don't win it, I don't want to be to blame."

A few weeks later, on June 27, those words would come back to haunt him when, with the Tigers trailing 6–1 in a game against Cleveland, Kaline slammed his bat into the rack after striking out against the Indians' Sam McDowell in the sixth inning, busting his little finger.

Kaline, who was hitting .328 with 15 home runs and 53 RBIs at the time, called it "the dumbest thing I ever did."

"It wasn't the strikeout alone," Al later explained. "The way the team was going and being behind again, I guess that's what touched it off. I don't feel as badly for myself as I do for the team. I'm afraid to go to the stadium and face them after this.

"When I get hurt, I don't fool around. It's a break or nothing," Kaline added. "But this was so unnecessary. I feel like a damn fool."

For much of the season, Kaline had been among the league leaders in batting average, RBIs, and home runs. At the time, there were only two active American Leaguers with five or more years of experience who owned lifetime batting averages of .300 or better. Mickey Mantle was one. Kaline was the other.

It would be a full month before Al would be able to return to the lineup on July 28. Meanwhile, in the wee hours of the morning on July 23, riots erupted on the streets of Detroit less than three miles from the fabled corner of Michigan and Trumbull, which left the city scarred, ill-tempered, and uneasy.

Ignited by a police raid on a *blind pig*, an illegal after-hours drinking and gambling establishment located at 9125 12th Street in an all-black neighborhood, the riots, which quickly spread and eventually encompassed more than 25 square miles of the city, resulted in 43 deaths, 7,231 arrests, 2,500 buildings burned or looted, and $200 million in damages.

At the time, it ranked as the bloodiest racial riot in American history. The scars are still evident on the streets of Detroit today.

"I don't want to use the word 'hatred,' but everywhere I went in the summer of '67, people were just against everything connected with the city—anti-black, anti-white, anti-police, anti-Tigers," recalled pinch-hitter Gates Brown, one of the team's three African American players.

The 34,000 fans at Tiger Stadium watching the Tigers engage the Yankees in a doubleheader on that muggy July 23 Sunday afternoon were largely unaware of the urban tragedy that was unfolding less than three miles away. Many who could see the black smoke billowing into the sky beyond the light towers atop the left-field stands wondered where the fire was and what was burning

Tigers general manager Jim Campbell and the team's flagship radio station, WJR, had ordered announcers Ernie Harwell and Ray Lane to ignore the smoke as the day's games dragged on.

The Tigers split their doubleheader with the Yanks, losing the opener 4–2 before winning the nightcap 7–3. When the second game ended, the public-address announcer advised fans, "The Grand River, Linwood, and Fenkell bus lines will not be operating this evening." That was when many first realized something serious and worrisome was happening.

The Lodge Freeway, a main thoroughfare north from Tiger Stadium to the suburbs, was shrouded in thick smoke. Gunfire could be heard. Looters ravaged shops that served the inner city, stealing what they could, then setting the stores on fire.

Before the sun set that Sunday afternoon, Mickey Lolich, who had started the first game of the doubleheader, had been ordered to report to his 191st Michigan National Guard unit, which was being hastily mobilized to safeguard the rest of the city. By nightfall, the portly left-handed pitcher, who hadn't even stopped to eat supper after he left the stadium following the game, was wearing a helmet and toting a rifle, his nerves on edge and his ample stomach growling.

The Baltimore Orioles, who had been scheduled to begin a three-game series in Detroit the next night, were ordered to stay home. To protect the players and any fans who might have come to the ballpark in spite of the danger, the Tigers' next two home games were moved to Baltimore, where they would be televised back to Detroit. The Tigers and city officials hoped that people would stop rioting in order to stay home to watch the ballgames.

The first game in Baltimore was rained out in the second inning. But the rioting in Detroit continued. It took five days for federal troops, National Guardsmen, and local police to restore order.

The riots were particularly painful for Willie Horton. As the Tigers' first bona fide black star, Horton was a hero within Detroit's large African American community.

As an impoverished youngster, Horton, who had grown up in one of the city's housing projects not far from the blind pig where the riots erupted, hung out at Briggs Stadium in Al Kaline's early years, hoping to be hired to help wash the Tigers players' uniforms or shine their shoes. When Willie was 12 years old, he landed a part-time job working in the Tigers' clubhouse.

"I thought the players were gods," Horton recalled. "I couldn't believe I could get that close to them. I'm no implanted player. I grew up here."

When Horton was 13 years old, without telling his parents, he slipped across the Detroit River to take part in an amateur boxing tournament in Windsor, Ontario. In the finals, Horton hammered his burly 18-year-old opponent into submission.

Horton was a 14-year-old high school freshman when he was selected for a summer All-Star Game, and he blasted a home run into the right-center-field bleachers at Briggs Stadium. "It scared me so much the umpire had to tell me to run," Horton recalled. "That was when everybody started talking about Willie Horton." That was three years after Kaline won his batting title.

The riots subsided, but with Kaline sidelined by his broken finger, the Tigers struggled, winning 14 games while losing 11. As one Detroit sportswriter wrote, "The Tigers without Kaline are like tomato juice without vodka—okay, but lacking in punch."

On August 17, in a game against Boston, Kaline connected for his 20th home run of the season and the 299th of his career, leaving him just seven behind the Tigers' all-time team leader in home runs, Hank Greenberg.

"Man, 'the Line' is the best hitter anywhere," declared relief pitcher John Wyatt, who would join the Tigers in 1968 but who was pitching for the Red Sox in '67. "You got to do some scufflin' with that guy. He just grin at me all the time like he know he gonna hang me out to dry. The Line, he just stay in there and 'swoosh!' You leavin' the game with an L."

However, the self-effacing Kaline didn't want to hear such talk.

"Beating Greenberg's record will have to wait until next year," Al told reporters. Then he added, "If I'm still with Detroit."

Meanwhile, the tightest pennant race in American League history was raging as five teams—the Tigers, the renaissance Boston Red Sox, the late-charging Minnesota Twins, the faint-hitting Chicago White Sox, and the long-shot California Angels—took turns clawing forward and then falling back, playing musical chairs at the top of the standings.

As late as September 7, four teams were essentially tied for the lead. Around the country, the press began calling it "the Great Race."

There were no playoffs, no wild cards in 1967. The two teams that finished first in their respective leagues' pennant chases would advance directly to the World Series.

On Friday, September 8, the Tigers, who were tied for first, went into Chicago for a four-game weekend series against the White Sox.

Mickey Lolich and Pat Dobson won the first two games. On Saturday, the Tigers rallied for seven runs in the ninth inning to turn a 3–0 defeat into a 7–3 victory. They were riding high.

But then the Tigers were shut out 6–0 and 4–0 in their Sunday doubleheader against the ChiSox as Chicago's Joe Horlen hurled a no-hitter in the opener. In 24 hours, the Tigers tumbled from first place to third. The race was that tight.

"From the high point of my baseball career to the low point, overnight," groused Kaline, who nevertheless enjoyed being legitimately involved in the pennant race so late in the season for the first time in his career.

At age 32, after 15 years in a big-league uniform, Al privately feared this might be his last, best chance to reach the World Series.

The Tigers limped home from Chicago, licking their wounds after the disappointing split in their four-game series. Bill Freehan, the most-often-hit batsman in baseball, had been plunked twice by the White Sox and had his arm in a sling. Denny McLain had wrenched his back. Adding insult to injury, the Tigers' bus driver got lost on the way to Chicago's O'Hare Airport, and their plane was more than an hour late taking off for the one-hour flight home.

To make matters worse, veteran Eddie Mathews, who had been hastily claimed on waivers from Houston in mid-August when third baseman Don Wert pulled a muscle in his leg, went home to Milwaukee for the off-day on Monday and fell down a flight of stairs, injuring his hand.

But again the Tigers rebounded, winning a pair at home against the Baltimore Orioles and then taking two in a row from the Washington Senators. Just that quickly, they were back on top by one full game—from first to third and back again in the space of a week.

In the opener against the Orioles, Kaline homered for the first time in nearly a month with Don Wert aboard to win the game 6–4. Al homered in the next game, too, as Mickey Lolich, who had lost 10 straight earlier in the season and set a team record by going 84 consecutive days without a victory, won his sixth game in a row when it mattered most.

The pear-shaped Lolich, whose ample belly drooped down over his belt, had been born right-handed. But a childhood accident forced him to learn how to use his left hand. "I pitch left-handed, I eat right-handed, and I think upside down," said the likable Lolich, who could always laugh at himself.

When the Tigers played at home, Lolich often rode his 250cc Kawasaki motorcycle to the ballpark, much to management's chagrin.

"I'm getting one for Kaline after the season," Lolich joked.

Upstairs in his third-floor corner office at Tiger Stadium, general manager Jim Campbell cringed.

On Friday, the Tigers trailed the Senators 4–1 with two outs in the eighth inning. Remembering what had happened the previous weekend in Chicago, many of the fans and some of the players found themselves thinking, *Oh, no, here we go again.*

But Jim Northrup singled to right, Norm Cash walked, and Bill Freehan belted a three-run homer, his 20th of the season—the most ever by a Tigers catcher. Suddenly, the score was tied. The Tigers were still alive.

An inning later, Willie Horton delivered a clutch two-out single to left, scoring Dick McAuliffe from second base with the game-winning run.

Horton, who despite his size and formidable strength always seemed to be hurting somewhere, was hobbled at the time by a bone spur on his left heel. "I'm not gonna feel good 'til I get this foot operated on," he said.

The pressure of the hectic pennant race had been particularly hard on him. "I can't sleep," Horton admitted. "Gates Brown and I sit up to three or four in the morning talking baseball. If I try to sleep, I can't."

Each of the Tigers coped with the mounting pressure in his own way.

"I get to sleep real easy," Dick McAuliffe deadpanned. "First, I take three tranquilizers, then..."

On Saturday, Earl Wilson, a stylish dresser who was well known in the clubhouse for his custom-tailored suits and snappy shoes, won for the 21st time as the Tigers whipped Washington 5–4. It was their fourth win in a row and their 11th in 14 games down the stretch since September 3.

Wilson, who died unexpectedly in 2005, was a proud, moody man. He was the most outspoken, some would say the most radical, of the Tigers' African American players. And he was often misunderstood.

"It's not that I'm cocky or stuck-up," insisted Wilson, who tied for the major-league lead with 22 wins for the Tigers in 1967. "I'm just nervous. The night before a game, I can't sleep. I keep waking up, thinking about the hitters. Then, when I get to the ballpark before the game, I'm plain scared. Not scared of losing—scared of failure. You know what I mean. You can win and still lose."

Suddenly the Tigers, who had fallen to third place a week earlier, found themselves alone in first for the first time since June 10.

On the streets outside Tiger Stadium, "Tag 'Em Tigers" bumper stickers became hot items. You could see them plastered everywhere.

On September 20, Denny McLain, who had won 20 games in 1966, was abruptly sidelined with what were initially diagnosed as dislocated toes. McLain claimed he had injured his foot at home when he awoke from a sound sleep in his easy chair and jumped up to chase away raccoons that were digging in his garbage cans outside. Two years later, that tale would resurface and take on a life of its own.

But during the hectic 1967 pennant chase, McLain missed most of the final two weeks of the season and a shot at another 20-win season before making a desperation start against the California Angels on October 1, the dramatic final day of the campaign.

The Tigers, on the advice of Ed Katalinas, the scout who had discovered and signed Al Kaline, had plucked McLain from the farm system of the Chicago White Sox, who failed to protect him in the draft because of his inability to throw a curveball. The Sox preferred to keep pitchers Dave DeBusschere and Bruce Howard.

"It took Charlie Dressen all of 15 minutes to teach me how to throw a curve," McLain would chortle years later.

Two days of heavy rain forced the Tigers and California Angels to play back-to-back doubleheaders at Tiger Stadium on the final weekend of the 1967 season.

The Tigers' situation was simple. If they could win three of those four games against the Angels, they would force a one-game, sudden-death playoff against the Red Sox for the right to represent the American League in the World Series.

The Tigers split Saturday's twin bill with the Angels. They won the opener thanks to Mickey Lolich, who had pitched his heart out since the riots, winning nine times in 10 decisions, including three consecutive shutouts. But they dropped the nightcap when the bullpen blew a four-run lead in the eighth inning.

Now Kaline and the Tigers needed to sweep the Angels in their Sunday doubleheader on October 1. It was do or die. When Joe Sparma was victorious in the opener, the season and a trip to the World Series rested on Denny McLain's gifted right arm in the nightcap.

But McLain, who hadn't pitched in 13 days, was still nursing that sore foot and lasted just two and two-thirds innings. Denny was long gone from the mound by the time the Tigers, trailing 8–5, came to bat one last time in the bottom of the ninth, with darkness descending on Tiger Stadium and the temperature dropping.

Tigers fans' hopes rose when Bill Freehan and Don Wert both reached base, bringing the tying run to the plate in the person of pinch-hitter Jim Price, still with nobody out.

But Price flied to left field, leaving the Tigers' fate up to scrappy Dick McAuliffe, who had knocked in three runs earlier in the game. McAuliffe, who would later be diagnosed with diabetes, was easily the most intense competitor on the team.

McAuliffe, with his unique Mel Ott–like batting style, had grounded into just one double play all year. That made him the perfect hitter to have at the plate in that situation.

Against all odds, McAuliffe bounced sharply to second base for a season-ending, dream-killing double play, and the Boston Red Sox, who had finished in ninth place the year before, grabbed the pennant by one game.

The Tigers were crushed. They had come so close.

Al Kaline, who had led his team with a .308 average, 25 home runs, 78 RBIs, and 94 runs scored, despite missing a total of 31 games because of injury, blamed himself and his busted finger for the Tigers' failure.

"I have to believe," Al said softly, "that if I had been in those games I missed because of the broken finger, I would have done something to help win a few of them. That's all we would have needed."

The Tigers' late-afternoon failure ignited a minor riot as frustrated fans stormed the field, throwing punches and stadium chairs, ripping up home plate and the pitching rubber, tearing up the sacred sod, and fighting with overwhelmed stadium guards, city police, and often one another. It was an ugly scene.

As dusk descended and the police struggled to restore peace, John Fetzer, the distraught billionaire owner of the Tigers—a graying reserved man not normally given to outpourings of emotion, who saw himself as the guardian of a sacred public trust known as the Detroit Baseball Club— retreated alone to his third-floor office at Tiger Stadium, sat down behind his desk, and privately bared his soul:

> On this infamous evening of October 1, 1967, there is no happiness in that section of Mudville near the corner of Michigan and Trumbull. The heroes have fallen and I am ill. I have been here for hours, but a few tears cannot wash away the hurt.
>
> As I tuned in on the waves of reflection, the brilliant lights of Tiger Stadium began to fade and I watched hundreds of fans give vent to their frustrations. They destroyed scores of stadium seats and piled the rubble on the dugouts. Still others clawed at home plate and the pitcher's mound, while a bedlam of confusion turned many more hundreds into a near mob scene with the elements of combat everywhere on the playing field.
>
> In stony silence, I thought of how desperately hard I had fought to build a winner in Detroit. It seemed that my long-sought goal was near fruition. I thought a pennant would have meant more to Detroit than all of the man-made remedies put together. I thought that 1967 would be a crowning year of glory for our city and that the world would soon forget our stormy past.
>
> But it was not to be. All season long it seemed as if a hexing magic was following each footstep. Every kind of injury stalked the ballclub. We were never able to use a full line of soldiers in the infantry. Time and again we would

charge, but the attack was short-lived. We just could never quite get going.

My thoughts turned to what I would say to the oracles. I knew they would surely come. They always do. But this time it was different. To be sure, they made the rounds. Everyone from the front office will be in the news—that is, everybody except the guy who wanted so much to do the thing Detroit wanted most. The fellow who spent a fortune trying.

I am glad to preserve my solitude. The plain unadulterated truth is the fact that I failed to win the pennant. Pennant winners are the only heroes, and the losers, even if only one game back, are destined to sit alone. Upon reflection, I wouldn't change that one bit because that's the American way. Rewards are sweet, and failure, well, John Fetzer has just died. This is his ghost speaking.

Inside the clubhouse, the Tigers players were similarly glum.

"All summer long, it was, 'Oh, well, we'll get 'em tomorrow,'" sighed dejected catcher Bill Freehan, summing up the feelings of the entire team. "Now there is no more tomorrow."

However, looking back at it now, Kaline has surprisingly fond memories of 1967.

"Was it disappointing? Yeah, it was disappointing," Kaline acknowledged. "I was getting older. I realized that may have been my last shot, so it was disappointing to me personally.

"But by the same token, that was the best team I ever played on. Up until then, all the other years, by the first of September, everybody was thinking, *Well, what am I going to do after the season is over?*

"Just to be on a team that battled so hard, right down to the last day, was a great feeling. That was something I had always wanted to do. It was a great experience just to be playing games in September that meant something."

13

"I Can't Get the Damn Cork Out"

When the 1968 baseball season dawned, the citizens of the riot-ravaged city of Detroit desperately needed something to feel good about. Something to bring them back together. Something to cheer. And the Tiger players desperately needed to win the pennant in order to feel good about themselves again.

Disappointed by their crushing last-day second-place finish in 1967, the Tigers reported to training camp the following spring determined to prove they indeed were—as they, to a man, had believed in their hearts the previous year—the best team in baseball.

Over the winter, Al Kaline severed his relationship with the Michigan Automotive Products Corporation, which he felt was consuming too much of his time, and accepted a position on the newly created Sports Panel of the Lincoln-Mercury Division of Ford Motor Company.

The members of the Sports Panel—including golf stars Arnold Palmer and Byron Nelson, track and field legend Jesse Owens, Green Bay Packers quarterback Bart Starr, racecar driver Dan Gurney, and professional bowler Billy Welu—would lend their names and their reputations to promote the cars that Lincoln-Mercury was producing.

Mostly, Kaline's job involved making appearances for the company and speaking to the public.

When Al's $93,000 contract from the Tigers for 1968 arrived in the mail, he signed immediately. He knew that, for him, the clock was ticking. And his time in the game was running out.

"A lot of players were hurt and had off years last season, and we were still in the running," Al reasoned. "It wouldn't take much improvement in each case to give us the extra punch we need this year."

Worried about his players' state of mind, manager Mayo Smith ordered the entire team, not just the pitchers and catchers, to report to training camp in Lakeland, Florida, a week early.

"I want to get us all started off together," Smith explained to reporters. "The theme is to generate that motivation just a little more, to start right off from scratch getting each and every man to believe that all he has to do is play just a little bit harder and we'll win it.

"I can't promise we'll win the pennant," Smith added. "But losing the pennant last year on the last day has done something to this team. The team really grew up last year."

Smith's strategy worked.

"Inwardly, we came out of spring training determined to prove that we were the best team in the American League," Mickey Lolich recalled.

The Tigers lost their season opener 7–3 to the Boston Red Sox. But then, with basically the same lineup that had fallen one game short the year before, they reeled off nine wins in a row, the organization's longest such string of successes in 19 years.

Three of those wins came by one run, also an encouraging sign. Three wins went extra innings.

"Those one-run games were the kind we weren't winning last year," noted manager Mayo Smith. "It's the mark of a winning team when you can pull out the close ones."

In fact, the 1968 Tigers would rally to win 40 games in which they were tied or trailing from the seventh inning on. Forty times out of 103 wins. And 28 times they won in their final turn at bat. They truly were amazing.

They became the Boys of the Summer of '68—back when Tiger Stadium was Detroit's sporting Taj Mahal and visiting players imbibed nightly at the

Lindell AC, a hole-in-the-wall tavern just a 10-minute walk down Michigan Avenue from the ballpark and, more importantly, within easy early morning stumbling distance of the Book-Cadillac Hotel, where most of the visiting teams resided.

Every day, it seemed, a different hero emerged for the Tigers. One day it was Willie Horton. The next day it was Norm Cash. Then it was Bill Freehan, then Gates Brown, then, of course, Al Kaline.

"Coming so close, like we did in 1967, then losing on the last day, was such a devastating thing that the guys were not going to be denied in '68," Kaline recalled.

"It was amazing how everybody participated and did their jobs. Everybody forgot about their batting averages and their win-loss records and their salaries. Everybody just gave 100 percent. Everybody did something to help us win. Every game.

"It was a great feeling just to be a part of that team. I had never been a part of a team like that before, where everybody had one goal, where everybody was just focused on winning. And I was never on another one after that."

"We just never gave up," agreed outfielder Jim Northrup, who knocked in 90 runs, tops on the team that year. "We got very confident. We felt if we were within two or three runs by the seventh inning, we were going to win the ballgame."

"I felt absolutely invincible that year," admitted Denny McLain, who rocked the baseball world with his 31 wins.

On May 19, Kaline, who was struggling to get his average up to .300, homered off Washington's Steve Jones, surpassing Hank Greenberg as the Tigers' all-time leading home-run hitter with 307 in his career.

"I'm glad it's over," Kaline admitted after the game. "Subconsciously, the thing was getting to me. I guess I was swinging for it on every pitch Jones gave me. Maybe now I can get back to hitting for average."

Then, on May 25, tragedy struck again when Al momentarily lost sight of a pitch from Oakland's Lew Krausse, instinctively threw up his right arm to protect his face, and was struck on the right forearm.

Kaline was immediately flown from Oakland back to Detroit where X-rays revealed a hairline fracture in his right arm. The prognosis was he would miss two to three weeks.

"These are the breaks of the game," a deeply disappointed Kaline said. "And I've had my share of them. But there's nothing I can do about it. There's no way to correct it."

The next day, Jim Northrup, who was playing right field and batting in Kaline's No. 3 spot in the order, was hit in the back of the head by a pitch thrown by the Athletics' Jack Aker. Northrup hit the dirt, dazed. When he got back on his feet, he charged the mound and a melee erupted.

As baseball brawls go, this one was a dandy. Veteran Eddie Mathews, who had been watching the game from the bench, punched Aker in the face three times. Manager Mayo Smith was kicked in the ribs.

With Kaline out of the lineup, the Tigers lost two games, then won five in a row. In early June, they won 10 out of 11. The aroused Tigers, who were in first place by two games when Kaline was hit by that pitch, won 30 of their next 43 games to pad their lead in the American League to eight and a half games by the midway point in early July. The rout was on.

On June 24 in Cleveland Northrup stepped up to the plate three times with the bases loaded. Twice he belted grand-slam home runs. On June 29 against the White Sox, he connected with the bases loaded again.

Northrup's Tigers teammates called him "Fox" or "Sweet Lips" because of his biting, outspoken comments. However, after those three grand slams, Tigers announcer Ernie Harwell took to calling him "Slammer."

Even without Kaline, their star right-fielder and team leader, the Tigers would not be denied. "We have a balanced ballclub, that's why we've been able to play over injuries," manager Mayo Smith told the press.

With the exception of Kaline, most of the 1968 Tigers were products of the team's farm system and had grown up together in the minor leagues. Fifteen of the Tigers were graduates of the team's sprawling Lakeland, Florida, minor-league complex, which had been constructed on the site of a former World War II airplane pilot training school and still included the hangars and old runways. Only Norm Cash and Earl Wilson, among the more prominent Tigers performers, had ever worn the uniform of another organization. They were a unique group.

"We all grew up together," recalled Mickey Lolich. "We were all friends. We knew each other's wives. We knew each other's families. It was great just to be around those guys.

"We always stuck together. On the road, when the games were over, we had our spots in every town. You always knew where to find us. And we always knew where to find one another.

"Nobody ever felt bad about a mistake they made in a game," Lolich continued. "Because we talked it out among ourselves. We were real close."

"We were like family," Jim Northrup agreed. "We barbecued together with our wives and kids. We partied together. When we had problems, we talked to each other. That's what made '68 so great for us. Maybe it's something that outsiders don't understand. But that group all knew each other for 10 years. When you accomplish something with your best friends, it makes it that much sweeter. That was the satisfaction, the thing that bonded us so closely.

"Hell, we even loaned each other money when things got tight—although we'd run the other way when McLain came along. He was constantly looking for a few bucks. He always said he needed money to 'buy a little something for the wife.' But it wasn't a loan with Denny. It was more like a gift.

"There was a closeness I don't believe can exist anywhere in professional sports anymore," Northrup continued. "It will never happen again. That's the sad part. It's unusual for one guy to stay with an organization for 10 years now. For 10 guys to do that is impossible. That makes it so much tougher. That '68 team really didn't need a leader because we were all just growing old together."

"Back in '68, we always used to joke that you could take a team picture in the hotel bar," recalled relief pitcher John Hiller, who three years later was felled by a heart attack. "You had a bad game, you had to take a drink to get over the disappointment. And if you had a good game, you sure as hell had to have some drinks to celebrate."

Willie Horton, Mickey Stanley, and Jim Northrup had starred together at the Tigers' Triple A subsidiary in Syracuse in 1964. They were known as "the Boys From Syracuse." Bill Freehan, Gates Brown, Mickey Lolich, Pat Dobson, and Ray Oyler had played together in Knoxville. Only Kaline had never set foot in the minor leagues.

And, unlike today, almost every member of the 1968 Tigers team was white. In 1968 the Tigers had only three black players—Willie Horton, who had been signed off the streets of Detroit; Gates Brown, whom they had scouted while he was serving time in an Ohio Penitentiary; and Earl Wilson, who was acquired in a trade with Boston midway through the 1966 season. A fourth African American, relief pitcher John Wyatt, was added late in the '68 season.

The only Hispanic in a Tigers uniform that summer was Julio Moreno, who pitched batting practice before the home games. For an international flavor, the Tigers had one Canadian-born player, pitcher John Hiller.

No one in the front office would ever admit it, of course—at least not on the record—but there were those in the organization who liked it that way.

Unfortunately, for the many long-suffering Tigers fans, the success of their favorite baseball team that summer was a well-kept secret. Both of Detroit's daily newspapers, the *Free Press* and the *News*, had been shut down by strikes in November 1967. They didn't resume publication until August 1968.

Even with Kaline out of the lineup for the entire month of June, the Tigers enjoyed a nine-and-a-half-game lead at the All-Star break. McLain was an unworldly 16–2.

McLain's roommate on the road—at least on those nights when Denny bothered to make an appearance at the team's hotel—was shortstop Ray Oyler. One day Oyler asked Denny if he thought he could win 30 games.

"Book it," McLain said, who chartered a plane and flew to Las Vegas for a day during the All-Star break, jetted to Houston where he pitched two scoreless innings in the All-Star Game, then flew back to Vegas for another day of fun and frolic before rejoining his Tigers teammates in Minnesota for the resumption of the regular season.

The 1968 Tigers were a fun-loving bunch. They played together, they partied together—and they won together.

"A bunch of us were sitting around playing poker on the bed in somebody's room one night, like we did a lot of nights, when Northrup caught McLain cheating," John Hiller recalled.

"Northrup jumped across the bed and grabbed Denny by the throat and was yelling, 'I'm going to kill you, you bastard! I'm going to kill you!'

"Gates Brown grabbed Northrup from behind and said, 'You're not going to touch him until after we win the pennant. Then he's all yours.'"

McLain, of course, went on to win 31 times that summer. With the '68 Tigers, winning always came first.

Late one night in the heat of the pennant race, Mayo Smith, who was well aware that many of his players enjoyed the nightlife on the road, as did he, pulled a surprise midnight bed check to make sure his boys were all in their hotel rooms where they were supposed to be.

Rather than send one of his coaches to knock on doors, Smith personally called each of his player's rooms on the phone. Somehow, possibly because Mayo had downed a cocktail or two himself that evening, he neglected to call pitcher Fred Lasher.

The next day, when Lasher learned he had been overlooked in the bed check, he confronted Mayo. "What about me?" the angry reliever asked. "I'm a part of this team, too, you know."

"I look back at all the jerks we had on that team—I don't mean that meanly, I mean it affectionately," said Hiller, who later bounced back from a heart attack in 1971 to become one of the most effective relief pitchers in Tigers history. "I just can't imagine another mix of personalities. We had more characters on that team than have ever been assembled on any one team anywhere.

"You forget about the games. You forget about the bobbles and the good plays and the good hits. What you remember are the pranks and the good times."

Like the time, according to Jim Northrup, when Gates Brown, who was well known for his appetite, heard his stomach growling early in a game.

"I leaned out of the dugout and asked a fan to go buy us a hot dog," recalled Northrup, ever the agitator. "I traded him a baseball for it. We did that all the time. Mayo never figured it out."

Only this time, before Brown could take his second bite of hot dog, Smith shouted Brown's name and ordered him to get up to home plate and pinch-hit.

"I offered to hold the hot dog for him, but you know Gates," Northrup said. "Once he's got his hands on something to eat, he's not going to let go."

Instead, Brown stuffed his hot dog inside his jersey and headed for the plate with his bat in hand. Of course, he got a hit. That was what he was paid to do. Gates, who was generally considered to be the best pinch-hitter in baseball at the time, led the American League in pinch hits in 1968 with 18.

According to Northrup, when the opposing pitcher tried to pick Brown off first base, Gates was forced to dive headfirst back to the bag, hot dog and all.

"When Gates stood up, he had a big splotch of mustard, about six inches across, on the front of his uniform," Northrup recalled. "Mayo went ballistic."

Although his playing time was limited because of the presence of Al Kaline, Willie Horton, Jim Northrup, and Mickey Stanley in the Tigers' outfield, Gates Brown was one of the most popular players on the team in the late 1960s.

As a youngster growing up in Crestline, Ohio, the burly Brown was fast for his size and better known for his feats on the football field than on the baseball diamond. By his sophomore year in high school, Brown, who in those days was known as William or Bill, had attracted the attention of football recruiters from gridiron powerhouses including the University of Michigan, Notre Dame, and Ohio State.

However, a youthful indiscretion landed Brown in the Boys' Industrial School for juvenile offenders in Lancaster, Ohio, for seven months. When Brown returned to Crestline, school officials refused to allow him to resume his high school football career, and Brown, his football dreams dashed, soon got into trouble again.

This time he was sent to the Mansfield, Ohio, Reformatory, where he served 22 months for robbery.

Signed by Tigers scout Pat Mullin—who had been one of the Tigers outfielders when Kaline broke into the big leagues—for a $7,000 bonus, Brown blossomed into a huge bargain, playing 13 seasons and collecting 107 career pinch-hits.

One day in the Tigers clubhouse, passing the time as players do before games, Willie Horton playfully asked Brown what classes he had taken when he was in high school.

"I took a little English," Gates replied. "I took some science. I took some hubcaps. I took some wheel covers."

"I first met Gator when we were playing in the Instructional League in Tampa, Florida," Horton recalled. "I was staying in a private home, and he was staying in another house two streets over.

"I'll never forget it. I was just a kid. I had just turned 20 years old. I called him on the phone. I said, 'Mr. Brown, this is Willie Horton.'

"He said, 'I'll tell you what, son. You better walk on over here and meet the Gator.' So I walked over to his house, and I see this guy sitting on the porch and he had a silver robe on. Sitting there on the steps he looked like a giant.

"He looked at me, and he said, 'You're that bonus player, ain't you? Was that real money they gave you?'

"One year in Minnesota we had one of those 11:00 in the morning games. Denny McLain was pitching, and Mayo put Gates in left field," Horton continued. "I'll never forget it. Bob Allison hit Gates right in the chest with a fly ball. Bang! Then Harmon Killebrew hits a high fly ball and Gates is yelling, 'I got it! I got it!' And the ball hits Gates right on the helmet.

"Gates comes into the dugout at the end of the inning and he tells Mayo, 'You know, I'm not supposed to be playing out there this early. I play poker at night.'

"Gates ended up winning that game with a hit in the ninth inning," Horton added.

Each of the '68 Tigers had a nickname, most of them awarded by free-spirited pitcher Pat Dobson.

Dobson himself was "Cobra." Mickey Lolich was "Condor." Norm Cash was "Beagle." Willie Horton was "Boomer." Denny McLain was "Dolphin." Bill Freehan was "Big Ten." Gates Brown was "Gator." Jim Northrup was "Fox." Earl Wilson was "Duke." Mickey Stanley was "Squirrely." Dick McAuliffe was "Mad Dog." Don Wert was "Coyote." John Hiller was "Ratso." Joe Sparma was "Square Deal." Jim Price was "Big Guy." Daryl Patterson was "Chief." Tom Matchick was "Pizza." Ray Oyler was "Oil Can." Wayne Comer was "Bush Hog." Al Kaline was simply "Line."

Norm Cash, who had joined the Tigers in 1960 in a trade with the Cleveland Indians, became one of Kaline's closest friends on the team.

"Norm was a special person," Kaline told me years later. "He was a fun guy to be around."

"Norm was a leader, too, like Al, but I don't think you'd want your son to be his type of leader," Willie Horton said. "Norm would call me at two or three in the morning, looking for something that was going on. But he was one of the best teammates I ever played with."

The team had its role players, too. Jon Warden made the leap from Double A Rocky Mount, North Carolina, to the 1968 Tigers primarily because he threw left-handed and could occasionally strike out hitters. "I was one of the last guys to make the team," he recalled.

Warden pitched in 28 games that season, winning four and losing one—and never appeared in the big leagues again. However, he has been able to call himself a world champion ever since.

"I got more mileage out of that one year in the big leagues than anyone who ever played the game," Warden admitted. "Being on that World Series team opened more doors than anything you can imagine."

It led to a job on ESPN and more banquets and speaking engagements than Warden cares to count. And Warden didn't appear in a single game during the World Series.

"It all happened so fast," Warden said. "One day, nobody knows who I am, then I'm on the roster of the Detroit Tigers, and we're fighting for a pennant. Next day, my arm is gone and my career is over."

When Kaline returned to the lineup on July 1, the Tigers were winning and the outfield of Willie Horton in left field, Mickey Stanley in center, and

Jim Northrup in right was clicking. Looking to keep all three of their bats in the lineup and not break up a winning combination, manager Mayo Smith called Al into his office and told him he wanted him to play first base in place of the slumping Norm Cash.

"First base?" the surprised Kaline asked.

"Sure," Smith said. "You can handle the job as well as anybody."

Without another word, Kaline borrowed a first baseman's mitt and headed for the field. Al had played 2,032 games for the Tigers up until that point. But never once had he played even an inning at first base.

Smith continued to play Kaline at first base as well as in right field and occasionally in left, whenever the manager wanted another right-handed bat in the lineup. Sometimes Al watched from the bench. Sometimes he pinch-hit.

It was a new role for Kaline, but the club was winning, and he wasn't about to complain.

It became increasingly obvious that the Tigers were headed for the World Series. Kaline was finally going to realize his lifelong dream.

Still, he couldn't help but wonder exactly what his role would be when the Tigers got there.

In the summer of 1968, Denny McLain was the toast of baseball. By 1972, he would be washed up at the age of 28. Eventually, he was disgraced by two bankruptcies and two stints in prison, where he would serve as much time behind bars as he did playing baseball in the big leagues. But in '68 McLain and Kaline were both heroes in Detroit. They were both stars. Both had been bonus babies. Personality-wise, however, they were polar opposites.

Kaline wanted no part of McLain's kinetic lifestyle. Like most of the other Tigers, Al quickly learned to tune out McLain and his antics. If they hadn't, Denny would have driven them crazy.

"You accept what he is, and you work with that," Tigers manager Mayo Smith admitted.

By 1968, McLain's life away from the pitcher's mound had become a whirlwind.

In those days, pitchers regularly worked with just three days' rest; at least most did.

"There wasn't much rest," confessed McLain, who jetted around the country between starts in a Lear jet; chugged complimentary Pepsi-Cola by the case; dyed his hair red; played the Hammond organ; formed his own paint company; schmoozed with the Smothers Brothers, Ed Sullivan, Bob Hope, and Steve Allen; appeared on the cover of *Time*; and recorded a couple of albums titled *Denny McLain at the Organ* and *Denny McLain in Las Vegas*.

"The days began at 7:30 in the morning," he admitted. "And they never ended."

On September 10, in a game against the California Angels in Anaheim, McLain notched his 29th win; went 3-for-4 at the plate with two RBIs to help his own cause; went out to celebrate with singer Glen Campbell after the game; went to Disneyland the next morning to book an off-season appearance; went to Capitol Records to pose for some publicity shots; taped the *Steve Allen Show*, on which he played both the organ and a game of catch; and somehow still made it back to the ballpark in time for that evening's baseball game.

However, sometimes Denny didn't show up at the ballpark at all between starts. "When you're doing well, certain liberties are extended to you," McLain explained smugly.

As the irrepressible McLain continued his relentless march toward 31 wins, few outside of the organization knew that Tigers general manager Jim Campbell had spent the winter between the 1967 and '68 seasons trying to trade McLain, whom he had deemed to be more trouble than he was worth.

At one point, Campbell thought he had a deal worked out with the Baltimore Orioles, swapping McLain for Hall of Fame shortstop Luis Aparicio. But that trade fell through.

Years later, Willie Horton recalled the first time he encountered McLain when the two were playing together in the Tigers' minor-league system in 1963.

"When I first met Mac, me and Mickey Stanley and Jim Northrup were playing in the minor leagues at Knoxville, Tennessee," Horton said.

"Well, Denny showed up wearing a mink coat. I had never seen a man wearing a mink coat. I said, 'Wow!'

"I'll never forget it. Right away, Denny said, 'I'm not here to stay. I'm just here temporarily. If you guys want to get out of here, you better get on my coattails. We're going to the big leagues.'

"Another year, down in winter ball, we went on a losing streak, and our manager Blackie [Wayne Blackburn] said, 'Well, boys, there ain't gonna be no more poker playin' on the bus.'" Horton continued.

"And Dolphin—we always called Denny 'Dolphin'—he said, 'Hell with that. We're going to play some poker. We're going to play off license plates. The first car comes toward you, that license plate, that's your hand. And the next one's mine.'

"If McLain would have just trained 10 percent—not 50 percent, just 10 or 15 percent—there's no telling what he would have done. But he didn't train at all. He just pitched. That's how much ability he had. For five years nobody could touch him.

"Maybe if Charlie Dressen had lived, maybe Denny would have done better, had a longer career or whatever. Because Charlie always stayed on him. He watched over him every minute.

"Denny is a good person," Horton added. "He was always a good person. But he's the type of person who was never satisfied."

"Money impresses me," McLain admitted. "I'm a mercenary. I want to be a billionaire."

Whenever McLain would pop off to the press, which was often, Kaline would just shake his head. But Al realized as long as the sportswriters were swarming around McLain, slurping up Denny's every outrageous word, they weren't bothering him.

More importantly for Kaline and for the Tigers in '68, Denny kept winning.

In McLain's third autobiography, *I Told You I Wasn't Perfect*, Denny alleges that Kaline sometimes gave less than everything he had on the field. After the book came out, McLain backed off, but only a bit.

"I wasn't being nasty to Kaline; I was just reporting what I saw," he told those who questioned his comments. "When there were 35,000 to 40,000 people in the ballpark, he was the best I ever saw. When there wasn't anyone in the ballpark, he hustled less.

"Of course," Denny added, "80 percent of Kaline was still better than 90 percent of the rest of the league.

"I don't regret anything I wrote, but I regret how my words about Kaline have been interpreted," McLain said. "I idolized Kaline. My heroes were Mickey Mantle, Ernie Banks, and Al Kaline."

Kaline stopped commenting on McLain years ago. It is a war of words that Al knows he cannot win, one in which he does not wish to engage.

On August 22, when Chicago's Tommy John barely missed Dick McAuliffe's head with one pitch and threw another behind him, the Tigers' high-strung second baseman charged the mound, igniting a brawl. John suffered a broken collarbone when McAuliffe's knee struck his left shoulder, and the pitcher was forced to miss the rest of the season. McAuliffe, who was known to his teammates as "Mad Dog," was suspended for five days. The Tigers were furious.

"The more I think of it, the madder I get," general manager Jim Campbell grumbled at the time. "It's the most unfair decision I've ever seen in baseball." What made Campbell mad was the attitude of American League president Joe Cronin, who imposed the suspension.

"We asked for a hearing, and all Cronin would say was, 'I'll give you a hearing, but I'm not changing my mind. The suspension is going to stick.' He prejudged the case, and we have no recourse."

"Mad Dog, what a ballplayer. Man, he was mean," Willie Horton recalled, referring to McAuliffe by his clubhouse moniker. "Nobody would go near him 20 minutes before a game. I've seen him get in arguments in the clubhouse. He'd snarl, 'What are you looking at?' He got in his trance or whatever he'd go through. He came to play every day. He really brought something to the table."

The Tigers proceeded to lose their next four games, each by a single run, and tied another that was called after 19 innings. Suddenly their seven-and-a-half-game lead in the American League pennant race had shrunk to five.

After the fourth loss, Bill Freehan marched to the blackboard in the clubhouse, grabbed a piece of chalk, and wrote, "Anybody who thinks the world ended today doesn't belong here."

The next day, with Earl Wilson on the mound, the Tigers blanked the Chicago White Sox 3–0 to end their losing streak.

On September 14, before a national TV audience and 33,688 at Tiger Stadium, McLain won No. 30.

Kaline, inserted in the game as a pinch-hitter for McLain in the bottom of the ninth inning with the Tigers trailing 4–3, walked and scored the tying run, making Denny's historic victory on Willie Horton's subsequent RBI single possible.

Kaline happened to be standing next to McLain in the Tigers dugout when Horton singled. On the cover of the next issue of *Sports Illustrated*, Al was pictured grabbing Denny in what appeared to be an uncharacteristic display of affection as the two men were about to rush out on the field.

In fact, according to McLain, Al was merely saving Denny from what could have been an embarrassing pratfall.

"When Horton hit it, I jumped up and banged my head on the dugout roof, almost knocking myself out," McLain later explained.

"Kaline caught me and all but carried me out of the dugout to join the celebration on the field. Kaline's holding me up as much as he's hugging me."

Dizzy Dean, who had tamed the Tigers so convincingly in the 1934 World Series, had been hired by the *Detroit News* to write a column about McLain's victory. But Dean was thrown out of the press box during the game by Watson Spoelstra, the beat reporter for the *News*, because Dizzy, while a Hall of Famer, was not a member of the Baseball Writers Association of America.

On September 17, with less than two weeks to go in the regular season, the Tigers, who needed only one win to clinch the pennant they had been deprived of the summer before, found themselves tied 1–1 with the New York Yankees in the bottom of the ninth.

With two out, Mayo Smith sent Al Kaline to the plate to pinch-hit for Norm Cash. Pitching carefully to Kaline, the Yankees' Steve Hamilton walked him. A single by Bill Freehan and a walk to pinch-hitter Gates

Brown loaded the bases, setting up a clutch, pennant-winning single by Don Wert, who was batting a paltry .198 at the time. It was typical of the way the Tigers had played—and won—all year.

Kaline skipped and hopped across home plate, setting off a celebration the likes of which the city of Detroit had not seen in nearly 23 years.

In the chaotic Tigers clubhouse, Kaline grabbed Jim Campbell and hugged him, just as Bill Freehan was dumping a bottle of champagne over the jubilant general manager's bald head.

Kaline grabbed a bottle of bubbly himself, but the cork stuck. "I've waited 16 years for this moment, and now I can't get the damn cork out!" Al exclaimed.

In the final season before baseball broke up each league into two divisions, the Tigers had led the American League for all but 14 days.

"We were just so confident that year," Kaline recalled. "I never played on another team that went out every day knowing that they were going to win. I can't tell you why that was. Maybe it was a holdover from the previous season when we lost a pennant we all knew we should have won. But it was great to be a part of it. Although, of course, it was a little frustrating for me, not playing all the time."

On September 19, Denny McLain won for the 31st time. McLain was beating the New York Yankees 6–1 when Mickey Mantle, who planned to retire at the end of the season, stepped up the plate in the top half of the eighth inning for what would be his final at-bat at Tiger Stadium. The Mick needed just one more home run to pass Jimmie Foxx for third place on baseball's all-time home-run parade.

As the fans stood and applauded in a final tribute to the Yankees great, Tigers catcher Jim Price, not wanting to infringe on Mantle's moment, walked slowly out to the mound.

"Let's let him hit one," McLain suggested, cocksure as always.

"I looked at him kind of funny for a moment, and I finally said, 'Uh, okay,'" recalled Price, now a Tigers radio commentator.

"When I got back to home plate, Mickey said, 'Hi, Jim. How ya doing?' Mantle always said hello, every time he came up to bat.

"I said, 'Mickey, we want you to hit one out.' Mantle took a step back, and he said, 'What?' Then he looked out toward the mound, and McLain nodded at him.

"I asked Mickey, 'Where do you want it?' Mantle said, 'High and tight, mediocre cheese.' So I signaled for a fastball, up and in."

Mantle took McLain's first pitch and fouled off a second. "That's when I knew I wasn't dealing with a Rhodes Scholar," McLain later joked.

"Then McLain grooved another one, and Mantle hit a bullet into the upper deck," Price remembered.

McLain was clapping as Mantle rounded the bases. As Mickey passed third, he looked at McLain and grinned. "When he got to the plate, he thanked me," Price said.

Somehow, the home-run ball found its way from the right-field seats back to the Tigers dugout. There, Al Kaline held up the ball for Mantle to see, then tossed it gently across the diamond toward the Yankees dugout.

Some said the triumphant 1968 Tigers saved the city of Detroit. Or, at the very least, brought the troubled citizens back together.

"I believe the '68 Tigers were put here by God to heal this city," declared Willie Horton, one of just three black stars on the team.

Ironically, the Detroit Tigers had been the next-to-last big-league team to integrate its ballclub. Not until 1958, 11 years after the debut of trailblazer Jackie Robinson, did a player of color take the field in Detroit.

"We were able to give people a positive diversion," Gates Brown said. "When I went into the neighborhoods, I heard people talking Tigers nonstop. None of that other stuff mattered, at least for the time being."

"I had a couple of police officers who worked at Tiger Stadium tell me that in 1967 there would be three or four guys standing on the street corner looking for trouble," Mickey Lolich said.

"In 1968, those same guys were standing on the corner, but they had a transistor radio and were listening to the ballgame. We, as a team, embodied what this city was all about. We were a blue-collar, working-class team who loved being a part of this city."

"Black, white, green, yellow, they were hugging each other," Denny McLain said.

"Let's be realistic," cautioned the late Earl Wilson. "A baseball team isn't going to cure the racial ills affecting a community. But we made everyone temporarily forget our differences and provided a little pride and a little hope.

"What I remember about that team in '68," Wilson added, "is that there were no divisions."

For Al Kaline, the pennant was a dream that had finally come true. However, Al wasn't sure he would even get to play in the World Series.

CHAPTER 14

Making Room

Despite their dominance during the regular season and despite Denny McLain's historic 31 wins, the Tigers made their long-awaited return to the World Series as 8-to-5 underdogs to the defending world champion St. Louis Cardinals, thanks in large part to the presence of Cardinals ace pitcher Bob Gibson. But when Al Kaline took the field at Busch Stadium in St. Louis on October 2, 1968, those odds were the furthest thing from his mind.

By 1968, Mickey Mantle, Kaline's contemporary, had played in 65 World Series games. Al Kaline had never played in one. In fact, Al had never even seen a World Series game in person.

"I promised myself a long time ago that the first World Series game I ever saw would be the one I played in," Kaline recalled. "I had watched the games on TV, of course. But I told myself I was never going to go to a World Series until I was playing in it."

Still, over the years, the thought, the dream, had endured.

"In the back of my mind I would wonder, *Man, am I ever going to get a chance to play in the World Series?*" Al admitted.

At long last, Kaline was finally going to get that opportunity. But where would he play? And how much? In the weeks leading up to the Tigers' return to the World Series for the first time since 1945, there didn't appear to be any room in the lineup for Al. To be perfectly blunt, the Tigers had won the pennant without him, and Kaline knew it.

When Al had been sidelined for five weeks with that busted bone in his arm, Jim Northrup had replaced him in right field and had played extremely well. When Kaline returned to active duty, manager Mayo Smith had alternated Al for a while with the slumping Norm Cash at first base. But Cash found his stroke at the plate after the All-Star break, batting .333 from July 27 until the end of the regular season, and the Tigers needed Stormin' Norman's booming left-handed bat in the lineup.

Kaline, in his 16th season, 16 times an All-Star, had become a glorified utility man. Al's batting average, which stood at .305 for his career coming into the season, fell to .287 in 1968. And when Kaline dropped a fly ball in August, he had heard a smattering of boos at Tiger Stadium for one of the few times in his career.

Smith knew he had to find a way to get Al back into the lineup for the World Series. It wouldn't be fair to leave the man who had been the team's best player since 1955 sitting on the bench. Kaline had waited his entire career, often suffering in silence, for this opportunity.

And as well as Willie Horton, Mickey Stanley, and Jim Northrup had performed in Kaline's absence, Smith knew the Tigers lineup was much more formidable with Al in it. The Tigers needed his presence. They needed his leadership. They needed his bat.

Smith thought briefly about benching third baseman Don Wert, who had only hit .200 during the regular season, and playing Kaline there. But Wert, a solid defensive player, was fielding as well as he ever had. And the Cardinals, with Lou Brock and Curt Flood, loved to run. Smith knew if he stationed Kaline at third base, St. Louis would try to bunt against him early and often—probably with considerable success.

Smith pondered his options. None of them were easy. Making Kaline's lifelong dream of playing in the World Series come true was going to require the boldest, ballsiest gamble any manager had ever made on baseball's biggest stage.

In retrospect, with the advantage of hindsight, moving Mickey Stanley to shortstop, shifting Jim Northrup to center field, and returning Al Kaline to right seems like the only logical, sensible move that Mayo could have made.

Oddly enough, Norm Cash, who had never made any secret of his disdain for his manager's baseball acumen, was the one who first approached Smith with the idea of moving Stanley from center field to short.

Smith was a hunch player. He liked to ride his ballplayers as long as he could when they were hot. Mayo listened as Cash laid out his plan. The more Smith thought about it, the more he liked the idea. It made sense, baseball sense.

Ray Oyler, the Tigers' regular shortstop, had batted .135 during the regular season. Aside from the pitcher—except in those games when the hard-hitting Earl Wilson was on the mound—Oyler was the only automatic out in the batting order. He was the Tigers' weakest link. But Smith kept his thoughts to himself.

As much as Kaline wanted to play, he—typically—tried to take his manager off the hot seat.

"I understood the kind of pressure Mayo was under because everybody was asking about me," Kaline recalled. "It seemed that every day in September there was some kind of story speculating on what would happen to me during the Series. 'Is Kaline going to play? Is he going to get in the World Series?'

"So after we clinched the pennant, I went into Mayo's office, and I told him, 'Look, Mayo, you know I want to play. But I know the spot you're in. Don't feel that you've got to play me. I understand the situation. It wouldn't be right to sit one of the kids because they're the ones who won it for you. They've battled all year. They got us here. I've just been sitting on the bench, injured or watching. I think you should go with the younger guys. They've earned it. They deserve to play.'

"Mayo just looked over and smiled and thanked me. 'Lemme think about it,' he said. Then he said, 'Why don't you take some ground balls at third base for a few days?' He never actually said so, but I think his original plan was to play me at third base.'

"That floored me. I had played one or two games there for a few innings in my career but never consistently. So I took some infield practice there. Then Willie Horton got hurt, and I went to right field. And, man, I really started to hit the ball. Because I really wanted to play. It was killing me. I wanted to force Mayo's hand, one way or another."

When a reporter, who had been tipped off by Kaline, asked Smith about Al's offer to ride the bench, the manager replied, "That shows you what kind of man Al Kaline is.

"It's one thing for him to tell that to a reporter," Smith continued. "But it's something else for him to come in and tell me. Keeping him on the bench has been the hardest thing I have ever had to do in my life."

"A few days later," Kaline recalled, "Mayo called me into his office along with a few of the other veterans—Norm Cash, Eddie Mathews, Bill Freehan. He asked us what we thought about moving Mickey Stanley to shortstop. That was the first any of us guessed what he'd been thinking."

The day after his conversation with Kaline and the other veterans, Smith went upstairs to the third-floor offices at Tiger Stadium to inform general manager Jim Campbell of the gamble he planned to take with his team's World Series chances. Mayo felt he owed his boss that much.

"Are you in a good mood?" Mayo asked when he walked through the door.

Campbell laughed. Of course he was in a good mood. The Tigers were going to the World Series.

"I'm going to play Mickey at shortstop," Smith said.

"Son of a bitch, are you serious?" the stunned Campbell fired back.

"If you say no, I won't do it," Smith said. "But Northrup will play center, Willie is in left, and Al will be in right. Once we get ahead, Oyler goes in and Mickey goes back to center."

Campbell thought about it for a moment, then said, "Well, I'll tell you, you've got us this far, so if you want to do it, then go ahead and do it."

Stanley was one of those rare guys everyone refers to as a natural athlete. He had been a pitcher in high school. It was no secret, as Bill Freehan put it at the time, that Stanley was "the best all-around athlete we've got."

Golf, tennis, basketball, billiards—you name it, and Mickey Stanley could play it. But shortstop? In the World Series?

"The shortstop thing just hit me out of the blue," Stanley admitted in an interview with former Tigers-beat-writer-turned-author George Cantor after Smith's daring gamble had become part of World Series lore. "I didn't have any inkling that this was going to happen. It must have been Cash. He always saw me fielding grounders out there during infield drills. But I was fooling around. I loved being on the field. I was just a big kid. I loved to play ball. Sure, Mayo had played me there a few times before. But to me, it was just like practice, to fill in, in an emergency or something. I think that Cash put a bug in his ear.

"We all knew something had to give about getting Kaline in the lineup. We'd heard maybe third base. The Cardinals had already announced that they would throw nothing but right-handers at us, so platooning Al at first base wasn't going to work."

Stanley, a Gold Glove winner in center field, often fielded ground balls at shortstop during batting practice in the regular season. It was a way to pass the time and burn up excess energy before the games. The kid in Stanley enjoyed it. It was a way of calming himself down.

"We were in Baltimore on the last Monday of the season [September 23], and Mayo called me up to his room at the hotel," Stanley recalled. "He told me that he was going to play me the last six games at shortstop, and if it worked out that I would start there in the Series."

"You're always popping off to me about how you can play shortstop, second base, and third base," Smith said, smiling. "Well, how would you like to play shortstop in the World Series?"

Stanley was stunned.

"Are you kidding?" Mickey asked.

"If you can play shortstop, I can put Kaline in the outfield, and I think our ballclub would be better offensively than it's ever been," Mayo explained.

Stanley gave Smith a boyish grin. "When do I start?" he asked.

As Kaline recalled, Stanley told his teammates, "I don't want to be the reason we lose. Everybody has to agree in order for me to do this."

"I wasn't concerned for myself, embarrassing myself, as much as I was afraid I'd let down the other guys," Stanley said later. "I wasn't afraid to do it. In fact, it was kind of flattering. If the ballclub had that much confidence in me, it must have meant something good."

A week before the World Series against the St. Louis Cardinals was to begin, Smith started Stanley at shortstop, moved Jim Northrup from right field to center, and put Kaline back in right field

"We'll see how Mickey does at shortstop," Mayo told Kaline.

Nobody made a big deal of it at the time. During the course of the season, Stanley had played first base in 15 games and second in one.

But when Baltimore's Don Buford barreled into Stanley on the front end of a double play, Mickey himself got worried.

"'Hmmmm,' I told myself, 'This is going to be interesting,'" Stanley recalled.

"Mayo told me I could do the job. But I wasn't so sure. To be taken out of center field and put at shortstop was like landing in alien territory."

That night, after the collision with Buford, Stanley phoned his manager in his Baltimore hotel room. "I asked Mayo if he was sure that this was what he wanted," Stanley recalled. "I said, 'I'm not worried for me. I'm worried for the other players.'"

"Mayo said, 'I know you can do the job. That's good enough for me. You're my shortstop.'"

Smith kept the full extent of his intentions secret from the media and from the public as Stanley and second baseman Dick McAuliffe worked out alone in the infield each afternoon before the gates opened and the press arrived at the ballpark. After one such workout, Smith called McAuliffe into his office and closed the door.

"What do you think?" Mayo asked. "Can he do the job?"

"Mayo," McAuliffe, intense as always, replied, "you've got to be kidding."

"Well, let's keep working on it," Smith ordered.

Mayo wasn't kidding.

However, McAuliffe wasn't the only Tiger who had his doubts.

"I thought he was out of his mind, I thought he had gone off the deep end," admitted relief pitcher Daryl Patterson. "But Mayo didn't give a hoot. He just did what he felt was right. He was a hunch guy. That was his hunch."

"I decided to just see what happened," Stanley said. "If I screwed up in the last six games of the regular season, who cared?"

Playing Stanley at shortstop in six meaningless regular-season games against the Orioles and Washington Senators was one thing. Starting him at shortstop in baseball's Fall Classic against the St. Louis Cardinals with the eyes of the world upon him was another.

Smith didn't reveal his intentions after the final game of the regular season. Even then, the move was shrouded in mystery. One of the Detroit newspapers ran a story saying Stanley would play shortstop in the World Series. The other Detroit daily declared that he would not.

No one in the national media that poured into St. Louis to cover the start of the Series could remember the last time a manager had made such a significant position switch—not because of an injury, but of his own volition.

When the Tigers' starting lineup for Game 1 was announced, Pee Wee Reese, the Hall of Fame shortstop who had found a second career in the broadcast booth, approached Smith in the Tigers' dugout.

"Mayo, you're not serious, are you?" Reese asked.

"The hell I'm not!" the Tigers' manager replied.

"You're damned if you do and damned if you don't," Smith explained to the writers who came calling. "But you have to make a decision. That's what they pay you for."

The night before the first game of the Series, Stanley, who was always the nervous sort anyway, asked his wife, Ellen, if he could have one of her sleeping pills. The morning of the game, he took a tranquilizer. At the ballpark, he threw up.

"I suppose," Stanley told renowned sportswriter Red Smith, "the first damn ball will be hit to me."

It was.

Stanley gloved Lou Brock's grounder and threw the speedy Cardinal out at first. "At least my knees stopped shaking after that," Stanley recalled. "I got the jitterbugs out. But the nervous feeling never really left me. It was always pretty hairy. I understood that Mayo had stuck his neck out a mile, and it was up to me to see that he didn't get it chopped off."

Stanley started the entire Series at shortstop. He batted only .214, no doubt in part because of nerves. But he made only two errors, both of which were questionable calls and neither of which mattered.

"I was scared stiff all the time," Stanley confessed years later. "I didn't want to let the guys down. I always felt that I got cheated out of my Series. It was no fun for me. I didn't enjoy the Series at all."

In the late innings, when the Tigers' victory in that game appeared secure, Stanley would return to center field, Jim Northrup would replace Willie Horton in left, and Ray Oyler would finish the game at shortstop. Al Kaline would remain in right, making the Tigers better defensively at all four positions.

Kaline played all seven games in right field. In the World Series at long last, Al batted .379, second only to Norm Cash's .385, and knocked in eight runs to tie Jim Northrup for the team lead.

Al's performance, as much as Mickey Lolich's three dramatic wins, was the difference in the Series.

"I think the whole damn World Series was Mickey Stanley playing shortstop!" declared Cash, with whom the idea had originated.

Funny how things play out sometimes.

If Tigers general manager Jim Campbell had succeeded in his efforts to trade Denny McLain to Baltimore for Hall of Fame shortstop Luis Aparicio prior to the 1968 season, Ray Oyler would not have been playing shortstop for the Tigers and Mayo Smith would never have dreamed of shifting Mickey Stanley from center field to short to replace Aparicio and make room in the outfield for Al Kaline. In that case, who knows how the World Series might have turned out?

And it was Kaline's performance in the 1968 World Series that elevated Al from a borderline Cooperstown candidate into a bona fide Hall of Famer.

CHAPTER 15

"Nobody Deserves It More"

The city of Detroit had been waiting for another World Series since 1945, when Al Kaline was just 10 years old. But no one was looking forward to the 1968 Series more eagerly than No. 6.

He wanted to participate, sure. The World Series is every player's ultimate goal. But privately, in the twilight of his career, Al still felt he had something to prove—to himself, if to no one else.

"I had always done pretty well against the National League in the All-Star Games, but in the All-Star Game, you never know if the guys are going all out," Al confided.

"In the World Series, you know everybody is going to let it all hang out. I really wanted to see how I could fare against the best players from the other league."

To this day, the '68 Tigers will tell you they were baseball's last true champions—the last real winners of baseball's Fall Classic before the postseason was diluted by playoffs and wild cards.

"You had to battle all year long to get to that point," Kaline explained. "But then you were there. Now, you have to get to the playoffs and get lucky to have a chance to get to the World Series."

As Kaline did so many times during the course of his career—so often that it became commonplace and expected—he rose to the occasion in his first and only World Series, batting .379 with two home runs and eight RBIs as the Tigers won their first world championship in 23 years.

"It was a joy and a delight just to play on that team," Kaline declared.

The 1968 World Series between Detroit and St. Louis was a rematch of 1934 when the Cardinals' Dizzy Dean brought the high-flying Tigers of Hank Greenberg, Charlie Gehringer, and Mickey Cochrane crashing back down to earth.

In 1968 it was Bob Gibson's turn to try to do the same. The hard-throwing, highly competitive Cardinals right-hander had won five World Series games in a row, beating the Yankees twice in 1964 and the Red Sox three times in '67. In six Series starts, Gibson had stuck out 57 of the best batters the American League could send up to the plate.

He had been about as close to unbeatable in the postseason as a pitcher can get. But the Tigers had a pitcher of their own who had been pretty unbeatable that season, too.

From the beginning, the 1968 World Series was billed as a battle between Denny McLain, the Tigers' brash 31-game winner and a throwback to the crazy days of Dizzy Dean, and Gibson, who had enjoyed a sensational season in his own right, compiling a 1.12 ERA with 22 wins and 13 shutouts.

It had been years since a World Series had featured two such out-standing, overpowering aces going head to head against one another. Rightfully, 1968 had been proclaimed the Year of the Pitcher in baseball.

In the World Series, except for Game 7, Gibson was his usual, unbeatable self, tossing three complete games and winning two of them, with an ERA of 1.67. Meanwhile, McLain, whose golden right arm had secretly been hurting since 1965 and had been repeatedly shot full of cortisone, failed in the first two of his three starts.

Instead it was Mickey Lolich—the pot-bellied left-hander who had long languished in McLain's shadow, playing second fiddle to the Tigers' flamboyant right-hander—who stole the show and the Series with three complete-game victories. No pitcher has been able to match that feat since.

Lolich, with his three wins, his 1.67 postseason ERA, and his 21 strikeouts, was named the World Series Most Valuable Player. No one could disagree with that.

But the 1968 Series also belonged to Al Kaline. Al was due. And he delivered.

Years later, Kaline would admit, "It was everything I dreamed it would be."

In his long-awaited first and ultimately only appearance on baseball's biggest stage, Kaline led his team to victory, delivering key hits in the crucial do-or-die Games 5 and 7 when the Tigers' backs were against the wall.

"Quite frankly, it put a lot of pressure on me," Kaline recalled.

"It took me so long to get to the World Series. Then, with the big buildup that the media gave it—'Kaline Finally Gets to World Series!'—I kept thinking, *Man, what if I screw up? What if I have a bad World Series?*"

The night before the first game, McLain had warmed up by playing the organ in the jam-packed lounge in the Tigers' Sheraton-Jefferson Hotel in downtown St. Louis, taking requests and dedicating a rendition of "Sweet Georgia Brown" to Gibson, who had spent a minor-league off-season barnstorming with the Harlem Globetrotters.

"I'm sick of hearing what a great team the Cardinals are," McLain boasted. "I don't want to just beat them. I want to demolish them."

But the highly hyped matchup between McLain and Gibson never materialized, as Gibson struck out a Series record 17 batters en route to a 144-pitch, 4–0, five-hit shutout in the Series opener.

One of those five hits belonged to Kaline, who delivered a double in the sixth inning with Dick McAuliffe aboard.

Gibson, who snacked on candy bars during the game, struck out seven of the first 10 batters he faced and retired Kaline, Norm Cash, Jim Northrup, Willie Horton, and Bill Freehan—the heart of the Tigers order—a combined 12 times.

In the ninth inning, to the delight of the 54,692 at circular cookie-cutter Busch Stadium, Gibson appeared to get stronger as the day wore on and struck out the side—Kaline, Cash, and Horton—to end the game.

"When I walked back to the dugout, everybody was up and cheering," Al recalled. "I knew those cheers weren't for me."

After the game, as the Tigers sat in somber silence in front of their lockers, rehashing the undressing they had just suffered in their minds, Cash suddenly started laughing out loud. Kaline, whose locker was next door to Norm's, turned and asked Cash what he found so funny.

"He looked at me," Kaline recalled, "and said, 'We just broke the record for most strikeouts, and I'm going to get $500 for going on the *Good Morning America Show.*'"

"In those days," Kaline added, "$500 was a lot of money."

Kaline, who admitted to feeling nervous when he stepped up to bat for the first time in his first World Series, struck out three times in that first game. Like many of the Tigers hitters, he appeared to be pressing. After waiting 16 years for this moment, who could blame him?

During a quiet dinner that evening, Kaline and Cash discussed Gibson's mastery over the Tigers and came to the conclusion they had all been uptight, overswinging, and trying too hard.

Before the start of Game 2, which pitted Mickey Lolich against the Cardinals' 19-game winner Nelson Briles, Kaline and Cash circulated among their teammates in the clubhouse and out on the field during batting practice, urging them to forget about trying to blast everything out of the ballpark and instead concentrate on swinging their bats the same way they had during the regular season. Do that, the two veterans told their teammates, and the home runs will happen.

Meanwhile, the bookmakers, taking into account the fact that the Tigers would have to face Gibson two more times if the Series somehow went the full seven games, had increased the odds against the seemingly overmatched Tigers to 14-to-5.

Lolich, who had won 10 and lost just two games down the stretch to finish with 17 victories for the season, had a boil lanced before the second game of the Series, and the antibiotics he received after the minor surgery left him feeling "sluggish and groggy."

"But once I began to warm up, I felt a little better," Lolich said later. "The antibiotics also relaxed me, and I wasn't nervous pitching in my first World Series."

Lolich felt so relaxed, in fact, that he belted a long home run to left field in the third inning. It was the first home run Lolich had ever hit in a decade of professional baseball. And it occured on baseball's biggest stage. The portly left-hander got so wrapped up in watching the flight of his masterpiece that he forgot to touch first base. First-base coach Wally Moses yelled at Lolich, and the pitcher had to retrace his steps.

"I had two strikes on me, and I told myself not to strike out," Lolich recalled. "When Briles started his motion, I began to swing the bat. The pitch hit my bat. I figured it was a fly ball. I ran to first, but I turned toward the dugout before I got to the bag."

"I still won't believe he hit a home run until I see the rerun," scoffed the sarcastic McLain, who suddenly found himself upstaged by a teammate he viewed with disdain.

Willie Horton and Norm Cash also homered, and Al Kaline—who personally killed a potential first-inning rally by the Cardinals with a gate-crashing catch of Orlando Cepeda's foul ball and a grab of Mike Shannon's drive to right—chipped in two hits and scored twice.

The Tigers had relaxed and, just as Kaline and Cash had promised, the big hits had come as they evened the Series with an easy 8–1 win.

As the Tigers trotted off the field with the Series tied at one win apiece, Kaline slapped Mickey Stanley on the back. "Now we go back to Detroit," Kaline said. "After all these years without a World Series, it should be something to see."

The city of Detroit was indeed alive as baseball's Fall Classic came calling for the first time since 1945. Bumper stickers and signs screaming "Sock It to 'Em, Tigers!" were everywhere.

As they had throughout the second half of the regular season, radio stations couldn't play the team's theme song often enough:

> *We're all behind our baseball team.*
> *Go get 'em, Tigers!*
> *World Series bound and pickin' up steam.*
> *Go get 'em, Tigers!*

Washington Boulevard, a mile from the ballpark and, at the time, still lined with hotels and fashionable shops befitting the heart of a major city, had been renamed Tiger Drive. Orange stripes had been painted down the middle of the street, and there were flags and banners everywhere.

A festive atmosphere prevailed. Tiger Stadium was jammed to the rafters as 53,634 turned out to witness the first World Series game played in Detroit since World War II.

However, in the Tigers clubhouse at the corner of Michigan and Trumbull, McLain and Lolich were both grousing about the three bases Cardinals speedster Lou Brock had so far stolen, running even in Game 2 when the Cardinals were far behind.

"It was definitely for his own self-glory," Lolich complained. "He wants to set a record for stolen bases or something. If it was Early Wynn or someone like that, the next time Brock came up, he'd be on his back on the first pitch."

Across the field, Brock simply smiled when he was informed of Lolich's criticism. "I've been in the dirt before," the future Hall of Famer said. "If he says it's for my self-glory, I'll do it anyway."

In fact, before the Series began, Brock had studied the moves of the Tigers pitchers to first base and felt confident he could run against them.

Brock's diligence paid dividends as he eventually stole seven bases during the Series—compared to none for the entire Tigers team.

As if to prove his point, Brock led off the top half of the first inning of Game 3 at Tiger Stadium with a walk—albeit a somewhat controversial one when the umpire awarded him ball four because Tigers pitcher Earl Wilson had allegedly wet his fingers—and promptly stole second. However, Brock was thrown out trying to steal third standing up on a Roger Maris strikeout.

In the bottom half of the third inning, with Dick McAuliffe aboard, Kaline brought the hometown throng to its feet with his first World Series home run, against the Cardinals' Ray Washburn, to give his team a 2–0 lead.

It would have been entirely appropriate if Kaline had emerged the hero of the first World Series game played in Detroit in 23 years. But that was not to be. After the Cardinals had chased Tigers starter Earl Wilson, broadcaster-to-be Tim McCarver homered in the fifth inning to put St. Louis on top to stay, 4–2. Orlando Cepeda also delivered a three-run homer in the seventh as the Cardinals rolled to a 7–3 win.

Game 4 brought a rematch of McLain against Gibson, both of whom swept the Most Valuable Player and the Cy Young Awards in their respective leagues during the regular season.

But first came the rain. A downpour began more than an hour before game time, leaving fans cooped up in their automobiles in parking lots surrounding the ballpark, in nearby saloons, or clustered together under the stands in the stadium, trying to stay dry and warm.

McLain had been regularly receiving injections of cortisone all summer to ease the pain in his right arm—a fact that had gone virtually unnoticed outside the Tigers clubhouse because Detroit's two daily newspapers were on strike most of the season. Team doctors had warned manager Mayo Smith that the shots would only work their magic for so long. Sooner or later, the medical people predicted, McLain would pay the price.

On this dreary October afternoon, after the start of the game had been delayed for 37 minutes, the Cardinals immediately jumped on McLain, just as they had done in the Series opener.

By the third inning, St. Louis was in front 4–0 and, with Gibson mowing down the Tigers hitters one after another, the rain, which had continued to fall, suddenly became the best hope of the Tigers' fans.

In the exposed center-field bleachers, the soaked spectators began chanting, "Rain! Rain! Rain!" silently praying for a postponement before the fifth inning, when the game, and the pounding that the home team was taking, would become official.

When the umpires huddled with baseball commissioner William Eckert and halted play, the grounds crew rolled the heavy tarp over the infield and the crowd cheered. In their clubhouse, the Tigers were aware that the weather forecast called for more rain, and they began looking forward to a fresh start on Monday.

During the delay, Denny McLain informed Mayo Smith that he couldn't possibly continue because he couldn't raise his throbbing right arm above his head. After the game, Denny would tell reporters that he was finished for the year. Regardless of what the Tigers did the rest of the World Series, he could not pitch again. Then he received another injection.

After a delay of one hour and 14 minutes, the two teams were ordered back out on the field, and the one-sided contest continued, albeit sometimes comically.

Bob Gibson, who had spent much of the delay in the St. Louis dugout eating ice cream bars, didn't appear too enthused about the resumption of play as he lobbed a few warm-up tosses in the bullpen.

Suddenly, as Cardinals bullpen catcher Johnny Edwards later revealed, Gibson said, "John, here they come."

According to Edwards, "He threw five pitches, and all of them were fastballs. They burned the hell out of my hand."

Gibson was ready.

While the Tigers repeatedly tried to slow down the game, conferring on the mound and backing out of the batter's box to clean the mud off their spikes, hoping the rain would intensify, the Cardinals padded their lead with two more runs in the top of the fourth. At the same time, the Cardinals were doing their best to try to speed up the game.

When Cepeda walked with two away in the top of the fourth, prolonging matters, the Cardinals dugout ordered him to half-heartedly try to steal second base. He did, and he was thrown out. Another half-inning was in the books.

Next, it was the Tigers' turn to stall. In the bottom of the fourth, Willie Horton, the Tigers' first batter, spent five minutes at the plate. He stepped into the batter's box, backed out, cleaned the mud off his spikes, and eventually headed toward the dugout hunting for the pine-tar rag. Finally, Gibson struck him out.

In the top of the fifth, when Julian Javier singled with two away, he immediately attempted to atone for his "mistake" by taking off for second. Tigers reliever Daryl Patterson whirled and threw to shortstop Mickey Stanley, who applied the tag, ending the inning.

The rain came and went the rest of the afternoon, but the game continued, eventually ending in a soggy 10–1 St. Louis romp as the Tigers managed just five hits off Gibson, two of them by Kaline.

Suddenly, the Tigers were not only battling the St. Louis Cardinals, they were battling baseball history.

Only two teams, the 1925 Pittsburgh Pirates and the 1958 New York Yankees, had ever rebounded from a three-games-to-one deficit to win the World Series.

One more loss and the Tigers would be eliminated—and humiliated. In Las Vegas, the odds against the long-shot Tigers were now 8-to-1.

In mid-September, when it had become obvious the Tigers were going to win the American League pennant, general manager Jim Campbell had approached Ernie Harwell, the team's highly respected 50-year-old radio play-by-play announcer, and asked him to select the national anthem singers for Games 3, 4, and 5, which were to be played at Tiger Stadium.

Harwell was the logical choice for that assignment. He knew the music business almost as well as he knew baseball, having himself written hundreds of songs, some 65 of which were recorded by artists such as Mitch Ryder and B.J. Thomas.

Harwell picked Margaret Whiting, Marvin Gaye, and an up-and-coming young blind Puerto Rican singer named Jose Feliciano to do the honors before the Tigers' three Series home games.

Actually, Feliciano was Harwell's second choice for Game 5. But country crooner Eddie Arnold was unavailable.

Campbell had suggested local plumber-turned-radio-personality Bob Taylor, who, billed as "Fat Bob the Singing Plumber," frequently performed the anthem at Tiger Stadium during the regular season. But Harwell settled on Feliciano, an avid baseball fan who had grown up listening to Mel Allen's broadcasts of the New York Yankees.

Feliciano was appearing at Caesars Palace in Las Vegas at the time. However, the singer, who was both flattered and honored to be invited, agreed to catch a red-eye flight to Detroit, sing the anthem, and then return to Vegas in time for his show that night.

On Monday morning, October 7, Harwell picked up Feliciano, his wife Hilda, and his guide dog Trudy at Detroit's Metro Airport and drove them to the ballpark, where Harwell personally escorted the singer into the Tigers' clubhouse.

"I was really looking forward to it," Feliciano said later. "It was my first World Series."

In the clubhouse, surrounded by the Tigers players, Harwell recalled, Feliciano "sang something like, 'C'mon Kaline, light my fire, Tigers got to have desire.'"

After Hall of Famer Goose Goslin, who had singled Mickey Cochrane home with the winning run in the 1935 World Series, unleashed the ceremonial first pitch, then Harwell led Feliciano and his guide dog into the outfield.

There, in a maroon suit and, wearing dark glasses, the 5'5" Feliciano strummed his guitar and sang a personalized, bluesy version of the national anthem that shocked the 53,634 fans at Tiger Stadium, provoked the wrath of many of the 50 million TV viewers tuned in around the country, got Jim Campbell censured by the American Legion, and nearly cost Ernie Harwell his job.

By today's standards, Feliciano's modifications to the anthem were modest and minimal. But 1968 was a time of social upheaval and racial strife in the country. Martin Luther King and Bobby Kennedy had been assassinated, and the Democratic National Convention had erupted in Chicago. The Vietnam War was raging. A year earlier, Detroit had been ravaged by riots just blocks from the ballpark, which left 43 dead and caused millions of dollars in damage.

Against that backdrop, baseball fans were in no mood for Feliciano's improvisation, no matter how innocuous it may now seem. The boos began even before Feliciano and Harwell left the field.

"I must have gotten a couple of thousand letters," Harwell recalled. "People called me all sorts of names, saying I was a communist. They didn't know that I had been in the marines for four years."

The switchboard at Tiger Stadium was immediately jammed with more than 2,000 complaints. In New York, NBC, which was broadcasting the game, was flooded with phone calls.

"Storm Rages Over Series Anthem," read the next morning's headline in the *Detroit Free Press*.

"I wasn't being disrespectful to the flag," Feliciano later told the *Free Press*. "I'm proud to be a Puerto Rican American. I owe everything I have to this country."

In the bullpen, Mickey Lolich, on whose left arm the Tigers' fast-fading hopes now rested, was just halfway through his warm-up tosses when the umpire told him it was time to play ball.

"I had a special routine for warming up," Lolich recalled. "I would go down to the bullpen 15 minutes before the game and throw a certain amount of warm-up pitches. Normally, I took 12 to 13 minutes to warm up.

"I got halfway through my routine, and all of a sudden they're doing the National Anthem. Jose Feliciano is singing, and it lasts forever. He goes on and on. I started cooling down.

"Then the umpire comes out and says, 'Come on, Mick. We gotta get the game started.' So I go to the mound, and all I can throw right away are fastballs."

The Cardinals, intent on ending the Series on the spot, jumped out to a 3–0 first-inning lead. But the Tigers, who appeared doomed, battled back thanks to fourth-inning triples by Mickey Stanley and Willie Horton, cutting the St. Louis lead to one run. Then Lou Brock, who had doubled, headed for home on Julian Javier's single to left in the top half of the fifth.

Willie Horton unleashed a long, looping throw that reached the plate on one hop. And when Brock failed to slide, Bill Freehan, who had done his best to block the plate, tagged the Cardinals speedster out.

To this day, Brock swears he was safe. "What did the umpire say?" Freehan retorts, whenever the question is raised.

"Every time I see him he says he thinks I never touched him," Freehan said. "And I say, 'I don't think you ever touched home plate.'"

"Was he out?" Horton asks, answering the question with a question. "Yeah, he was out. I got the ring."

Case closed.

Mayo Smith later called it the turning point in the game—and the Series. "But at the time you had no idea that's going to happen," Freehan admitted. "You just try to make a play."

"People talk about Brock not sliding," Jim Northrup noted. "But Willie still had to make a perfect throw and Freehan had to block the plate. They all did their jobs."

As Horton later revealed, before the Series began, even as Brock had been busy studying the Tigers' pitchers, the Tigers had been busy studying Brock.

"We studied film on Brock, and we knew he always went in standing up at home coming from second base," Horton explained. "I think he was so successful throughout his career that coaches would relax as he came around third base and he didn't get any help from the hitter on deck. I would say that was the play that did it for us."

"If Brock scored, we might never have gotten out of the inning," Northrup agreed.

In the seventh inning, with the Tigers still trailing 3–2, Mickey Lolich, a .114 hitter during the regular season who had suddenly discovered how to swing a bat, blooped a base hit to shallow right field. That brought left-hander Joe Hoerner, who had shut down the Tigers in Game 3, out of the Cardinals bullpen, this time to replace Nelson Briles.

Hoerner had suffered a heart attack in 1958. When doctors told him he could never pitch overhand again because the muscles around his heart were too weak, he had developed a rather unique delivery that was somewhere between sidearm and underhand.

Now, Dick McAuliffe greeted Hoerner with a single past first, advancing Lolich to second, and Stanley walked to load the bases.

The stage was set. Next up: Al Kaline.

The 53,634 at sold-out Tiger Stadium rose to their feet in anticipation as Kaline stepped into the batter's box. This was it. The bases were loaded, there was one out. The Tigers, down three games to one in the Series, trailed the Cardinals 3–2. The game and the World Series were on the line.

The fans knew it, and Kaline knew it, too. After 16 years of waiting, this was his chance, probably his last chance. It was now or never.

Mickey Lolich, who was perched on third base, later remembered thinking, *This is Al Kaline, 16 years in the big leagues, never played in the World Series.*

"I knew it was the perfect spot for him. I wanted Al to get a base hit for my sake, naturally, and for the team's sake," Lolich said.

"But not so much for myself and for the team, but for himself. If anybody could get that hit, I wanted it to be Al Kaline."

In his book, *The Tigers of '68*, former Detroit sportswriter George Cantor, who covered Kaline in 1968 and was on duty at Tiger Stadium that afternoon, wrote, "In Kaline's long career, this may have been the defining moment."

Cantor continued, "Many of the corporate and VIP fans who had been given tickets for the first two games of the Series had jumped off the boat for this one. The people who loved the game were in the ballpark this Monday, and they screamed for their longtime hero with passion that could not be contained. This is where it had all been leading, their adulation for him for all these long hopeless seasons. It was all this moment. Kaline could not fail them now.

"If there had been noisy afternoons before in this ballpark's long history, they were eclipsed by the din that filled it at this moment. The light towers seemed to sway from the sheer volume of it. The big crowd pleaded with him not to fail them now.

"Hoerner got ahead on the count, and Kaline fouled off one pitch after another on the corners. This was Six, one of the smartest hitters in baseball, fully focused on what had to be done. Hoerner finally made one pitch a little too good. Kaline, who always described himself as a 'mistake hitter,' pounced on this mistake. He lined it to right center. Lolich and McAuliffe came racing home and the Tigers went ahead.

"If there had been noise before in this game, in this season, it was nothing compared to this. The stands had become a cauldron of hysteria. The Line had come through with everything on the line. The last 15 years had been redeemed, stamped 'paid in full.'"

"I was looking for a fastball," Kaline later recalled, "because that's the way Hoerner pitched me before."

And Hoerner obliged. Kaline got the fastball he was waiting for, outside the plate, where the Cardinals had been pitching him all Series, and he socked it into right-center field to drive the tying and winning runs home.

When Kaline jogged out to right field for the start of the eighth inning, the capacity crowd stood again and cheered in tribute. Kaline tipped his cap. "It sent goose bumps up and down my back," he admitted.

"When I saw all those people standing, it's hard to describe the way you feel. You try to pay them back because they've been good fans, and I wanted so much to have them see us win one game here after the way they'd treated us all season."

And Kaline wasn't alone in those feelings.

"You know, you sort of get goose bumps when you see him do well," admitted Kaline's teammate and friend, catcher Bill Freehan.

"Somehow, I enjoy hitting with men on base," Kaline told the reporters who crowded around his clubhouse cubicle after the game, which the Tigers won 5–3. "I just don't seem to get the same incentive when they're not there.

"The main thing was, I didn't want to hit into a double play. I was trying to hit the ball up the middle or to right. I just wanted our club to go out there today and play good baseball. We represent the American League, and I didn't want to see our league embarrassed. We had to win this one, and we did. Now our only concern is winning the next one.

"The fans in Detroit have been just great when you consider it's been 23 years since they had a winner. I don't know if we'll win this thing or not, but we're going to fight right down to the wire. I know I will."

The Tigers still trailed in the Series, three games to two. And when the scene shifted back to St. Louis for Game 6, everyone wondered who would be the Tigers' starting pitcher. Everyone assumed they had seen the last of Denny McLain, who had been pounded in his first two outings. Privately, Tigers manager Mayo Smith had, in fact, promised himself as much. Good riddance.

On the field during the off-day workout at Busch Stadium, Smith was talking to a gaggle of reporters when one of them asked the identity of the team's Game 6 starter.

"I'm not sure," Mayo admitted. "Maybe Earl Wilson."

Just then, McLain walked by. From behind the wall of reporters, Denny looked over at his manager and winked.

"I didn't say anything to reporters," Smith later recalled, "but I thought to myself, *By God, there's my pitcher.*"

McLain, unpredictable as always, his aching arm eased by yet another injection of cortisone, made it look ridiculously easy this time as the Tigers rolled to a 13–1 victory to even the Series at three wins apiece.

"I remember the Cardinals coming out and watching us taking batting practice before the sixth game," recalled Kaline, who homered and singled twice in the rout, driving in four runs to boost his RBI total to eight. "They were all joking and having a lot of fun.

"Then all of a sudden we scored 10 runs in the third inning, and those guys weren't joking around anymore."

"When we went out and got 10 runs in one inning, we all knew the Cardinals were just waiting to get beat," Jim Northrup agreed. "And we were going to beat 'em."

Even as that rout in the sixth game of Series was unfolding, Mayo Smith, who was already looking ahead to Game 7, approached Mickey Lolich in the Tigers dugout.

"Can you pitch tomorrow?" the manager asked.

"Well, Mayo," Lolich replied, "it's only two days' rest."

The truth was, Lolich's rubberlike left arm felt dead.

"Well, I really want you to start tomorrow," Smith persisted. "I want you to pitch five innings. Do you think you can pitch five?"

"Yeah, I guess so," Lolich replied.

Although Lolich had pitched admirably, turning in two complete-game victories in the Series to keep the Tigers' hopes alive, nobody in their clubhouse was taking anything for granted. Especially not with glowering Bob Gibson due back on the mound for the Cardinals.

"This guy is not Superman," Mayo Smith told his team before Game 7, referring, of course, to Gibson. "He's beatable.

"But even if we don't win," the Tigers manager added, "We've had a helluva year."

"Mayo," first baseman Norm Cash piped up, "I don't know about him not being a Superman. He's dressing in a phone booth over there."

Kidding aside, it was a different Cardinals team—and a different Tigers team—that took the field for the seventh and deciding game.

"I noticed in the fifth game, after we threw Brock out at the plate, a little bit of the aggressiveness of the St. Louis hitters changed," Lolich recalled. "When we blew them away in the sixth game and when I went out to pitch in the seventh game, their hitters were totally different.

"They had become defensive hitters. They started swinging at bad pitches. When I saw that, I started keeping the ball down, and I actually started to go below the strike zone. And they were swinging at it. They were under a tremendous amount of pressure in the seventh game, and I knew by the second inning that if we could just score, which was going to be difficult because we were up against Gibson, we had a very good chance of beating them."

Still, no one expected Lolich to pitch like he did.

"I was absolutely sure we were going to win that game," Bob Gibson admitted years later. "I knew that Lolich wasn't exactly what you'd call a finely tuned athlete. He had to be dog-tired on two days' rest."

Mayo Smith's mandate to Lolich had been to pitch five innings. But as the game progressed and it became obvious the Tigers actually had a chance, Mayo wanted more.

"When I came in after the fifth inning, he [Smith] asked me if I could go one more, which I did," Lolich recalled. "When I came in at the end of the sixth, he said, 'Can you go one more?'"

With two out in the seventh inning, Jim Northrup, who had belted a grand-slam home run in Game 6, broke up a scoreless pitchers' duel between Lolich and Gibson with a two-run triple over Curt Flood's head in center field, driving in two runs. The normally smooth-fielding Flood initially started in on the ball, then slipped on the soggy field and almost dropped to one knee when he tried to pivot. Bill Freehan followed with a double, sending Northrup home with an insurance run.

"When we scored those three runs in the seventh, Mayo asked me if could finish the game," Lolich recalled.

"I said, 'Yeah.'"

The Tigers had done the impossible, coming back from a three-games-to-one deficit to beat Bob Gibson in the finale 4–1, sending Mickey Lolich, all 210 pounds of him, leaping into catcher Bill Freehan's waiting arms.

More than 40 years later, the photograph of Lolich jumping on Freehan following the final out of the '68 Series remains a classic.

"That was the most famous picture of my career—and you can't even see my face," Freehan groaned years later. "My back's never been the same since."

"The main reason I did that was because I didn't want him to jump on me first," admitted Lolich, who later owned and operated a doughnut shop in a Detroit suburb, showing up every morning before dawn to prepare the day's supply of doughnuts himself.

"It was a good thing that picture was taken then," Lolich added. "Bill would never be able to lift me now."

In the jubilant Tigers clubhouse, John Fetzer, the staid Tigers owner, who 12 months earlier had penned that melancholy ode to the disappointing 1967 season, yanked a bottle of champagne out of Mickey Stanley's hands and shouted, "Hey! Gimme a swig of that!"

"There's no feeling in sports like winning a World Series," Fetzer declared.

"I've never been this happy in my life. Never! Never! Never!" exclaimed Willie Horton. "I looked over the left-field roof in the seventh inning, and there was Rudolph the Red-Nosed Reindeer!"

Then Willie began walking around the locker room, singing "Jingle Bells."

"We are the greatest ballclub in the world!" proclaimed pitcher Earl Wilson.

"All my life, someone else was the big star and I was No. 2," said Lolich, who was born a right-hander but who learned to use his left after he broke his collarbone in a childhood bicycle accident. "I've just been a working stiff. Pot-belly. Big ears. There's always been somebody ahead of me. A hitter like Al Kaline. A pitcher lke Denny. It was always somebody else— never Mickey Lolich. But now my day has finally come."

It had been a World Series filled with pivotal turning points: Mickey Stanley's gutty performance at shortstop, where he made just two errors, neither of any consequence, allowing Al Kaline to remain in the lineup; Mickey Lolich's three gallant wins, upstaging both teammate Denny McLain and Cardinals ace Bob Gibson; Lou Brock's failure to slide in Game 5; and Curt Flood nearly falling down in center field on Jim Northrup's triple in Game 7.

But no Tiger put on a bigger or a better show than Al Kaline, who, after waiting for 16 years, personally turned around the Series in the crucial fifth game, batting .379, with two home runs among his eleven hits, and driving in eight runs.

Eyeing the mob of reporters jockeying for position around Kaline's locker in the champagne-soaked Tigers clubhouse afterward, Jim Northrup declared, "Nobody deserves it more than he does."

In 1968 the average salary for a Major League Baseball player was $22,000. Kaline was the highest-paid Tiger at $93,000. The total payroll for the '68 world championship team was just $980,000. For winning the World Series, each Tiger player received an extra $8,300, after taxes.

"Hell, the paper boy cashed my Series check for me," the always outspoken Jim Northrup later quipped.

"Without sounding too conceited, the '68 Series was what made me famous," Mickey Lolich recalled. "I actually had a better year in 1971, but nobody remembers that. All that anybody remembers is the World Series. I sometimes kid people that that was the only week I ever pitched in baseball. It might just as well have been."

After the World Series, some of the Tigers set out to cash in on their success.

Denny McLain played the organ at the Riviera casino in Las Vegas, serving as the opening act for Shecky Greene.

Jim Northrup tried to market a 1969 calendar featuring pictures of him and some of his Tigers teammates—in the nude.

"Burt Reynolds had posed naked for *Ms.* magazine or something, and I said, 'Hell, I'll get 11 other ballplayers to do the same thing, and we'll sell more calendars than they can make,'" Northrup explained decades later.

"But I could only come up with nine guys. We were three short. A lot of the guys wanted to do it, but they knew they would have real problems with their wives at home.

"We weren't going to show anything," he continued. "You know, you pose with your hand or your arm in a certain place. Today, everybody would say, 'Ho-hum.' But back in those days, that just wasn't done. Can you imagine the commotion we would have caused?"

Kaline had a much calmer, quieter off-season in mind for himself.

"I didn't do anything special, I just stayed around the house, played a little golf until the weather got too bad," he recalled. "I didn't do many appearances. Of course, back in those days, you didn't get much money for it anyway."

Thirty years later, many of the 1968 Tigers, including Kaline, gathered for the team's annual Fantasy Camp at Tigertown in Lakeland, Florida. There, out-of-shape stockbrokers and schoolteachers paid $2,995 apiece for the privilege of wearing the sacred Olde English D and rubbing shoulders for a week with their hallowed heroes of yesteryear.

"The older we get, every time we get together, you wonder if you'll ever see all these guys again," Kaline admitted that February in a sentimental moment away from the field. "We're all getting to that stage where you never know from day to day if you'll ever see everybody again.

"It's at times like this that I really miss Norm Cash," Kaline said softly. "Every time I think of Norm, I get a smile on my face. He was a great teammate. He never got all the credit he deserved. He would have really enjoyed this.

"I think about 1968 all the time. I think about the tremendous amount of fun I had. The more you talk about it, the more things you remember. What I remember is a great bunch of guys who put a tremendous amount of effort into winning.

"People bring things up all the time, but I don't reminisce about the games or particular plays or at-bats," Kaline continued. "I reminisce about the feeling when we won it.

"Seeing just how big the World Series was. I had played in a lot of All-Star Games, and there was always a lot of media there. But I couldn't believe how big the World Series was and how much attention you got, just by being a part of it."

CHAPTER **16**

"Thanks for the Memories"

When the world champion Tigers gathered with their wives in late March 1969 for their annual spring-training dinner party, the team debuted the 1968 highlight film, which of course included plenty of scenes from both the dominating regular season and the dramatic World Series.

When the cheers and whistles subsided, Al Kaline felt obligated, as the team's leader and elder statesman, to make a brief speech.

"We had a lot of fun last year," he said, addressing the audience filled with his teammates and friends. "You saw it in those pictures. Let's make this year just like last year. Let's everybody in this room pull together and do it again."

However, as Kaline and the Tigers would soon discover, repeating in baseball is much easier said than done.

In 1969 the American and National Leagues were each split into two divisions. The Tigers found themselves in the AL East, along with the New York Yankees, Boston Red Sox, Baltimore Orioles, Cleveland Indians, and Washington Senators.

In late April the Tigers appeared on national TV for the first time since the World Series. By then Mickey Mantle, who had recently retired, was part of the broadcast team, doing the pregame show.

During batting practice, Mantle was sitting in the Tigers dugout, visiting with Bill Freehan, when Kaline saw the two talking and walked over.

"Al," Mantle joked, "you don't realize how easy this game is until you get up in that broadcasting booth."

Kaline laughed, never dreaming that in seven years that was exactly where he would be.

Between the 1968 and '69 season, Denny McLain had purchased an airplane at a reported cost of $80,000 and was taking off into the wild blue yonder as often as possible—much to the chagrin of the Tigers management, which couldn't do anything to keep him grounded. Denny's teammates soon dubbed him "Sky King."

As so often happens with teams the season after they win the championship, the Tigers struggled to live up to expectations in 1969. Although Kaline was hovering around .300 at the plate in mid-May, the team was under .500 in the standings and Tigers fans, who had been spoiled by the previous year's success, were already growing restless.

The players shared their fans' frustration. On May 15, Willie Horton, who was mired in a miserable slump and frequently the target of the boos that could increasingly be heard at Tiger Stadium, stormed off the field after going 0-for-3 against the Chicago White Sox, ripped off his uniform, walked out on the team, and disappeared.

The Tigers suspended Horton without pay, and Willie missed a two-game series against the Twins in Minnesota. Horton met privately with general manager Jim Campbell, whom Willie always viewed as a surrogate father, and explained that his exit had been due not only to the boos but also to some personal problems that were never publicly disclosed.

"I made a big mistake, and I'm sorry," Horton said. "I just hope the fans and the ballplayers will forgive me."

Restored to the lineup on May 20, Horton went 2-for-5 with three RBIs.

On June 1 Al Kaline was presented with the Fred Hutchinson Award, given annually to the big-league player who displayed the sincerity, character, dedication and competitiveness of the former Tigers manager. Hutchinson died of throat cancer in 1964. The award, which was instituted the following year, had previously gone to Mickey Mantle, Sandy Koufax, Carl Yastrzemski, and Pete Rose.

To Kaline, that meant a lot. To this day, other than relief pitcher John Hiller in 1973, Kaline remains the only Tigers player ever to receive the award.

"I was amazed. I just couldn't believe it," said Kaline, who broke into the big leagues under Hutchinson in 1953. "Fred Hutchinson was my friend and my first manager in Detroit. He's the one who put me in the lineup for the first time."

On June 16, Kaline belted a two-run homer to help beat the New York Yankees 3–2. The Tigers were in third place, nine games behind the Baltimore Orioles.

Denny McLain, who had spent the past several days in the hospital recovering from food poisoning, had been discharged just in time to pitch a complete game, strike out five, and hold the Yankees to six hits, in typical McLain fashion.

After the game home-run hero Kaline sat alone and largely unnoticed in front of his locker as the sportswriters surrounded McLain in hopes of getting a good story or at least a few juicy quotes.

"Hey, Al," one of the veteran writers joked, "maybe you didn't hit a home run. Maybe it was our imagination. Maybe that's why nobody wants to talk to you."

"No," Kaline fired back, loud enough for McLain to hear. "It's just that I'm around all the time. You don't get a chance to talk to Denny much."

A year later, when Denny McLain was suspended for the first half of the 1970 season for consorting with bookmakers, manager Mayo Smith was asked almost daily about his absent ace. But Smith, who could already read the writing on the wall and realized his own big-league career was almost over, refused to throw Denny under the bus.

Instead, Smith would point with pride to the World Series ring he wore on his finger and say, "See this? He helped put that there."

That was true. But the same thing could just as honestly have been said about Al Kaline or Mickey Lolich. And neither of them ever sought or received the special privileges that were granted to McLain.

The special treatment that the Tigers manager accorded his prima donna pitcher did not sit well with some of the other players—especially in 1969, when the team wasn't winning.

Smith had two sets of rules—one set for Denny and one set for the rest of the team. On days when McLain wasn't scheduled to pitch, he would come and go as he pleased while the other pitchers were required to be at the ballpark every day. On nights when he was pitching, Denny would often show up 20 minutes before the start of a game. Other players had to report two and a half hours before the first pitch. When McLain was taken out of a game and replaced by a reliever, he often dressed and left the stadium immediately—something the other Tigers pitcher were usually not allowed to do.

"Mayo did grant Denny lot of privileges that the other players didn't have," Kaline admitted in retrospect. "And I think he was wrong in doing that.

"But it didn't bother me personally. I judge a man by what he does on the field, and there was never any doubt that Denny gave 100 percent when he pitched. But those privileges did bother a lot of the younger players.

"Finally, the players asked Norm Cash and me to talk to Mayo. We were the senior members of the team. We did, and Mayo recognized the problem. But he said he was afraid to crack down on Denny because he might quit on the team and that would destroy morale even more."

Major League Baseball, which traced its origins back to the barnstorming 1869 Cincinnati Red Stockings, celebrated its centennial year in 1969, and fans in Detroit were invited to vote for the "The Greatest Tiger Team of All-Time."

When the fans' all-time Tigers lineup was announced in June, it included five players who were in the Hall of Fame and two who were still playing: Al Kaline and Denny McLain.

Other members of the All-Time Tigers team were first baseman Hank Greenberg, second baseman Charlie Gehringer, third baseman George Kell, shortstop Billy Rogell, catcher Mickey Cochrane, outfielders Ty Cobb and Harry Heilmann, and pitcher Hal Newhouser.

With the memory of the 1968 World Series still fresh in fans' minds, Kaline actually outpolled Cobb, receiving 16,115 votes to Ty's 14,211.

However, Cobb was voted the Greatest Tiger Ever. Kaline finished a distant second.

The Tigers ended the 1969 season in second place, 19 games back, as Kaline batted .272 with 21 homers and 69 RBIs.

The following spring, the 1970 season began without Denny McLain. The prodigal pitcher was suspended for the first half of the season by baseball commissioner Bowie Kuhn for his alleged involvement in a Mafia-linked bookmaking operation dating back to 1967.

Shortly before training camp opened in the spring of 1970, *Sports Illustrated* broke a shocking story that claimed McLain had helped finance a Flint, Michigan, bookmaking operation run by a gambler with alleged Mafia connections. The exposé, in the February 23, 1970, edition of the magazine, was titled, "Baseball's Big Scandal—Denny McLain and the Mob."

Many feared that baseball's biggest betting scandal since the infamous Chicago Black Sox threw the 1919 World Series was about to explode.

The story also alleged that McLain's mysterious foot injury at the height of the 1967 pennant race was the result of a Mafia enforcer stomping on Denny's toes in an effort to convince him to pay his supposed bookmaker-partner $46,000 to offset some losses that their illicit business had incurred.

McLain had claimed he injured his foot when he was awakened in his living room by the sound of raccoons rooting around in trashcans outside and jumped to his feet to investigate. Denny said his foot had fallen asleep and he twisted his ankle getting up.

With McLain on the brink of bankruptcy, under investigation by both the Internal Revenue Service and the Michigan Corporation and Securities Bureau, and facing various lawsuits, the emphasis was hardly on baseball when Al Kaline and the Tigers reported to Lakeland, Florida, to begin training for the 1970 season.

Kaline got off to very good start, including a 5-for-5 game against Minnesota, and by May 6 he was batting .344. "In the four years I've been with the club, Al has never swung the bat better," declared Wally Moses, the Tigers' wizened hitting coach. "He's concentrating on every pitch. Let me tell you, that boy is some kind of hitter."

August 2, 1970, was officially designated Al Kaline Day at Tiger Stadium. All agreed it was a long-overdue, much-deserved honor for the Tigers superstar, who by that point was in his 18th season with the team.

But, typically, Kaline dreaded the thought of having to listen while one speaker after another paid tribute to him and his career. That just wasn't Al's style.

"Don't get me wrong," Kaline modestly told a reporter who asked about the upcoming ceremonies, "but I'll be glad when it's all over and I'm back at first base or in the outfield, playing ball as if nothing happened."

Fans were given commemorative Al Kaline Day buttons, Cherry Street behind Tiger Stadium was renamed Kaline Drive, and Michigan Governor William G. Milliken issued a proclamation, making Kaline's day a statewide event:

> One night, slightly more than 17 years ago, a young Detroit Tiger fielder made his first entry into a major-league game and a baseball legend had its start. Since that time in 1953, the legend has grown to become an institution. For virtually every Michigan resident, whether sports fan or not, the name Al Kaline signifies baseball as immediately and fully as does the name Tiger or the image of a diamond.
>
> In baseball, the thrill of the game is captured in memories of unforgettable plays or the long lists of records which detail batting averages, RBIs, or fielding percentages. However, mention of the name Al Kaline does more than any record book because to countless thousands around the world that name recalls a matchless athletic grace on the field and a warm profound humility off the field. As he is a leader to teammates by example, 'The Line' provokes rich emotions in baseball fans who hold in deepest respect his athletic abilities and his constant effort to do the very best that is within him.

Al Kaline Day in Tiger Stadium, on Sunday, August 2, 1970, is the first such commemoration for an active Tiger player in nearly three decades. It is fitting that baseball should so honor a man who for so long has brought honor to the game. However, this tribute cannot and must not be limited to the confines of this stadium.

Therefore, I, William G. Milliken, Governor of the State of Michigan, do hereby proclaim Sunday, August 2, 1970, as AL KALINE DAY in Michigan, calling on all Michigan residents and sports fans everywhere to pause in honor of a great athlete and a great man who means so much to so many.

Although 53,863 fans—the largest crowd at Tiger Stadium since 1961—had turned out a month earlier on July 1 for prodigal pitcher Denny McLain's return from exile, only 40,113 showed up on Al Kaline Day, a sweltering summer afternoon, to pay homage to the greatest player many of them had ever had the privilege of watching play.

An anxious Kaline sat in the Tigers dugout as dignitaries such as baseball commissioner Bowie Kuhn and American League president Joe Cronin, himself a Hall of Fame ballplayer, sang Al's praises on the field.

"All choked up, No. 6?" chided Jim Northrup, who was watching the show from the dugout and who understood the agony his friend Al was going through.

"When I go out there," Kaline said softly, "I just hope I don't miss the top step of the dugout and fall flat on my face."

When he was finally called upon to speak, with his family standing on the field behind him, Kaline called it, "The greatest day of my life."

"There have been so many people who have helped me to get to the big leagues and who have helped me stay there, it would be impossible for me to acknowledge them all," Al told his audience.

"I can still remember back to June 1953, and I can honestly say I thank God I chose to play for the team here in Detroit as I did. I will always remember this day, and I will always remember you, the fans, and the support you have given me—and I say that from the bottom of my heart."

Then Mel Torme sang a personalized version of "Thanks for the Memories," written especially for Al Kaline Day:

> *Thanks for the memories*
> *Of sunny afternoons*
> *Beaming August moons*
> *Good field, good hit are words you fit*
> *You left St. Louis in ruins*
> *We thank you, so much*
> *Thanks for the memories*
> *Of records you have set*
> *The list is growing yet*
> *Your golden mitts and booming hits*
> *And throws we can't forget*
> *We thank you, so much*
> *You came here when you were eighteen*
> *And the years have quickly passed*
> *But you've earned our highest rating*
> *And countless friends amassed.*
> *So thanks for the memories*
> *Of a batting title won*
> *A Series job well done*
> *All Star Games and Halls of Fame*
> *That wait to add your name*
> *We thank you, so much.*

However, there was precious little for Tigers fans to cheer about the rest of that 1970 season—and precious little for Kaline to enjoy.

"It was one bad thing after another," Kaline said at the time. "How can anyone do his best in an atmosphere like this? We got so far behind that after a while nobody seemed to care what happened—and I was as guilty as anyone else.

"At the end of the season, I was so disgusted I didn't care if I ever played another game of baseball," Kaline admitted.

The season ended the way it began, with Denny McLain again suspended by commissioner Bowie Kuhn, this time for carrying a handgun and violating his probation.

In between, many of the Tigers players flat-out quit on manager Mayo Smith. At the conclusion of the season, Smith, a hero just two years earlier when he brazenly shifted Mickey Stanley from center field to shortstop and the Tigers won the World Series, was allowed to resign rather than be fired.

"The fans in this city wouldn't know a ballplayer from a Japanese aviator," Smith grumbled on his way out the door, convinced he had been scapegoated for the failures of his players.

To some degree, Smith was right.

"Anybody who paid to see us play in that final month was robbed," Kaline admitted.

"We quit like dogs," Jim Northrup agreed.

It hardly came as a great surprise that the Tigers fell under .500 for the first time since 1963 and into fourth place, a remote 29 games behind the Baltimore Orioles.

As a result, the Tigers—who had for years made a habit of hiring conservative managers and promoting loyal company men who were not likely to rock the boat—departed from that tradition in 1971 when they turned over the team to fiery Billy Martin, who had a history of fighting with the front office and, in at least one instance, with one of his own players.

The laissez-faire approach of Mayo Smith had failed, and the Tigers desperately wanted to try to coax one more championship out of the aging nucleus of the 1968 team, including Al Kaline.

Kaline was the only player remaining on the Tigers roster who personally knew Martin from Billy's brief tour of duty with the Tigers as a player in 1958. And Al was determined to keep an open mind where his new 42-year-old manager, his senior by just six years, was concerned.

In baseball, whenever a team changes managers, it is fashionable to extol the merits of the incoming skipper and to thrash his predecessor. But Kaline was too forthright to fall into that trap.

"I know Billy Martin real well, and I want to learn as much as I can under him," Kaline said at the time. "I admit I was pretty low at the end of last season. But when they hired Billy, I felt I wanted to stay around. He puts everything into the game, and that's the way I like it.

"There's no question in my mind Mayo Smith wasn't to blame for what we did last year. He gets the blame for letting Denny get out of hand, but that's it. To blame Mayo for the way we played is ridiculous. It's easy to put the blame on a man who has been fired, but we didn't play good baseball. It's as a simple as that. We didn't have a good attitude—none of us. And this wasn't just in the final six weeks. It was all year.

"I thought Mayo Smith was a mighty big man to take all the things he had to take and not strike back at people," Kaline continued. "He was a good man to play for. But as it is in every sport, you always have some players who take advantage of a nice guy, and that is what happened on our club."

During spring training in 1971, when Martin asked Kaline to tutor some of the young Tigers players, Al was delighted.

"I never had that responsibility before," he said. "I don't know if I can help anybody or not. I don't know if I'll be able to communicate. But if Billy wants me to try, I will."

On Opening Day 1971, Billy Martin had a brainstorm. He batted Kaline second in the order.

"A bird flew in and gave me the idea," Martin quipped.

The Tigers won the opener 8–2 behind the six-hit pitching of rubber-armed Mickey Lolich as Kaline went 1-for-4.

By April 16, 36-year-old Al Kaline, in almost constant pain because of a pulled muscle in his leg, was nevertheless batting .471. "The guy is a professional pro," Martin raved.

But despite the hitting of Kaline and Norm Cash and Martin's constant prodding, the Tigers lacked the pitching to make a serious run at the title.

This time, however, the Tigers didn't quit. In fact, they were the winningest team in the league during the final five and a half weeks of the season. Even so, they had fallen so far behind that they could only climb as high as second place, 12 games behind Baltimore.

That clinched it in Kaline's mind, not that there was ever any real doubt. Al was coming back in '72.

"I enjoyed this year," Kaline said after hitting .294. "The way we finished leaves a good taste in your mouth. I'm definitely going to be there. I want to be a 20-year man in the league."

CHAPTER 17

The $100,000 Man

Longtime Detroit Tigers general manager Jim Campbell pushed the button on the cassette player, leaned back in his recliner, and folded his hands across his ample belly as he settled in to listen to the precious tape for the umpteenth time:

> *...And Jim Northrup comes to bat now against Gibson...Now the set by Gibson, we're ready...Here's a swing and a fly ball to center...Here comes Flood, digging hard... He almost fell down!...IT'S OVER HIS HEAD!...Cash is rounding third...He scores...Willie Horton rounding third... He scores...Northrup goes into third base...Detroit leads, two-to-nothing.*

Until the day Campbell died of a heart attack at age 71 in 1995, sadly exiled from the baseball team that had been his whole life, he kept that cassette of Hall of Fame announcer Ernie Harwell's call of the glorious Game 7 of the 1968 World Series close at hand.

Campbell played the tape often when he was alone and when friends stopped by his downtown Detroit high-rise apartment. And no matter how many times the Tigers GM played that tape, it never failed to put a smile on his face.

"How 'bout that, huh?" a grinning Campbell would exclaim, giving a little fist pump as if he was listening to the broadcast of the game live for the very first time.

"Another triple for Northrup. Way to go, Jim! I knew you could do it."

Then Campbell would quickly click off the cassette player, lest Ernie Harwell change his mind.

There was no bigger fan of the Detroit Tigers than Jim Campbell, the balding, overweight, pigeon-toed, pipe-smoking baseball lifer whom Willie Horton affectionately called "Buddha." There was no bigger fan of Al Kaline than Jim Campbell, either. And the feeling was mutual.

"Jim was one of those special people you meet in your life who is true baseball," Kaline remembered. "He loved the Tigers. His whole life was the Detroit Tigers and baseball.

"What I always respected about him was the fact that his word was his bond. You didn't have to sign a piece of paper, you didn't have to sign a contract. If he told you he was going to do something for you, he did it. He'd fight for you, if he had to, in order to keep his word.

"I had all the respect in the world for Jim. His only concern was for the team and for the organization."

Nevertheless, Campbell kept that 1968 audio tape tucked away, out of sight and out of mind, whenever any of his players, including Al Kaline, came knocking on the door to his wood-paneled third-floor office at Tiger Stadium to talk contract.

Yesteryear's base hits, even in the World Series, don't win today's ballgames. Or pay today's bills.

And that was Campbell's job: building a winner—and paying the bills.

The cold, calculating, conservative, colorless Campbell fought a never-ending battle to keep the baseball team that he guarded as carefully as if it were his own financially in the black.

Al Kaline was the bell cow of Jim Campbell's Tigers teams. Kaline was also the hammer Campbell used to keep the salaries of the other Tigers players in line.

Some of other players resented the fact that their earning power was limited by the salaries that Kaline accepted—salaries which, many believed, did not reflect Al's true value or the changing baseball market in the late 1960s and early 1970s.

Denny McLain, the Tigers' 31-game winner, made a mere $30,000 as the American League's Most Valuable Player and Cy Young Award winner in the world championship season of 1968. And when McLain marched into Campbell's office that winter and demanded $100,000 for 1969, the Tigers' general manager told him bluntly, "I can't give you Kaline money."

It was a familiar refrain, one that other Tigers stars—including Mickey Lolich, Norm Cash, Willie Horton, and Jim Northrup—all heard repeatedly over the years.

Invariably, the player would eventually hang his head, maybe mutter an epithet or two under his breath, and sheepishly withdraw his request for a significant pay increase.

No one dared argue with Campbell's logic. No one dared declare themselves worth more money than Al Kaline—not even when Al was accepting less than the market dictated; less than, many believed, he deserved.

"Unfortunately, I didn't realize that he would use me in negotiations with other players," Kaline said in retrospect, long after Al had retired and Campbell had passed away.

"I should have realized it, I suppose. Maybe I was naïve. But I just wanted to play baseball. I was doing exactly what I wanted to do, I was making a living, and I thought the Tigers were paying me reasonably well.

"I understood later that some players were very concerned that I signed too early and didn't try to get more money so they could get more.

"If I had it to do over again, I might have fought for a couple thousand more dollars just to make their salaries better," Al said. "But I'm not apologizing for it, because I thought I was paid well. If you're doing something you love, money shouldn't be the biggest thing you're concerned about. I can't take it back."

Al Kaline's position as the Tigers No. 1 star and the team's highest-paid player would remain secure until the day Al retired in 1974.

During the winter between the 1962 and 1963 seasons, Rocky Colavito, whose ego was without equal in the Tigers clubhouse, decided he deserved more money than Kaline, whom Colavito once referred to as "a little tin god." Suffice it to say, that was not meant as a compliment.

That was Jim Campbell's first season as the Tigers' general manager, and Colavito, who had come to the Tigers from Cleveland on the eve of the 1960 season opener in exchange for reigning American League batting champion Harvey Kuenn, was a matinee idol and a marquee figure, a big-league star who was accustomed to getting his way.

Colavito was the Tigers' biggest home-run threat since Hank Greenberg, who had himself become embroiled in a salary dispute with Tigers management in 1947, forcing a trade to the Pittsburgh Pirates where Greenberg became baseball's first $100,000-a-year ballplayer.

Now Colavito was determined to test the Tigers' new GM.

Colavito had batted .273 in 1962 with 37 home runs and 112 RBIs.

Kaline had hit .304 that year with 29 HRs and 94 RBIs.

In the months leading up to the 1963 season, a war of wills broke out, both behind closed doors and in the newspapers. The baseball world and the entire Tigers team, including Kaline, was watching.

It was Campbell, the rookie general manager, against the slugger the fans called "the Rock."

"I made up my mind it was him or me," Campbell admitted a decade later.

Although he watched the battle in silence from the sidelines, Kaline was very much on the minds of the men on both sides of the bargaining table.

"What I offered Colavito was fair," Campbell later insisted. "But he [Colavito] had a lot of ideas about contracts that were way out of line. At the time, I was just fed up with all the nonsense. I figured now was the time to get it all over with.

"A player is never going to get as much as he'd like when it comes time to sign. And I'm not going to sign him for as little as I'd like. There has to be a meeting of the minds. But when I reach a certain point, fuck it. I think most of my higher-priced players know when I've reached that point."

Colavito eventually capitulated, but not before a heated, five-day spring-training-camp holdout during which Colavito vowed never to speak to Campbell again.

Campbell made Colavito's promise an easy one to keep. At the end of season, he traded the prima-donna slugger along with relief pitcher Bob Anderson to Kansas City for defensively solid second baseman Jerry Lumpe, plus pitchers Dave Wickersham and Ed Rakow. The penny-pinching Campbell even threw in an extra $50,000 to sweeten the swap.

The message had been sent: don't mess with Jim.

Campbell was old-school, a throwback to the days when players played the games and ballclubs paid those players whatever they pleased. In the 1970s, when players began hiring agents to negotiate their contracts, Campbell refused to speak to those agents or even let them set foot in his office.

As a result, Kaline never had an agent. "We weren't allowed to," Al recalled with a small smile.

Pitcher Earl Wilson was the first Tigers player to seek negotiating help. He hired Boston-based agent Bob Woolf. But because Woolf was not welcome in Campbell's office or even in the ballpark, when Wilson went in to talk contract each winter, he would continually excuse himself, claiming he had to use the restroom, and scurry down the third-floor corridor to phone Woolf with Campbell's latest offer.

"Campbell must have thought my bladder had shrunk or something," Wilson chuckled.

Years later, when Wilson told Campbell the truth, the Tigers' general manager chortled, "I suspected something was up because you're not that goddamned smart."

Without free agency, without any real leverage, the players were totally overmatched at the bargaining table.

Mickey Lolich, like McLain, made $30,000 in 1968. After Lolich won three games in the '68 World Series, Campbell offered him a $10,000 raise to $40,000. "It was better than digging ditches," Mickey admitted after accepting the offer, albeit reluctantly.

In 1967 Tigers pitcher John Hiller made the major-league-minimum salary, which, at the time, was still $6,000. That winter, Campbell mailed him a contract for $12,000. "Of course, I signed it right away," Hiller recalled. "I couldn't believe they were doubling my pay."

Only later did Hiller learn the minimum salary had been raised to $10,000 that winter. "So I actually only got a $2,000 raise," he said.

When pitcher Hank Aguirre informed Campbell that he was not going to sign his contract unless he received a raise, no matter how small, the Tigers general manager obliged by adding a penny to his last offer. Aquirre laughed—and signed. That was the way baseball did business in those days, especially the Detroit Tigers.

"We knew the owners were making money—we just didn't know how much," Jim Northrup said. "And we had no way of finding out."

And Jim Campbell was not about to tell them.

"I guess, over the years, I have developed a reputation for being scotch," Campbell admitted one evening over dinner at the London Chop House, then one of downtown Detroit's ritziest restaurants—on the ballclub's expense account, of course.

"I'm not ashamed of it. I watch every penny around here, and I'm proud of it. If I spend any of Mr. Fetzer's money, I spend it as if it were my own."

As Northrup recalled, "Jim Campbell would always say, 'Do you want to play baseball or not? If you don't like what I'm paying you, go out and get a job.'"

When McLain threatened to sit out the 1969 season if he didn't get the $100,000 that he demanded, the Tigers' boss, who had offered Denny a salary of $50,000, laid it on the line.

As McLain recalled, "He said, 'Okay, Denny, do what you have to do. But before you walk out, I'll just tell you this: my final offer is $60,000. You've got five minutes to sign this contract. After five minutes, every minute that goes by that you don't sign, it goes down a thousand dollars.'"

McLain looked at Campbell. He knew he was beaten. "Give me that contract," McLain grumbled. "Where's the pen?"

As much as Jim Campbell liked and admired Al Kaline, as much as he appreciated what Al had done for the team and had meant to the franchise over the years, he could never bring himself to completely bridge that gap between boss and ballplayer. Not even for Al.

Unlike some general managers, you never saw Campbell on the field before the games. You never saw him in the clubhouse palling around with the players, patting them on their backs.

Campbell had his place, and the players had theirs.

"Look, I'm as big a fan as you'll find," Campbell once told me. "I can't wait until I come to work in the morning, and I hate to leave at night. I love to be around the ballpark. I don't ever want to lose my enthusiasm as a fan.

"But I can't afford the luxury of being close friends with the players. I don't draw a wall between us, but we each have our own place in the organization. My primary responsibility is to John Fetzer. The Tigers are a very valuable asset in his organization. My primary responsibility is to protect that asset."

Nevertheless, during the winter between the 1970 and '71 seasons, Campbell summoned Kaline to his office and offered Al a contract that called for a salary of $100,000—a first in the annals of the Detroit Tigers Baseball Club.

Even more incredible was the fact that Kaline—who had argued for more money in previous years when he felt he deserved it and had accepted cuts in his salary without complaint when he felt they were warranted— turned down the unprecedented six-digit deal. But there was more to that oft-repeated story than that.

"It wasn't like the Tigers had offered me $100,000 originally and I turned it down," Kaline recalled, debunking another Detroit urban legend.

"I had made $96,000 in 1970, and I didn't have a good year. After the season, they sent me a contract for 1971 at the same $96,000 salary, which I thought was fair. So I signed it and sent it right back.

"At the time, $100,000 was the magic number. That was it. Ted Williams and Mickey Mantle had made $100,000. Actually, they got a lot more than that. But that was the ultimate number back then. Anybody who made $100,000 was supposed to be a superstar, a Mantle or a guy of that stature. The Tigers had never had a $100,000 ballplayer, and the media was saying I should be the first.

"Jim Campbell called me in after I had signed that first contract for $96,000 and sent it back and said, 'We want to give you $100,000 next year.'

"I told Jim, 'No, we have a contract. I'll live up to that. I'll have a better year next year. If you want to give me $100,000 then, that'll be fine.'"

The truth is, the Tigers were merely trying to generate some favorable off-season publicity and get the team's name in the news in the middle of winter. The front office considered that additional $4,000 a small price to pay.

"I couldn't take it," Kaline explained. "I really hadn't had what I considered a good year in 1970. I felt they were just giving me the $100,000 because I had been around for so long. I wasn't going to try to gouge somebody just because I had been around for a while."

So, Kaline played for $96,000 in 1971, and, true to his word, he had a better year, batting .294, tops on the team and his best average since 1967, with 15 home runs and 54 RBIs.

And on December 20, 1971, when Kaline made his annual off-season visit to Tiger Stadium to wish members of the front-office staff a Merry Christmas, Al finally became the Tigers' first $100,000-a-year man—long after six-digit salaries had become commonplace throughout most of the rest of the game.

"I never would have asked for it," Kaline said. "But Jim Campbell said Mr. Fetzer wanted me to have it."

It marked the first time the Tigers had officially, publicly, revealed a player's salary.

"I don't know if I actually deserve $100,000 off what I did this year," Kaline admitted at the time, modest as always. "But at least I feel better about it."

"If he hasn't earned $100,000, then nobody has," Campbell declared, grinning from ear to ear.

At the press conference at Tiger Stadium to announce the historic signing, Kaline confided, "I hope this won't be my last year. I want to keep playing as long as I feel I can help the team."

Campbell also confirmed the fact that Kaline had turned down the Tigers' belated offer of $100,000 the winter before.

"It would have taken a lot of heat off of last year if we could have told the whole story of what happened with Al's contract—why we weren't paying him $100,000," the Tigers' general manager said. "But Al didn't want it that way. It's his contract, and it's his business."

Times have since changed—both for baseball and for the Detroit Tigers.

In 2000, the Tigers threw an unprecedented eight-year $148 million offer at outfielder Juan Gonzalez—only to have Gonzalez unceremoniously throw that record offer back in Tigers owner Mike Ilitch's face.

During the 2009 season, 433 out of 818 players on the major-league rosters—a whopping 53 percent—made $1 million or more. Eighty-six of those players made $10 million or more.

In 2009 the average big-league salary was $1.15 million—more than 10 times what Al Kaline, who certainly was never considered average, made in his most profitable year.

However, as salaries have soared, the chasm between the highest- and lowest-paid players has widened too, often separating teammate from teammate.

During Kaline's playing career, the gap between the paychecks of the Tigers' best-paid stars and the lowest-paid rookies was never more than about $90,000. In most cases, it was a lot less.

In 2009, while Tigers rookies such as Ryan Perry were making the major-league-minimum $400,000, Magglio Ordóñez was hauling in $18 million—45 times as much.

No matter how hard some players may try to downplay the money, that can make it difficult for teammates to relate.

Today's behemoth contracts and budget-busting salaries can't help but make Al Kaline occasionally muse about how much money he might be making if he was playing today. He certainly is not bitter. But, understandably, it gives him pause.

"I hope the players appreciate the fact that a lot of people struggled to make the game what it is for them right now," Al said. "I truly hope these players appreciate what has been given to them. I hope they realize that a lot of guys did a lot of suffering to get them where they are today.

"But I have no bad feelings whatsoever toward today's players and the money they're making, I really don't. I just hope the players think about the fans. I hope they think about the game.

"All that those salaries mean is that the owners made an awful lot of money when I was playing," continued Kaline, who in his most financially rewarding season only received $103,000—roughly one-fourth of the major-league minimum today.

"I worry about what's going to happen to baseball 10, 15, 20 years from now," Kaline said. "We can't let baseball become a corporate game.

"The way salaries are going, we're going to price baseball out of the reach of the working man. The way salaries are going, pretty soon it's all going to be luxury suites.

"The Players Association has got to step in. They've got to say, 'God, this is ridiculous.' The owners can't stop it. That would be collusion. But everybody can't make $6 million, $7 million, $8 million a year."

Kaline shook his head.

Then he added, "And to play a game that all of us said we'd play for free."

CHAPTER 18

One Last Chance

The 1972 season got off to an inauspicious start—both for big-league baseball and for Al Kaline and the Detroit Tigers.

Shortly before midnight on Friday, March 31, less than a week before the Tigers were scheduled to take the field in Boston for their regular-season opener against the Red Sox, players all across baseball walked out on strike for the first time in the history of the game.

The worm was turning. The pendulum of power was shifting. For more than 100 years, baseball's owners and general managers had ruled the sport, deciding how much, or how little, each player would be paid as well as where they would play and when their careers would end.

But now—tentatively, almost reluctantly in some cases—major-league players were finally flexing their muscles off the field, led by their combative mustachioed union boss, Marvin Miller.

Many players weren't even certain they needed a union—or wanted one. Nevertheless, although few in baseball saw it or wanted to see it coming, the players were taking control of the game, their game, bit by bit.

Following the Tigers' Friday-evening exhibition game against the Boston Red Sox in Lakeland, Florida, on the last day of March 1972, the players milled aimlessly around the uneasy Marchant Stadium clubhouse, anxiously waiting for word to arrive from the all-important union meeting that was taking place in Dallas, Texas. There, the players' representatives, including the Tigers' veteran backup catcher Tom Haller, had gathered with

Marvin Miller to take a strike vote—a vote that would change the face of Major League Baseball forever.

No one quite knew what to think. No one quite knew what to do. No one had ever been down this road before.

In his small clubhouse office, where a larger-than-life photo of a snarling Ty Cobb hung on the wall behind his desk, Tigers manager Billy Martin seethed as he chugged beer after beer. Clearly, the volatile Martin was taking this threat of a strike personally.

The Tigers had won 16 games and lost nine under his tutelage that spring. They were ready to play. They were ready to win. How dare the players, his players, whom he had painstakingly prepared all spring for a run at the American League pennant, think of betraying him now?

Then came a timid tap on Martin's open office door. It was veteran second baseman Dick McAuliffe, whose own fiery disposition had earned him the nickname "Mad Dog."

Several of the Tigers, bored with waiting, had decided to pass the time by playing cards in the clubhouse. But, ballplayers being ballplayers, they felt obligated to seek their manager's permission first—even as they stood on the brink of shutting down the national pastime. Old habits die hard.

"Skip," McAuliffe asked softly, "is it okay if some of us play cards?"

"Go ahead," Martin snapped.

Then, when McAuliffe was out of earshot, the Tigers manager quietly cursed again.

When word finally arrived from the union meeting in Dallas that baseball's players, including Al Kaline and the Tigers, were officially on strike by a unanimous vote of 47–0 by their representatives, the bewildered players quickly scattered.

Some went back to their hotels or rented houses, although with Opening Day just days away, most of their families had already packed up and gone home. Several players sought solace in nearby saloons.

Why not? There would be no early morning workout tomorrow. No need to get a good night's sleep.

"I guess I got you guys ready for a summer vacation," Martin snarled sarcastically as he headed out the clubhouse door to get drunk himself.

Tigers general manager Jim Campbell, so old-school that he refused to even speak to agents, much less negotiate his players' contracts with them, was equally livid.

Each spring, Tigers management rented a full-sized moving van to haul the team's equipment—and the players' personal belongings—to Florida in early February and then back to Detroit at the end of March when the team broke camp.

But early on the morning of April 1, with news of the strike against baseball still sinking in, Campbell marched from his modest Tigertown office across the abandoned airplane runway to the parking lot in front of the Marchant Stadium clubhouse. There the GM ordered workmen to immediately remove all of the players' personal belongings, including their luggage and their kids' bicycles, from the team's huge truck.

"Santy Claus is dead," the fuming general manager declared.

Effective immediately, Campbell decreed, the Tigers' spring-training locker room, which contained all of the players' bats, gloves, and uniforms, was officially off limits to the striking players. The Tigers players were barred from their own ballpark.

Uncertainty eerily filled the air in Lakeland, Florida, on that overcast Saturday morning. There were many, many questions but no answers.

How long would the strike last? How would the players, who after five weeks of spring training were primed for Opening Day, stay in shape on their own? Would they continue to receive expense money? The team's charter flight had been put on hold. How would the players get home? What about their salaries for the regular season?

The striking players soon found out they were on their own.

Only Al Kaline dared enter the darkened Marchant Stadium clubhouse that morning. Jim Campbell wouldn't throw out the team's superstar.

Kaline, who had enjoyed a tremendous spring, batting .358 with three home runs and nine RBIs, gathered some bats, balls, gloves, and spikes and personally hauled them to the diamond at Kathleen High School, on the far west side of Lakeland.

There, five days away from what was to have been their season-opener, on a Saturday when the Tigers had been scheduled to engage the Red

Sox before a sellout spring crowd in Winter Haven, Florida, a handful of confused, concerned players held an impromptu practice session on their own on an otherwise empty high school field.

The players changed from their street shoes into spikes in their automobiles. They wore T-shirts and shorts or blue jeans. Kaline played shortstop. Jim Northrup was on the mound. A sportswriter shagged fly balls in right field. The whole scene was surreal.

When the issues involving the funding of the players' pension fund and their right to salary arbitration were eventually resolved and the strike was settled on April 14, it was decided that the 86 games that had been postponed would be permanently canceled because the still-outraged owners were unwilling to pay the players for the days they had spent on strike.

As a result, the Tigers would play 156 games in 1972, instead of the standard 162. The Baltimore Orioles, most people's pick to win the title in the American League East, would play 154 games. The Boston Red Sox and New York Yankees would each play 155.

"I hope nobody wins or loses the pennant by a half a game," Jim Northrup noted—prophetically, as it turned out.

After a slow start, caused no doubt by the players' strike, Kaline became the driving force behind the Tigers' march to the American League East title as goading manager Billy Martin and the front office sought to coax one more title out of the aging remnants of their '68 championship team.

On August 13, with the Tigers in second place, one game off the pace and mired in a four-game losing streak, the unpredictable Martin approached Kaline in the locker room before the first game of a doubleheader against the Cleveland Indians. Martin held his baseball cap in his hand. In it, on tiny folded scraps of paper, the manager had penned the names of the eight players he planned to employ in his starting lineup in the opener.

"Okay, we're picking the batting order out of the hat today," Billy announced. "Pick a player, Al."

"Are you kidding?" asked Kaline, who was sidelined with an injury at the time.

"Nope. Pick one out," Martin ordered.

Kaline reached into the manager's cap and pulled out the first name. It was Norm Cash. Martin wrote the name down, then asked several other players to do the same.

Slugging Stormin' Norman batted leadoff that day, and faint-hitting shortstop Eddie Brinkman hit cleanup. The Tigers won 3–2, snapping their losing streak.

The Tigers lost the nightcap, and they lost the following day, too. But those facts were conveniently forgotten as Billy Martin took more bows for his managerial genius.

Down the stretch, when it mattered most, Kaline collected 22 hits in his final 44 at-bats.

In a book titled *Kaline*, author Hal Butler wrote, "Injured for much of the season and burdened by an unspectacular batting average, Kaline regained his top form that September. In the clutch, when there was no longer a margin for error, Kaline performed like a 20-year-old rather than a 20-year veteran. He lifted the Tigers into the playoffs against Oakland and acquitted himself brilliantly in the five-game showdown series."

On September 27, Kaline came through with two singles, a sacrifice fly, and two RBIs as the Tigers overcame a five-run deficit and topped the New York Yankees 6–5. The next day, Al made several spectacular catches in the outfield and went 2-for-4 in a 3–2, 12-inning loss. In the must-win three-game sweep of Milwaukee that followed, Al went 7-for-14 with three RBIs as the Tigers outscored the Brewers 30–10.

Then, in a three-game showdown against the Red Sox at Tiger Stadium, with a trip to the postseason on the line, Kaline went 3-for-4 in the series opener as the Tigers prevailed 4–1. In the clincher, Kaline came through with a seventh-inning game-winning RBI single off Boston's Luis Tiant and scored an insurance run before a crowd of 50,653 as the Tigers claimed the title in the American League East by half a game, thanks to the strike-made unequal schedule.

Afterward, the streets outside Tiger Stadium were gridlocked with cars and wide-eyed, screaming fans, some of whom, whether from joy or from juice, were barely able to stand.

Inside the champagne-drenched Tigers clubhouse, TV cameras carried the players' celebration live. There, mild-mannered shortstop Eddie Brinkman looked a camera in the eye and declared, to the delight of all of the Tigers fans watching the party vicariously at home, "We really beat those fuckers!"

In the playoffs, the Tigers encountered the Oakland A's, who had beaten them eight times in 12 games during the regular season.

In the first game of that best-of-five elimination, Kaline, batting second behind Dick McAuliffe, belted an eleventh-inning home run off future Hall of Famer Rollie Fingers to briefly give the Tigers the lead, only to be charged with an error when his throw from right field in the bottom half of the inning struck Gene Tenace of the A's, allowing the winning run to score.

"I went from hero to goat quicker than ever before," Al admitted after the game.

The A's won the second game 5–0 behind the three-hit pitching of Blue Moon Odom to grab a two-games-to-none lead in the series. When Tigers relief pitcher Lerrin LaGrow, acting on orders from manager Billy Martin, threw at Oakland's speedy Campy Campaneris to start the seventh inning, hitting him on the foot, the A's shortstop hurled his bat at LaGrow, igniting a full-scale brawl.

The Tigers kept their flickering hopes alive with a 3–0 win at home in Game 3, thanks to the 14-strikeout pitching of Joe Coleman. Kaline did his part, going 2-for-3. And Al singled and scored the tying run as the Tigers rallied for three runs in the tenth inning of the fourth game to even the series at two wins apiece, 4–3.

Suddenly, the Tigers and their fans, recalling their 1968 Series comeback, began making plans and buying tickets for the World Series and what would be Kaline's second trip to the Fall Classic in five years.

However, it was not to be as the A's won Game 5 2–1 in a pitcher's duel between the Tigers' Woodie Fryman and Blue Moon Odom at Tiger Stadium.

Kaline, two months shy of his 38th birthday, finished the season with a .313 average, his best since 1961. It marked the 19th year in a row that he appeared in at least 100 games.

"I have always referred to Al Kaline as 'Mister Perfection,'" said his appreciative manager, Billy Martin, who had prodded the pieced-together Tigers to half a pennant.

"He does it all—hitting, fielding, running, throwing—and he does it with that extra touch of brilliancy that marks him as a super ballplayer.

"Although he is a regular outfielder, Al fits in anywhere, at any position in the lineup and any spot in the batting order," Martin continued. "I like to send him to the plate in the No. 2 slot because he is the best there is at moving up the runner. He can bunt, hit behind the runner to right, or belt it out of the ballpark."

Unfortunately, that would be Kaline's last season above .300. He batted .255 in 1973 and finished with a .262 mark in 1974 to see his career average dip below .300 to .297.

The 1972 season would also mark the Tigers' last appearance in the postseason until they won the world championship in 1984. The team finished a disappointing third in 1973, and the front office finally got fed up with Martin's antics and fired him. In 1974, Kaline's final season, the Tigers limped home in last place in the American League East.

CHAPTER 19

3,000 Hits

There are certain magic numbers in baseball—500 home runs for a slugger, 300 wins for a pitcher, and 3,000 base hits.

Babe Ruth, the legendary Sultan of Swat, never reached the latter milestone. The Bambino collected just 2,873 hits in his still-storied career. Ted Williams, Al Kaline's boyhood idol who considered himself "the greatest hitter who ever lived," finished his war-interrupted career with 2,654 hits. Joe DiMaggio, the epitome of baseball elegance to whom the young Kaline was often and unfairly compared in Al's early years, owned only 2,214 hits when he hung up his spikes. Barry Bonds, Lou Gehrig, Frank Robinson, and Rogers Hornsby, to name just four of baseball's finest batsmen, are not members of baseball's exclusive 3,000-Hit Club.

But Al Kaline is.

At the conclusion of the 1973 season, Kaline was briefly tempted to retire. In his heart, he knew the end was near. But, more than anything, Al now wanted to reach 3,000 hits.

He had played in the World Series. He had played in the big leagues for more than 20 years. He had achieved his two earlier goals. And now, going into 1974, he was only 139 hits away from 3,000. Suddenly Al wanted that more than he had realized—more than he had previously been willing to admit.

"People ask me, was it my goal to play in the majors for 20 years? Was it my goal to get 3,000 hits someday? Lord knows, I didn't have any goals," Kaline told *Sports Illustrated* at the time.

"I tell them, 'My only desire was to be a baseball player.'

"I never wanted to be a flashy personality or anything like that," Kaline continued. "I'm a straight actor. That's the way I am, and that's the way I played the game. I was blessed with a good body that didn't put on weight, and that helped, too.

"But most of all, I never looked ahead at anything else. I had no desire to have a big job during the off-season. My only concern was to keep myself in shape for the spring. You can't blame guys today for always looking ahead to what they'll do out of baseball. But you can look ahead too often and forget what you should be doing now. You forget what got you here.

"I could hang on for a few more years, but I won't," he said. "This is a young man's game and, like everything, it comes to an end."

But first Al had one last bit of unfinished business to wrap up.

Before Kaline departed for spring training in 1974, *Detroit Free Press* columnist Joe Falls, a longtime Kaline chronicler and admirer, and I met Al for breakfast one morning. Falls and I wanted to write a book, a diary, detailing Kaline's quest for 3,000 hits.

Al agreed, on one condition: if, for any reason, he didn't reach 3,000 hits in 1974, if he became injured or mired in a lengthy slump and fell short of his goal, the book would go straight into the nearest trash can. It would never see the light of day.

As always, Kaline's pride was showing. He didn't want the whole world sharing his misery, his anguish, if for any reason he didn't make it. He didn't want to be embarrassed.

Under those conditions, Falls and I regretfully declined to proceed. Like Kaline, we felt confident he would reach 3,000 hits that season. But we didn't want to waste a summer's worth of work if he failed to get there.

By 1974, much of the joy had gone out of the game for Kaline, who realized the inevitable end to his days as a player was approaching.

"It was kind of tough to play on a team where a lot of your friends were gone," Al recalled. "We won in '68, but now they were bringing a lot of young guys in, which I knew they had to do. But for a veteran, senior guy on the ballclub to go through that was kind of hard.

"You want to be able to play for something in September. And, of course, we weren't able to do that."

The game Kaline had so eagerly and easily embraced since he was a young boy had become a chore.

"I knew I had certain skills then, and that made me unbelievably relaxed and confident," he said, recalling his younger years.

But, as happens with every athlete, those skills had been eroded by age.

"There was one time when I struck out four times in a game against Steve Busby in Kansas City, that I thought about quitting," Kaline admitted.

"I called my wife that night, and I said, 'Man, I've never struck out that many times.' But she convinced me it was just one game."

In 1974 Kaline was relegated to the role of designated hitter in his quest for 3,000 hits. That took him out of right field, where he once felt so much at home, and forced him to sit idle on the bench between at-bats, often with nothing to do but think.

As so many big-league players before Kaline and since have discovered, the DH is not an easy role to play.

On August 20, aware that the overpowering Nolan Ryan would be on the mound for the California Angels in Anaheim that evening, Kaline confronted the fact that his slowing reflexes made it unlikely he would be able to catch up with Ryan's famed fastball.

When Al arrived at the ballpark late that afternoon, he walked into Tigers manager Ralph Houk's office and asked to be taken out of the lineup.

It was hardly his proudest hour.

"I've got one regret, and it still haunts me to this day," Kaline admitted. "I'm ashamed of myself to say it, but I asked out of a game when I was 39 years old. I went to Ralph Houk, our manager, and I said, 'I can't play today. I can't hit this guy.'

"I could have played. I could have taken an 0-for-4, and it wouldn't have bothered me one bit. Instead, somebody else had to take that 0-for-4 for me. That still bothers me."

In fact, Bill Freehan replaced Kaline as the Tigers' designated hitter that night. He went 1-for-3. Gene Lamont, in turn, replaced Freehan behind the plate. He went 0-for-4.

"I still have bad dreams about that," Kaline confessed. "That was embarrassing."

Late in the 1974 campaign, I asked Kaline if he would like to play right field one last time, possibly in the final game of the season. I thought it would serve as a fitting farewell.

"No way," Al replied tersely. "I have no desire to ever play the outfield again.

"I can't reach balls I used to catch," he admitted, "and I don't want to embarrass myself."

There was that pride again.

Kaline knew he was no longer the superstar he had once been. And he wasn't satisfied with being anything less.

As the hits piled up and Al inched ever closer to the magic number of 3,000, he grew edgy and more moody. He wanted the chase to be over. He was looking forward to retirement.

But baseball had been his whole life. What would he do next?

"Baseball is the only job I've ever had," he admitted in an interview with *Sports Illustrated*.

"It got me out of the slums of Baltimore. It gave me everything I have in life. It gave me a challenge every day of my life. What do I do without that challenge?

"I've always been realistic about the outside world. It's a real jungle. Here I am in this little padded room where everything is great. Out there, it's different. Oh, I could take a job with the Tigers, or in business, but I don't know if I want that. I only know that I'm not worrying so much about getting my 3,000th hit as I am about what I'm going to do after it."

Appropriately, on September 24, 1974, with his proud parents, Nicholas and Naomi, in the stands at Baltimore's Municipal Stadium, Kaline collected his milestone 3,000th hit in his hometown, not far from the sandlots where he had first learned to play the game.

The Tigers' schedule called for them to finish the season with seven games at home against the Red Sox and Orioles. There was speculation Kaline might sit out the remaining road games so that he could collect his 3,000th hit at home, in front of the Detroit fans at Tiger Stadium.

But the furor that had erupted earlier that year over Hank Aaron's bid to break Babe Ruth's record at home in Atlanta instead of on the road was still fresh in the minds of the Tigers' front office.

"I had mixed emotions because I wanted to get it in Detroit really bad," Kaline admitted. "But Jim Campbell called me on the phone and said, 'You know what? Get it as soon as you can. You never know what kind of crazy things can happen.'

"Fortunately, we were playing in Baltimore at the time, which was the second-best place for it to happen. I had my family there, my parents. And a lot of my old school friends, guys I had played ball with, were there, too. I would have hated to disappoint them."

At 8:20 PM on September 24, in the 2,827th game of his career, leading off the fourth inning against the Orioles' Dave McNally, Kaline sliced a double to right field that was fair by at least two feet—a clean hit all the way—to become just the 12th man in baseball history, the first American Leaguer since Hall of Fame second baseman Eddie Collins nearly a half-century earlier, and the first Tiger since Ty Cobb, to collect 3,000 hits.

"I almost forgot to run when I hit the ball," Kaline admitted with a sheepish grin in a hastily arranged press conference after the game. "The ball was really curving foul. It was plenty fair when I first hit it, but I didn't think it was going to make it.

"When I got to second base, I said a little prayer of thanks for letting me play all these years and get all those hits."

The game was immediately halted amidst a standing ovation, and Kaline walked over to the box seats alongside the Tigers dugout, where members of Al's family and some baseball dignitaries were seated.

Kaline handed his bat and the ball to American League president Lee MacPhail, who promised to deliver those items to the Hall of Fame in Cooperstown.

However, at Kaline's request, the celebration was brief. Three minutes after Kaline made contact with that Dave McNally fastball, Al was back standing on second base.

Once there, though, Kaline remembered the strange phone conversation he had had with McNally months earlier, while the Tigers were still in spring training.

"Dave and his brother were interested in buying a Ford dealership that had become available in Montana," Kaline recalled. "Dave called me during the winter and asked, 'Do you know anyone at Ford Motor Company?' Of course, at the time, I was very close to Lee Iacocca, who was the president of Ford. So I told Dave I'd call Iacocca on his behalf.

"To make a long story short, Dave got the dealership, and when he called me back to thank me, he said, 'By the way, I had a dream that you got your 3,000[th] hit off me.'

"And that's exactly what happened, six months later," Al said.

"It was eerie."

As Kaline sat in the visitors' clubhouse at Baltimore's Memorial Stadium, sipping half a glass of champagne after the game, he tried to put his latest accomplishment into perspective.

"This definitely ranks above the batting championship," he said. "Any time you win a batting championship, there's a lot of luck that goes with it. But when you get 3,000 hits, I don't think anybody can say you were just lucky. You've had to withstand the pressure of all those seasons and injuries and everything. To me, that really means something.

"But," he quickly added, smiling, "nothing will surpass winning the World Series."

Now Al Kaline could retire in peace.

He was tired of the travel and the grind. After 22 seasons, he'd had enough. Once he reached 3,000 hits, there was no point in punishing his body any further by continuing to play. He had nothing left to prove.

"I'm just happy it's finally over," he said. "It seemed like a big black cloud had been lifted from me as soon as I got it."

Now Al didn't have to worry anymore about whether or not to play again in 1975 just to reach the 3,000-hit plateau.

"Once I got close, I was sure I was going to get there that season, sooner or later," Al recalled years later. But in baseball, you never know.

In fact, Kaline collected two hits that night to climb past the late Roberto Clemente and into eleventh place on baseball's all-time hit parade at 3,001, as the Tigers lost 5–4 to the Orioles.

When the team returned home, the Tigers honored Kaline in ceremonies at the ballpark. Tigers owner John Fetzer presented him with a wheelbarrow filled with 3,000 silver dollars. And for the first time in their long history, the Tigers announced plans to retire a uniform number. Appropriately, it would be Kaline's No. 6.

On October 2, 1974, at Tiger Stadium, Al Kaline played his final game. Unfortunately, the handful of die-hard fans—well below the announced attendance of 4,671—who showed up at the ballpark on that cold, blustery afternoon for an otherwise meaningless game against the Baltimore Orioles, never got a chance to actually say good-bye.

Hoping to conclude his career with home run No. 400 or at least with a base hit, Kaline struck out looking against the Orioles' Mike Cuellar in the first inning and flied to left in the third.

As he trotted back to the bench, eyes down, Al decided that was it.

"It was one of those horrible days. I had already told myself if I had gotten a base hit I was going to ask to be taken out because I wanted to leave on a high note," he recalled.

"But I hit a line drive to left field for an out, and when I walked past Ralph Houk in the dugout I said, 'Ralph, that's it. Take me out.'" That was it. That was all. After 22 years and 3,007 base hits, it was over.

"I took myself out of the game," admitted Kaline, whose sore shoulder was hampering his swing at the time. "And that was one of the most disappointing days of my life.

"I took myself out of the game, not realizing that a lot of people were there to see my last game. Maybe I'm too naïve, but I already knew I was going to retire, and I just thought, *That's it. It's over.* I didn't even think about the fans. When Ben Oglivie had to pinch-hit for me in the fifth inning, he got booed. I was sitting there in the clubhouse, and I could hear them booing. That has ranked up there with my biggest regrets. It wasn't his fault."

"I have enough respect for Al to do what he wanted to do in a game like this," explained Houk, who initially caught some heat from the press for so unceremoniously removing Kaline from his final game. "With a hitter as great as he is, you don't send him back out there when he says he's had enough. I think I owed Al that much."

Nevertheless, what should have been a memorable moment instead became a sad occasion.

"I remember my wife waiting for me at our car out in the players' parking lot after the game—and she was crying," Al said.

Kaline concluded his career with 3,007 hits, 399 home runs, 1,583 RBIs, 10 Gold Gloves, and 18 invitations to the All-Star Game, where he batted .324 and was a flawless 1.000 in the field. Al would have liked to have walked away from the game with a .300 career average, but his average slipped in his final two years and he finished at .297.

He was the model of consistency. Over the course of his 22-year career, he batted .292 during the month of April, .295 in May, .295 in June, .296 in July, .298 in August, .307 in September, and .333 in his two trips to the postseason, where it mattered most.

Asked once how he would assess his big-league career, Kaline said simply, "I showed up, I played, and I loved it."

Were it not for all of those injuries, Kaline would surely have been the first American League player ever to collect 3,000 hits and 400 home runs. Instead that honor went to Boston's Carl Yastrzemski.

"If I had known I was going to get that close, I would have tried to hit more homers instead of moving guys over," Kaline later quipped when his near-miss became a big deal. Of course, he was only kidding. That wasn't the way he played the game.

"You know, baseball is a game that you measure in failure," Kaline once mused. "You fail seven times in 10 at-bats and you're a great player. Where else in life can you fail that often and be a success?

"I played 22 years in Detroit and won only once. That means there were a lot of seasons we came up empty."

When Al quietly walked away at the end of the 1974 season, sports-writer Joe Falls, who would himself later be inducted into the writers' wing of the Baseball Hall of Fame, summed up Kaline's career in one telling paragraph:

"Al Kaline, magnificent ball player, decent person, family man, who for 22 years conducted himself with great presence as a Tiger player. Not an Aaron. Not a Mays. Not a Mantle. He never pretended that he was. He was a man who simply went into the right field corner, played that double-carom shot and fired the ball into second, holding the runner at first. He didn't hit them upstairs because he couldn't. He wasn't strong enough. But he could line it into left, or maybe up the alley, and two runs would score. And he would do it day after day."

No doubt Kaline could have continued to serve as the Tigers' designated hitter for a couple more seasons, piling up hits and home runs, further enhancing his place in baseball's record book. But Al wanted none of that. He was through.

In 1978 he was invited to play in an Old-Timers Game in Cleveland. Quickly and quietly, he declined. He told the Indians he would appear on the field if they wished. He would smile and wave to the crowd when he was introduced. But he would not swing a bat or chase after a fly ball.

"I have too much respect for that uniform ever to do anything to embarrass it," Al later explained.

In 1975, the season after Kaline took off his spikes and put away his trusty glove, the Tigers lost 102 games, 19 of them in a row. I bumped into Al at the ballpark one evening that summer and remarked, "You should never have retired. You can still play better than two-thirds of these guys who are out there today."

Kaline smiled. "Maybe you're right," he said softly. "But I couldn't still play the way I wanted to play."

To Al Kaline, that was what mattered. Anything less just wouldn't have been him.

CHAPTER 20

"The Proudest Moment of My Life"

Only the greatest of the greats are ushered into baseball's Hall of Fame the first year that the hallowed gates of Cooperstown are opened to them. Even the legends aren't always admitted immediately. For reasons that often defy logic, many superstars, some with impeccable credentials, aren't deemed to be deserving the first time that their names appear on the ballot.

Joe DiMaggio, against whom Al Kaline was sometimes measured early in his career, was not officially anointed a Hall of Famer by members of the Baseball Writers Association of America the first time that his name came up for Cooperstown consideration. As special as Joltin' Joe was, it took the Yankee Clipper three tries before it got into the Hall.

The great Lou Gehrig wasn't elected the first time he was eligible, either. Neither were Tris Speaker, Tigers slugger Hank Greenberg, Charlie Gehringer, or Jimmie Foxx.

For Al Kaline, his selection in 1980, the first time that his name appeared on the annual Hall of Fame ballot, was a tribute to Al's abilities, his achievements, and, maybe most of all, to his unwavering excellence, game after game, year after year.

Although I had covered Kaline for the final five years of his career and certainly considered him a legitimate Hall of Famer, I wasn't at all certain he would be elected the first year that he was on the ballot.

Nineteen-eighty was also the first year that I was eligible to vote in the annual election, which is limited to those who have been active members of the BBWAA for at least 10 seasons. Needless to say, I welcomed the opportunity.

I voted for Kaline, of course. In my mind it was a no-brainer. But I wasn't sure that enough of my often cynical colleagues around the country, many of whom, especially on the East Coast, often looked down patronizingly upon middle-America Detroit, harbored a similar appreciation for what Kaline had accomplished in his career or for what he had meant to his team and his town for 22 years.

Given that bias, plus the fact that, since the inaugural group of undisputed Hall of Famers—Babe Ruth, Ty Cobb, Walter Johnson, Christy Mathewson, and Honus Wagner—were inducted in 1936, only nine players—Stan Musial, Bob Feller, Ted Williams, Mickey Mantle, Jackie Robinson, Sandy Koufax, Warren Spahn, Ernie Banks, and Willie Mays—had been pronounced Cooperstown worthy on their first try, I thought Al's chances of election in 1980 were 50–50, at best. After all, as Kaline himself had often admitted, he was no Musial, no Williams, no Mantle, no Mays.

As I sat at my desk in the sports department of the *Detroit Free Press* on January 9, 1980, I remembered how, just one year earlier, 23 allegedly intelligent veteran baseball writers among the 432-man electorate had left Willie Mays, a bona-fide Hall of Famer if there ever was one, completely off of their ballots—even though, under the rules, they were allowed to vote for as many as 10 players.

As outstanding as Kaline had been during his career, he couldn't match Mays' speed or power or charisma. And Al never had the influential, often shamelessly partisan New York media to trumpet his feats.

If 23 voters could, supposedly in good conscience, completely ignore the great Willie Mays, how many of them might snub Al Kaline, at least his first time around?

I went into the office early on the day that the election results would be revealed. Because of my newspaper's deadlines, I knew that, once the official announcement was made in New York, I would only have a few hours to write both my column and the lead story on Kaline's election—

or rejection. I wanted to be prepared either way. I wanted to make my stories as good as possible. After all, I would be writing about Al Kaline. He deserved nothing less.

So I gathered enough information for two stories—one hailing Kaline's deserved election to baseball's Hall of Fame and the other lamenting the fact that he didn't make it.

Kaline's credentials for Cooperstown were certainly considerable.

At the time, only three members of the Hall of Fame—Tigers icon Ty Cobb, Al's childhood hero Stan Musial, and the incomparable Willie Mays—had played in more games than Kaline's 2,834.

Only Ty Cobb, Hank Aaron, Stan Musial, Tris Speaker, Cap Anson, Honus Wagner, Eddie Collins, Willie Mays, Nap Lajoie, and Paul Waner had collected more hits than Al's 3,007. And of those, all except Aaron, Musial, Mays, and Kaline had played in baseball's Dark Ages when the game was decidedly different.

Nevertheless, I was more than a little surprised—as was Kaline—when he was named on 340 of 385 ballots cast, receiving 88.3 percent of the vote.

Al had needed just 289 votes to be elected. It was a landslide. When Mickey Mantle was elected in 1974, he had received 88.2 percent of the vote.

After finding out the night before the results were officially announced that he had made it, Kaline, who had been sworn to secrecy, flew incognito to New York with his wife Louise. Kaline made his airline reservation using the pseudonymous name Al Hamilton, Louise's maiden name.

To keep the media in the dark, Jack Lang of the Baseball Writers Association of America reserved a three-bedroom suite in a New York hotel under his own name for the Kalines and the other electee, Dodgers great Duke Snider.

Underappreciated Chuck Klein, a slugger from the 1920s and '30s, and longtime Boston Red Sox owner Tom Yawkey, the nephew and adopted son of lumberman Bill Yawkey (who owned the Tigers shortly after the turn of the 20th century) were also to be inducted in 1980, courtesy of the Veterans Committee.

Mindful of the big day that lay ahead, Kaline went to bed that night at 11:00 PM. However, he couldn't fall asleep. Al thought about his early days as a skinny high school freshman. Now he was in the Hall of Fame.

"I don't think my vocabulary can express what I felt," Kaline later admitted. "I was very, very shocked. To go in on the first ballot was a huge, huge honor.

"For whatever reason, some great players don't get enough votes on the first ballot. I can't believe some writers didn't vote for Ted Williams or for Willie Mays. Knowing all the great players who didn't make it on the first ballot, I thought my chances of making it were nip and tuck. You hope so, but I told myself I wasn't going to get my hopes up too much because I didn't want to be disappointed. I had confidence I would eventually make it. But I thought it might take awhile.

"I wasn't as good a player as I wish I could have been," Kaline confessed when the results were announced. "I strived to be the best, but I fell short. But it wasn't because I didn't try.

"I really never thought I would choose an individual thing that happened just to me over a team thing like the World Series. But I would have to say this is the biggest thing that has ever happened to me.

"All my life, as long as I live, as long as my kids live, my name will always be there," he said. "Every time there is an election, my name will be mentioned."

Sunday, August 3, 1980, Induction Day at Cooperstown, was a day Al Kaline will always remember.

"I'll never forget when I walked in the back room before we went on stage, with all those Hall of Famers, with Ted Williams and Mickey Mantle and all those great players who I idolized growing up," Kaline said. "Here I am, in the same room with them—not in their same class, but a Hall of Famer with them."

Al's aging mom and dad were seated in the audience for the ceremonies at quaint Cooperstown in upstate New York. Kaline was thankful for that. His wife, Louise, and their two sons, Mark and Mike, were also there, of course, as were Al's two older sisters.

"It was one of those hot days at Cooperstown, and you're out there sitting in the sun all the time," Kaline recalled. "My dad had his coat on, and I knew he had to be hot. I was afraid he was going to pass out. I was up there on the stage, and I kept looking down at my dad from the stage, and I was mouthing the words, 'Take your coat off.'

"But he was so proud. He always wore suspenders, and he was too embarrassed to take his coat off and have everybody see his suspenders."

"We at least wanted to live 'til Al got in the Hall of Fame," Al's mother, Naomi, said. "We started saving money a year ago to go to Cooperstown."

After all of the preliminaries, Kaline, a man of so few words early in his playing days, stood up on the stage along with most of baseball's greatest living luminaries and delivered his acceptance speech:

> It is a great honor for me to be up here today with all these great people in baseball. But two in particular— growing up as a youngster in Baltimore and wanting to be a lot like them, or as close as I possibly could—were more or less my inspiration in going on in baseball. Of course, the great No. 9, Ted Williams, and Stan Musial, No. 6, my heroes.
>
> You know, ever since my induction last January, I've been tossing around in my mind exactly what it means to be elected to the Baseball Hall of Fame. Of course, there are the obvious answers. Whether or not I truly deserve the honor, my name always will be linked with those of the greatest hitters, pitchers, fielders, managers, and coaches baseball has ever enjoyed. That's an almost indescribable thrill and honor.
>
> But there is more to it than that. What it boils down to is the interest, confidence, patience, care, loyalty, and love of many persons—people who took time to share their qualities with me, to help me reach this greatest of honors, which all players dream of.

I don't want to bore you with a lot of long lists of acknowledgments of many persons you might not even know. But if you bear with me for a few moments, you'll see that without these people there would be no way I'd be standing here today.

First, my lovely wife, Louise. Unless you're in baseball, it's very difficult to understand and appreciate the role a wife plays for a player. For all of the time I was on the road and all of the evenings in Detroit when I was playing a game, she was at home playing mom—and mom and dad— to our two sons. For all of the support when I was fighting a slump and the encouragement when I was fortunate enough to be in a streak, thanks Louise. For all of the fame and glory one derives from playing baseball, it isn't worth a thing without someone to share it with.

It must not be easy, growing up and going to school while the old man is fighting a batting slump, which might hurt the pennant of the home team. But they were always there with words of encouragement, the prizes of my life, my sons, Mark and Mike.

When I was a youngster, life was a baseball game. There was nothing more exciting than a good old game of ball. I played a lot of ballgames growing up in Baltimore, every day from spring to fall. I never would've had that chance to prepare for a career every boy dreams of without the love and hard work of two people, my mom and my dad.

The business side of baseball has changed over the years, but I was so fortunate to play my entire career for a man—almost play my entire career for a man—whose high moral convictions never have changed. They reflected what baseball truly is all about. As owner of the Detroit Tigers, baseball and I owe you an awful lot. Thank you, Mr. Fetzer.

There's another man with the Tigers who too often receives more criticism than the praise he really deserves for the difficult decisions he's made over the years...the president and general manager of the Tigers. Thanks, Jim Campbell.

My first manager in the big leagues was Freddie Hutchinson in 1953. Ralph Houk was my last in 1974. There were 12 others in between. I learned something from all of them, and I respected all for the patience they showed with me. Managing is not the easiest job in baseball. Managing is the easiest job in baseball to second-guess and the hardest for which to gain respect. Thank you, many.

Regardless of what anyone tells you, a player is only as good as those other players around him. I can't tell you how lucky I've been to have played with some of the fellows I did. Maybe we didn't win a lot of pennants, but the Tigers were always there. Without naming all of those who helped shape my career, please accept the hearty thanks, guys.

A young man gets an opportunity to play professional baseball only if a scout sees something in him that most others ignore. I was very lucky that the scout who showed the most interest in me happened to work for the Tigers... for signing me and pulling for me all the way, thanks, Mr. Katalinas.

For Mr. Katalinas to see me, I needed a chance to play, and sandlot teams are only as good as their coaches. Coaching in the sandlots is a labor of love. The only reward is the appreciation one gets for seeing a few kids have a good time. So thanks to those fellows who gave me that opportunity and taught me how to make baseball a rewarding career.

Often a player is too eager to accept praise and too reluctant to accept criticism voiced daily in newspapers, radio and TV. But without such public exposure, baseball wouldn't be the game that it is today. To the writers who voted me into the Hall of Fame and all the members of the media who displayed a special feeling toward baseball, thank you very much.

Next to my family, the friends I have been fortunate to make in Detroit and around the country are my most valuable possessions. They are too numerous to mention all, but you all know who I mean. For all your kindness, thank you very much.

Most of all, I would like to particularly thank Tiger fans everywhere, but especially those who supported me my entire career in Detroit. We've had our highs and some lows, but through it all Detroit fans have stuck with the Tigers to prove they are the best in baseball.

I was fortunate enough to spend my entire 22 years in the Tigers uniform. I wouldn't have wanted it any other way. Your support helped me to reach whichever accomplishment I was able to achieve. You know, I've been very lucky. In fact, sometimes I feel I've been one of the luckiest people in the world.

I've played on All-Star teams with the greatest players in the game. I was able to finish with over 3,000 hits. I played on a world championship team. But most of all, for 22 years, I was able to make my living playing the game that has been my whole life.

Being inducted into the Baseball Hall of Fame is an accumulation of numerous successes and thrills for which I'm indebted to a countless number of people. If there is one accomplishment for which I am particularly proud, it is that I've always served baseball to the best of my ability. Never have I deliberately done anything to discredit the game, the Tigers, or my family. By far, being inducted into the Hall of Fame is the proudest moment of my life. You can

be sure I will make every effort to live up to the obligation
associated with this honor.
Thank you.

Although Kaline had traveled to Cooperstown with the Tigers when they played in the Induction Weekend exhibition game at Doubleday Field, he had never toured the museum that is the centerpiece of baseball's Hall of Fame.

When he finally took the time, Al was amazed at all of the artifacts that were on display, helping to chronicle the history of the game. His plaque would hang on the hallowed wall there, too.

Now, each summer, Kaline returns to Cooperstown, New York, on Induction Weekend to rub shoulders with the best of baseball's best and to welcome the new members into the club. He wouldn't think of missing it. There is nowhere else he would rather be.

"I'm still in awe when I go back there and see some of the great players," Kaline admitted after he returned from the 2009 induction ceremonies that honored Rickey Henderson, Jim Rice, and former Tigers coach and manager Joe Gordon.

"Willie Mays, Hank Aaron, Bob Feller, just seeing all those guys—guys who, when I was growing up, I thought, *Those guys are the greatest.* Just to be in the same room with them, to be considered one of them—even though I know I'm not. I mean, I'm in the Hall of Fame, but I'm not like a Willie Mays or a Hank Aaron.

"I'm in that exclusive club that is so, so difficult to get into. That means so much, not only to me, but to my family, my kids and my grandkids, and to all those friends who helped me along the way."

CHAPTER 21

58 Years...
and Counting

Al Kaline, a towel modestly wrapped around his waist following his postpractice shower, is sitting in front of his locker in the Detroit Tigers' spring-training clubhouse at Marchant Stadium, momentarily lost in his thoughts. The crowded, noisy locker room is filled with young ballplayers, many of them barely one-third Al's age, guys who, in some cases, are young enough to be his grandkids.

None had even been born when Kaline began his big-league career, when he began living his dream, in the summer of 1953. Yet many of them are already multimillionaires, far richer than he, thanks to the changing nature of the game.

Nevertheless, it is here that Kaline, the septuagenarian, the Hall of Famer, still feels most at home—in the locker room, in the dugout, and out on the field. In baseball.

Not all former stars are so fortunate.

The tragedy of Mickey Mantle was that he never was able to truly enjoy being Mickey Mantle, and all that that entailed, until the very end, when it was almost too late. Joe DiMaggio never stopped suspecting that people, even close friends, were trying to take advantage of him. And that jaded him. Until the day he died, Ted Williams privately felt guilty about his shortcomings—not as a ballplayer, but as a father.

Al Kaline, on the other hand, is completely at peace—with himself, with his life, and with his legacy.

"He's very, very comfortable with himself," said Kaline's close friend Joe Colucci. "He and his wife, Louise, have a great life. He's very happy with everything that's going on in his life.

"And he loves the Tigers," Colucci added.

And it shows.

Henley Field in Lakeland, Florida, the ballpark where Kaline reported to his first spring training in 1954 along with Harvey Kuenn, Walt Dropo, Frank Bolling, Ned Garver, Billy Hoeft, and Steve Gromek, still stands, just a mile south of the Tigers' current spring home.

Except for three years during World War II when travel was restricted, the Tigers have gathered in Lakeland to get in shape each spring since 1934, the year Kaline was born. Today, Al still makes his winter home in Lakeland.

Palm trees line the aptly named Al Kaline Drive, the road leading from busy Lakeland Hills Blvd. to Marchant Stadium, where the Tigers have conducted their spring training since 1966. Out back, beyond Marchant Stadium's center-field wall, players take extra batting practice on Al Kaline Field.

In 2007, Kaline's grandson, Colin, was drafted by the Tigers on the 25th round. But, rather than immediately embark on a professional career, Colin Kaline, who looks remarkably like his famous grandfather did when Al first joined the Tigers, elected to enroll at Florida Southern College in Lakeland and play baseball for the Moccasins.

Each spring Kaline puts on a uniform and serves as an instructor during training camp, making it a point to introduce himself to the new Tigers players, especially the rookies. When a player is called up to Detroit during the regular season, Al does the same. It's a little thing, a simple gesture, but it means a lot to those kids.

Kaline remembers how, back in 1953, when he himself was a skinny, scared kid, some of the Tigers players did the same thing for him. He remembers how much a few words of welcome from a veteran such as pitcher Ted Gray meant to him.

When the Tigers traded for speedster and reserve outfielder Josh Anderson in the waning days of the 2009 training camp, Kaline was one of the first to welcome Anderson to his new team.

"That was cool," admitted Anderson, who at 26 was hardly a wide-eyed kid.

"Meeting a Hall of Famer.... It's hard to know what to say."

The next day, rookie pitchers Rick Porcello, just 20 years old and two years removed from high school, and Ryan Perry, age 22 with just 14 professional games in the low minor leagues under his belt, both made the Tigers' 2009 team.

Before that day's exhibition game against Atlanta, Tigers manager Jim Leyland called both players into his office, closed the door, and, trying to keep a straight face, informed them both that they were being sent down to the minor leagues.

Then, it being April 1, Leyland shouted, "April Fools!"

Following batting practice, Kaline talked to the two new rookie pitchers, too.

"I've been in your situation. I was here when I was 18 years old," Kaline told them, after first offering his congratulations. "I know what you're going through.

"Respect the major leagues. But don't fear it. You're going to be riding in jets and staying in great hotels. But don't forget the reason you're here. Don't worry about the names on the backs of the uniforms. If you make your pitches, you can get Babe Ruth out."

Clubhouse hijinks have been part of baseball since Ty Cobb wore short pants. And Kaline still enjoys that part of the game, too.

Wearing eyeglasses out of deference to his years, Al is sitting in front of his locker in the clubhouse early one spring morning, reading the newspaper, when pitcher Jeremy Bonderman tiptoes up behind him and grabs the newspaper, pulling it three feet away from Kaline's face.

"Maybe you can see it better this way," Bonderman says, laughing.

Kaline laughs, too. He snatches the paper from Bonderman's grasp and swats it at the pitcher's backside as Bonderman walks away, grinning.

If I am standing in the Tigers clubhouse talking to a player or another writer when Kaline happens to walk by, more often than not he will give me a hard shove. Boys will be boys.

Appropriately, a larger-than-life steel sculpture of Al Kaline stands beyond the left-field wall at Comerica Park, along with statues honoring Ty Cobb, Charlie Gehringer, Hank Greenberg, Hal Newhouser, and Willie Horton. A mile or so away, a deserted street bearing Al's name borders the site of what was once Tiger Stadium.

Unlike some teams, most notably the New York Yankees, the Tigers were reluctant to retire any player's number. For years, they defended that position, pointing out that Ty Cobb, the most famous Tiger of them all, had never worn a number during his days in Detroit.

When the Tigers retired Al's No. 6 on August 17, 1980, following Kaline's election to the Hall of Fame, it was a franchise first.

Since then, the Tigers have also retired No. 5 in honor of slugging great Hank Greenberg and No. 2 to pay tribute to their superb second baseman Charlie Gehringer. Five years after pitcher Hal Newhouser was voted into baseball's Hall of Fame by the Veteran's Committee in 1992, the Tigers retired his No. 16. And they honored hometown hero Willie Horton by retiring No. 23, which had more recently been worn by Kirk Gibson.

But no number in Tigers history is more cherished than No. 6.

During the baseball season, Kaline usually arrives at Comerica Park at least three hours before the game. He enjoys nothing more than mingling with the players, talking baseball. They all look up to him. Many call him Mr. Kaline.

But such recognition isn't why he is there. Baseball is in his blood.

From his earliest days, Kaline was always a student of the game. He studied plays and players. He took it all in. He still does.

During batting practice, he stands behind the back of the cage, scrutinizing the various players' swings, just as people scrutinized his swing more than half a century ago.

Baseball players have changed. They have gotten bigger and stronger. But the game remains the same.

Once the games begin, Kaline sits in one of the executive suites on the third-base side of the press box and watches the action with the rest of the Tigers brass.

On one such night, Mike Ilitch, the Tigers' billionaire owner, was squinting, trying to read the out-of-town scores on the outfield scoreboard.

"What's the score in that Chicago game?" the 80-year-old Ilitch asked Kaline, who was seated at his side.

"They're winning 3–1 in the sixth inning," Kaline told him.

"You can still see that?" Ilitch asked incredulously.

Kaline smiled.

"Yeah, I can still see it," Al said.

Kaline still has the eyes of a great hitter.

"Even to this day, my eyes are really good," he later said without sounding boastful. "I can see a fly ball off the bat and judge it. I was always able to see the ball coming off the bat real good. That helped me a lot as an outfielder.

"I don't think anybody can ever describe exactly what makes a good hitter. But I think it must have something to do with being able to pick the ball up a little quicker when it comes out of the pitcher's hand. If you can see the spin a little quicker, it gives you a little extra time to react to it."

Kaline is a better interview today than he ever was as a ballplayer, especially during the early years. He is more quotable, more accommodating, more at ease.

Beginning in 1976, one season after he retired as a player, through 2001, Kaline spent more time in the Tigers' TV broadcast booth—26 years—than he did on the playing field. Most of that time was spent alongside his friend and fellow Hall of Famer George Kell, who helped smooth out some of the remaining rough edges and make Al more comfortable with the spoken word.

In 2002, after serving as an advisor to Tigers owner Mike Ilitch—who as a young man had played in the team's farm system—Kaline became a special assistant to Tigers president and general manager Dave Dombrowski, offering input on possible trades, roster moves, and other matters of importance.

The amazing thing is, until Kaline was invited to join the front office on June 18, 2001, as part of an advisory committee created by Ilitch, nobody in the Tigers organization had ever asked Kaline's opinion about much of anything.

"In the back of my mind, I'm thinking, *Why all of a sudden, now?*" Al admitted at the time. "I'm still the same guy who could have been helping the ballclub for 25 years.

"In all the years I was with the Tigers, very few people ever asked for my input. The first one who ever did was Bo Schembechler."

Schembechler, the famed former University of Michigan football coach, was the Tigers' president under owner Tom Monaghan from 1990 to 1992.

Incredibly, in retrospect, when Kaline hung up his spikes in 1974, the Tigers didn't even offer him a job.

"Maybe it was my fault," Kaline said modestly. "I was never a pushy guy. I would never go ask for anything. I wouldn't ask, 'Is there a scouting job or a coaching job?' I was always laid-back. I never asked for anything.

"I always figured I would pay my own way. I didn't want anything given to me. I wanted to earn it. I figured, 'If they want you, they'll come get you.'"

Before he retired in 1974, Al Kaline had repeatedly said he didn't want to manage. He wasn't about to spend several years riding the buses, sleeping in lumpy beds, and living on greasy cheeseburgers in the bush leagues, waiting for a big-league summons to arrive.

And Tigers general manager Jim Campbell had vowed he would never hire a major-league manager who hadn't already proven himself and paid his dues.

Kaline might have made a great manager. Or not. The world will never know because Al never got the chance to try.

"They never asked me," he admitted. "Jim Campbell once mentioned that I'd have to go down to the minors for several years, and that didn't have much appeal to me. I never saw the sense in it.

"It got to the point where I figured that if I had to ask, it wouldn't have been worth it. And besides, if I asked and they didn't want to do it, how were they going to tell me no? It would have been too embarrassing for everyone."

Kaline had no interest in becoming a coach, either, trying to scrape by on $17,000 a year—the going rate for coaches when Al retired—plus, of course, all of the meal money he could pocket by dining on clubhouse cold cuts and overcooked kielbasa when the team was on the road.

No, thank you. Al Kaline was too proud to do that.

I long suspected that, decades ago, Kaline would have loved to have been the Tigers' general manager. But Jim Campbell was not about to budge from that job when Al retired. And Campbell's boss, Tigers owner John Fetzer, had no interest in making such a change.

Instead, paired with fellow Hall of Famer George Kell, Kaline became the Tigers' color commentator in 1976. He soon became a fixture in the TV broadcast booth, just as he had been in right field for all of those years. Fans too young to have ever seen Al hit or throw came to know him as the voice of the Tigers.

Some ex-players are naturals behind a microphone. They just open their mouths and let the witty observations and analysis flow. Al Kaline was not one of those guys.

Kaline, who had gone straight from high school to the big leagues, struggled on the air at first. He felt uncomfortable. He wasn't a polished speaker. He had never received any training in that regard. And, by nature, he was never a glib or talkative guy.

Kaline certainly knew the game. And he definitely had plenty to say. But he didn't always know the best way to say it.

As a result, during his first years in the booth, he was often criticized in print and mocked in private for his grammatical errors and fractured syntax during the Tigers telecasts.

The attacks hurt. Al didn't like playing the broadcasting buffoon. So he worked hard to hone his skills and master his performance behind a microphone, just as he had done so many years earlier on the baseball diamond.

In the late 1970s, a fan wrote to me, complaining about Kaline's lack of polish on the air. I still remember my response.

"If you ignore how he says things but pay attention to everything he says," I wrote, "I guarantee you will learn something new about baseball every game."

"When Al first started broadcasting, I think he felt a little insecure," George Kell, Kaline's broadcast partner who passed away in 2009, admitted in his autobiography.

"That's natural. He was such a great player and always performed to such a high level, I think he was wondering if he could meet such high expectations in a new profession.

"Al was afraid he might hurt someone's feelings in the clubhouse. He knew all the players' wives watched the games. He was concerned they'd get upset and tell their husbands about something he might say. He wanted to be friends with everybody.

"'You can't do it that way,' I told him. 'You can still be friends with the players. But you have to report the games the way they are played. You don't have to single someone out and persecute him. You don't have to say so-and-so isn't doing his job. If so-and-so makes an error, though, you have an obligation to tell the truth. You're not up there to cover up. You're not a shill. You're a professional broadcaster.'

"Al Kaline is not the type of person who would deliberately embarrass someone under any circumstances," Kell continued. "He's too much of a gentleman.

"Because Al knows the game so well, though, he's able to analyze when a player makes a mistake. Al also is quick to point out some little good thing that a player does to help a team that a fan might not even notice.

"When I first knew Kaline as a player, there had been some talk about him possibly becoming a manager when his career was finished. To be honest, I never thought of him as a managerial type. Even after my first year in the booth with him, I wasn't convinced he would have made a good manager. My opinion changed, though. After spending more time with Al, I'm convinced he could have managed the Tigers and would have done a terrific job.

"Al Kaline knows baseball like no one else knows the game," Kell said. "And I witnessed an incident in the clubhouse that proved to me he had the guts to manage a team.

"Before a game, Kaline and I were in the Tigers clubhouse when Kirk Gibson started to needle Al about something he had said on the air about Gibson the previous night.

"Al can take good-natured ribbing as well as anyone. When it reached a certain point, though, Al put a stop to it in a hurry.

"'You do your job as well as I do mine, and we won't have any problems,' Kaline told him. 'All I do is report what happens on the field. You made a mistake, and I reported it. There's no hard feelings.'

"Gibson got quiet quickly because he knew Al was right.

"Once in a while, Al would go quiet on me," Kell went on. "When he saw too many bad plays happening in front of him, it seemed like he got bored with the game. I learned how to draw him back in. I'd say something like, 'That was quite a play in right field. I never would have thought about throwing the ball back here.'

"Then Al would take over. He'd explain the play from A to Z. He's that smart about baseball.

"Al Kaline would have made a good manager. I'm glad he chose the broadcast booth, though, because it was an honor to work with him for all those years."

As Kaline's confidence in the broadcast booth grew, so did his candor on the air.

"Al absolutely loved George Kell. He loved him," said Kaline's longtime friend and confidant, businessman Joe Colucci. "When George wasn't feeling good, Al would pick up George's suitcase and put it on the plane. He had so much respect for George, for the great person that he was, as well as the great professional."

On September 27, 1999, Kaline, wearing his familiar No. 6, brought the lineup card to home plate before the start of the final game ever played at venerable Tiger Stadium.

By then, the green wooden seats that Kaline so fondly remembered from his early years were long gone. And the ballpark, which had been home to big-league baseball under one name or another since 1912, was rapidly deteriorating.

Christened on April 20, 1912, six days after the sinking of the *Titanic*, the ancient ballyard at the corner of Michigan and Trumbull had been the scene of Babe Ruth's 700th home run in 1934, a 480-foot blast off Tommy Bridges; historic All-Star Game home runs by Ted Williams in 1941 and Reggie Jackson 30 years later; as well as home to the Tigers' pennant-winning teams in 1934, 1935, 1940, 1945, 1968, and 1984 and four world championships.

Kaline, of course, was among the 65 former Tigers stars who were fêted in ceremonies surrounding the team's final game at Tiger Stadium. Kaline sat next to baseball commissioner Bud Selig.

"If any player defined the spirit of the Tigers in the second half of the century, it was No. 6," legendary Hall of Fame announcer Ernie Harwell told the crowd.

The 76-second standing, screaming ovation that followed caused Kaline to step back from the microphone, look down, shuffle his feet, remove his cap, and bow his head.

On his cap bearing the cherished Olde English D, Kaline had inscribed the initials J.C. and N.C.—tributes to the late, longtime Tigers general manager Jim Campbell and to Norm Cash, Al's deceased friend and former teammate.

Kaline wanted to share this day with them.

"I'll leave here with more memories of Tiger Stadium than anyone else ever had," he confided in a quiet moment earlier in the day. "Because I've worn a Tiger uniform longer than anyone else.

"That's the way I'm trying to look at it. That's the way I'm trying to get through this day.

"Forty-six years," Kaline said softly as he continued to ponder the significance of the moment at hand. "Forty-six years. I can't even comprehend how many games that has been."

Dan Petry pitched for the Tigers from 1979 through 1987, and again in 1990–91. He was a member of the 1984 world championship team. Petry now makes his home in suburban Detroit and occasionally fills in on the Tigers telecasts.

On one such occasion, in May 2009, Petry bumped into Kaline in the corridor outside the broadcast booths at Comerica Park.

The two ex-Tigers chatted for a while, as former ballplayers will do, before Kaline asked, "Did you get the message I left for you a while back?"

Petry was taken aback. He looked genuinely embarrassed.

"No, I didn't get it," he stammered, struggling to apologize. "If I had, I certainly would have returned the call."

"It was no big deal," Kaline said as the two men shook hands and went their separate ways.

But Petry, who himself won 125 games in the big leagues and was a star in his own right, was still mortified. He shook his head and said, "Can you imagine anyone getting a message from Al Kaline—from Al Kaline!—and not calling him back?"

Incredible.

Sources

Bak, Richard. *A Place for Summer*. Wayne State University Press, 1998.

Butler, Hal. *Al Kaline and the Detroit Tigers*. Henry Regnery Company, 1973.

Cantor, George. *The Tigers of '68*. Taylor Publishing Company, 1997.

Detroit News. *They Earned Their Stripes*. Sports Publishing, LLC, 2000.

Falls, Joe. *Detroit Tigers*. Collier Books, 1975.

Falls, Joe. *The Detroit Tigers*. Walker & Company, 1989.

Freehan, Bill. *Behind the Mask*. The World Publishing Company, 1970.

Hawkins, Jim and Dan Ewald. *The Detroit Tigers Encyclopedia*. Sports Publishing LLC, 2003.

Kell, George with Dan Ewald. *Hello Everybody, I'm George Kell*. Sports Publishing, LLC, 1998.

Nicholson, Lois P. *From Maryland to Cooperstown*. Cornell Maritime Press, 1998.

Index

About the Author

Jim Hawkins is a graduate of the 1950s' Knot Hole Gangs in his native Superior, Wisconsin. He began collecting baseball cards in 1953, the same year that Al Kaline broke into the big leagues. He began covering Kaline and the Detroit Tigers as a 25-year-old rookie reporter in 1970, back in the days when sportswriters pounded typewriters; filed their daily stories via Western Union; and traveled, dined, and occasionally drank with the guys on the team.

As the baseball beat writer and columnist, first for the *Detroit Free Press* and later for *The Oakland (Michigan) Press*, Hawkins was there when Kaline signed his historic $100,000 contract and when Al collected his 3,000th base hit. The first vote that Hawkins ever cast as a member of the Baseball Writers Association of America's Hall of Fame electorate was, appropriately, for Al Kaline.

This is Hawkins' seventh book and his fifth about the Tigers, including a biography of Mark "the Bird" Fidrych and the autobiography of Ron LeFlore, which was published in three languages and made into a TV movie starring LeVar Burton.

B
Kaline,
A.

1004-050-2495
Hawkins, Jim
Al Kaline: The
biography of a
Tigers icon